JOHN ORMOND'S O

WRITING WALES IN ENGLISH

CREW series of Critical and Scholarly Studies
General Editors: Kirsti Bohata and Daniel G. Williams (CREW, Swansea University)

This CREW series is dedicated to Emyr Humphreys, a major figure in the literary culture of modern Wales, a founding patron of the Centre for Research into the English Literature and Language of Wales. Grateful thanks are due to the late Richard Dynevor for making this series possible.

Other titles in the series

Stephen Knight, *A Hundred Years of Fiction* (978-0-7083-1846-1)

Barbara Prys-Williams, *Twentieth-Century Autobiography* (978-0-7083-1891-1)

Kirsti Bohata, *Postcolonialism Revisited* (978-0-7083-1892-8)

Chris Wigginton, *Modernism from the Margins* (978-0-7083-1927-7)

Linden Peach, *Contemporary Irish and Welsh Women's Fiction* (978-0-7083-1998-7)

Sarah Prescott, *Eighteenth-Century Writing from Wales: Bards and Britons* (978-0-7083-2053-2)

Hywel Dix, *After Raymond Williams: Cultural Materialism and the Break-Up of Britain* (978-0-7083-2153-9)

Matthew Jarvis, *Welsh Environments in Contemporary Welsh Poetry* (978-0-7083-2152-2)

Harri Garrod Roberts, *Embodying Identity: Representations of the Body in Welsh Literature* (978-0-7083-2169-0)

Diane Green, *Emyr Humphreys: A Postcolonial Novelist* (978-0-7083-2217-8)

M. Wynn Thomas, *In the Shadow of the Pulpit: Literature and Nonconformist Wales* (978-0-7083-2225-3)

Linden Peach, *The Fiction of Emyr Humphreys: Contemporary Critical Perspectives* (978-0-7083-2216-1)

Daniel Westover, *R. S. Thomas: A Stylistic Biography* (978-0-7083-2413-4)

Jasmine Donahaye, *Whose People? Wales, Israel, Palestine* (978-0-7083-2483-7)

Judy Kendall, *Edward Thomas: The Origins of His Poetry* (978-0-7083-2403-5)

Damian Walford Davies, *Cartographies of Culture: New Geographies of Welsh Writing in English* (978-0-7083-2476-9)

Daniel G. Williams, *Black Skin, Blue Books: African Americans and Wales 1845–1945* (978-0-7083-1987-1)

Andrew Webb, *Edward Thomas and World Literary Studies: Wales, Anglocentrism and English Literature* (978-0-7083-2622-0)

Alyce von Rothkirch, *J. O. Francis, realist drama and ethics: Culture, place and nation* (978-1-7831-6070-9)

Rhian Barfoot, *Liberating Dylan Thomas: Rescuing a Poet from Psycho-Sexual Servitude* (978-1-7831-6184-3)

Daniel G. Williams, *Wales Unchained: Literature, Politics and Identity in the American Century* (978-1-7831-6212-3)

M. Wynn Thomas, *The Nations of Wales 1890–1914* (978-1-78316-837-8)

Richard McLauchlan, *Saturday's Silence: R. S. Thomas and Paschal Reading* (978-1-7831-6920-7)

Bethan M. Jenkins, *Between Wales and England: Anglophone Welsh Writing of the Eighteenth Century* (978-1-7868-3029-6)

M. Wynn Thomas, *All that is Wales: The Collected Essays of M. Wynn Thomas* (978-1-7868-3088-3)

Laura Wainwright, *New Territories in Modernism: Anglophone Welsh Writing, 1930–1949* (978-1-7868-3217-7)

Siriol McAvoy, *Locating Lynette Roberts: 'Always Observant and Slightly Obscure'* (978-1-7868-3382-2)

Linden Peach, *Pacifism, Peace and Modern Welsh Writing* (978-1-7868-3402-7)

John Ormond's Organic Mosaic

Poetry, Documentary, Nation

WRITING WALES IN ENGLISH

KIERON SMITH

UNIVERSITY OF WALES PRESS
2019

www.uwp.co.uk

British Library CIP Data
A catalogue record for this book is available from the British Library.

ISBN: 978-1-78683-488-1
e-ISBN: 978-1-78683-489-8

The right of Kieron Smith to be identified as author of this work has been asserted in accordance with sections 77 and 79 of the Copyright, Designs and Patents Act 1988.

THE *A*SSOCIATION FOR
*W*ELSH *W*RITING IN *E*NGLISH
*C*YMDEITHAS *L*LÊN *S*AESNEG *C*YMRU

Typeset by Marie Doherty
Printed by CPI Antony Rowe, Melksham

For Eileen

CONTENTS

SERIES EDITORS' PREFACE

The aim of this series, since its founding in 2004 by Professor M. Wynn Thomas, is to publish scholarly and critical work by established specialists and younger scholars that reflects the richness and variety of the English-language literature of modern Wales. The studies published so far have amply demonstrated that concepts, models and discourses current in the best contemporary studies can illuminate aspects of Welsh culture, and have also foregrounded the potential of the Welsh example to draw attention to themes that are often neglected or marginalised in anglophone cultural studies. The series defines and explores that which distinguishes Wales's anglophone literature, challenges critics to develop methods and approaches adequate to the task of interpreting Welsh culture, and invites its readers to locate the process of writing Wales in English within comparative and transnational contexts.

Professor Kirsti Bohata and Professor Daniel G. Williams

Founding Editor: Professor M. Wynn Thomas (2004–15)

CREW (*Centre for Research into the English Literature and Language of Wales*)
Swansea University

CREW

Acknowledgements

This book stemmed from doctoral research at CREW (the Centre for Research into the English Literature and Language of Wales), Swansea University, during 2010–14. My heartfelt thanks to my two supervisors, Gwenno Ffrancon and M. Wynn Thomas, for giving me the opportunity to embark on that project, and for their encouragement during those years and beyond. I take full responsibility for the unwieldiness of the finished thesis. This book is a substantial revision of that document, and its current shape was informed by the comments and suggestions of my two examiners, Dai Smith and Damian Walford Davies, who graciously pointed out some whopping errors of fact and judgement. That said, fresh errors in this book should be attributed to me alone.

I look back fondly to my time at CREW, particularly the ideas (and pints, often both) shared with Rhian Barfoot, Georgia Burdett, Clare Davies, Nia Davies, Gareth Evans, Anthony Howell, Sarah Morse and Ugo Rivetti. My gratitude also to Kirsti Bohata and Daniel G. Williams, who, unlike some of the others named, offered consistently sound advice.

The work would not have been possible without the cooperation of the archivists at BBC Cymru Wales in Llandaff, Cardiff, who gave me access to Ormond's films and facilitated their transfer to the Richard Burton Archives at Swansea University.

Diolch to Hannah Sams, who translated the Patagonia films.

I am grateful to Hywel Francis, Phil George and Colin Thomas, all of whom took the time to talk to me at various stages of the project. Those conversations enabled me to view Ormond's work from a far more informed perspective. My warm thanks in particular to Rian Evans, who gave the manuscript considerable time and attention, and helped tease out further nuances of the background to the films and the form they took.

Finally, thank you to my family, for your unfailing encouragement and support.

Note on cover image: every effort has been made to trace the source of the cover image and obtain permission for its use. I would be grateful if notified of the source and/or its copyright holder in order to credit them in future reprints or editions of this book.

ABBREVIATIONS

Quotations from the poetry of John Ormond are taken from John Ormond, *Collected Poems*, edited by Rian Evans (Bridgend: Seren, 2015). References to this will be made within the text using the abbreviation *CP*, followed by the page number.

1

INTRODUCTION: 'WELSH THINGS TO BROADCAST ABOUT'

JOHN ORMOND THOMAS

John Ormond Thomas was born on 3 April 1923 in Dunvant, a small village a few miles outside Swansea. He was the son of Elsie Thomas and her husband Arthur, a shoemaker. Despite its proximity to a (then) prosperous Swansea, Dunvant was at that time a sheltered place with a 'rural outlook',[1] and the Thomases, like many other families in Wales at that time, lived within the influence of the local chapel. For the Thomases, this was the Welsh Congregationalist Ebenezer, which stood just two hundred yards from the family home. Thankfully for the inquisitive John, Ebenezer was not entirely the staid, straitlaced institution that it looked. As Rian Evans has noted, the chapel had 'a cultural life rich even by Welsh standards: choral singing, oratorio performances, theatrical productions and discussion groups were all part of the normal calendar'.[2] Yet even with this activity, as the young boy grew older, he became increasingly aware of a world of wider experience beyond the village. One summer weekend, the Dunvant-born artist Ceri Richards, then living in London, turned up at Ebenezer for the Sunday morning service. The young Ormond was astounded: 'His hair was not cut in the short-back-and-sides manner of all the other men in the polished pews that day, but left perhaps an inch longer. Instead of dark serge he wore a tweed sports-jacket and grey flannel trousers.'[3] In 1930s Dunvant, Richards must have seemed a creature from another planet. The rebellious artist represented something significant yet, at that time, inexpressible: 'the feeling [was] there but not the vocabulary to express it'.[4] Later, when he could find the words, Ormond suggested that Richards on that day threw into relief the 'narrow, literal'[5] Nonconformist world he felt he inhabited.

Over the coming years, Ormond began to extend his cultural lexicon. This necessitated trips outside the village. He made regular bus journeys to the 'Tiv', the cinema in nearby Gowerton,[6] and during lunchtimes at Swansea Grammar School he would hurry down to the Glynn Vivian Art Gallery. A decisive moment came in 1941, when one evening he read two poems from a Penguin poetry anthology he had found in the window of Morgan and Higgs's bookshop in blitzed Swansea: Wilfred Owen's 'Exposure' and Dylan Thomas's 'The force that through the green fuse'.[7] 'Life was never to be the same again', he later said.[8] In the same year, he won a scholarship to University College Swansea to study Philosophy and English, twin subjects that suited his expanding interests. Through his Philosophy lecturer, Rush Rhees, he encountered Ludwig Wittgenstein, whose ideas were to influence him significantly. Meanwhile, Ormond was developing ambitions as a poet. Although he spoke some Welsh – sufficiently later to complete translations of early Welsh verse, such as 'To a Nun' and 'The Hall of Cynddylan' – his work, whether on paper or on screen, would be in the English language. He began writing and publishing, first in the University College magazine *Dawn*, and later in Keidrych Rhys's journal *Wales*. By 1943 he had contributed to an anthology with two other young poets, John Bayliss and James Kirkup.[9] While his early poems were often perhaps a little too heavily informed by Dylan Thomas in style,[10] and while his friend Vernon Watkins was probably right, a little later, to advise him that he 'ought not to publish any further collection until [he] was thirty',[11] his early verse offered a sure indication of the creative ambition that was to drive his life's work.

Though Ormond's primary ambitions were as a poet, upon leaving university he sought out work as a journalist. He made the move out of Swansea upon graduation, initially to Essex to take a job at the *Brentwood Gazette*. However, he wasn't to be at the newspaper long. He had around this time sent a selection of poems to Tom Hopkinson, then editor of the photojournalist magazine *Picture Post*. Reading the poems, Hopkinson immediately offered him a job as a staff writer, and Ormond soon moved into London to work for the magazine, writing articles on a range of topics covering the people, places, politics and culture of post-war Britain. On beery jaunts in Soho he made informative new creative acquaintances with some of the major poets of the day – George Barker, Cecil Day-Lewis and, naturally, Dylan Thomas – but it was at the magazine that he began to ply a new trade. There, matching words with images, he learned to think like a camera. He remained in London until 1949, when he moved back to Swansea to take a job as sub-editor on the *South Wales Evening Post*. Back in his hometown, he enjoyed friendships with Dylan Thomas, Vernon Watkins, and the rest of the Kardomah Gang, but finding himself frustrated with the monotony of newspaper work, he began looking for other outlets for his creativity. Things were to improve. In 1955 Tom Hopkinson, by then features editor at *News Chronicle*, invited him to write verse captions to the weekly 'Saturday Picture' taken by some of the great photographers of the era. In the same year, a major opportunity arose: Ormond was appointed the role of Television News Assistant at the fledgling Welsh National Region of the BBC in Cardiff – 'not a Television News Assistant but the one and only one', he later recalled. The impression he made there evidently impressed his superiors; by 1957 he had been made head of the new BBC Wales Film Unit, and by 1961 a senior documentary producer.

Here, Ormond was no mere reporter, but a film-maker, a role that carried with it an entirely different set of freedoms and responsibilities, along with a certain, and not inconsiderable, professional cachet. Ormond was well equipped for such a role, and over the decades that followed he honed a distinctive style of 'personal documentary'[12] that blended his journalistic eye with the sensibilities that informed his poetry: humour, plain-speaking egalitarianism, an eye for irony, and a love of the arts. He produced films on an impressive range of topics, spanning history, culture and contemporary Welsh society. Moreover, alongside his professional success at the BBC, he continued to pursue the poetic ambition of his youth. It was in part the creative labour of documentary film-making that recharged his energy as a poet of the 'Second Flowering' of anglophone writing in Wales in the mid-1960s.[13] This was a culturally fertile time, and the friendships he struck up with other Welsh writers of this era – Meic Stephens, Glyn Jones, Alun Richards, Ron Berry, among many others – fed into his creativity in verse and on screen in intriguing ways. Having rebuilt confidence in his poetry with the support of such friends, in 1969 he published his first solo collection, *Requiem and Celebration*, in 1973 his second, *Definition of a Waterfall*, and in 1975 he won the Cholmondeley Award.

However, Ormond was always balancing his work as a poet with the creative demands of filmmaking, with the result that, while his output on screen was nothing short of prolific, his work on the page in these years was comparably slim. This was to be the source of some regret; he later mused that,

> if I'd spent even a tenth of the time and imaginative effort in trying to write a poem as I put into making a film – directing it, writing it, arranging it, supervising the cutting to a twenty-fifth second of it – then I'd probably have more poems.[14]

It seems to have been partly this sense of artistic frustration that led him to take such pleasure basking in the light of Tuscany in the years of his retirement from the BBC. He had visited Arezzo with the BBC in 1963 to produce the film *From a Town in Tuscany*, and it was here, he later recalled, that he had been inspired to return to poetry after so many years. In the small town of Cortona, a place where 'long-felt ideas and long-heard music seem [. . .] to cohere',[15] he settled more comfortably into being the poet he had always felt himself to be. He recalled a conversation with an Italian couple with whom he had become acquainted:

> Last year, the courtesies exchanged, the usual enquiries about our families and respective healths done, the old couple's curiosity could be hidden no longer. What did I do, they wanted to know [. . .] Now, I said something I am normally reluctant to say at home, and this is the essence of my being here and my joy in it: 'Sono poeta,' I said [. . .]: 'I am a poet'.[16]

Having found a long-sought-for sense of creative ease, he came to view Cortona as a home from home, and wrote several poems in honour of it. Sadly, he had in an earlier visit to the region contracted Lyme disease which undermined his health somewhat in later years. He died of a stroke at the University Hospital of Wales, Cardiff, on 4 May 1990. He had published some one hundred and forty poems and produced over fifty films in his illustrious, and fruitfully dualistic, creative career.

TV AUTEUR?

While much of Ormond's work certainly lends itself to biographical interpretation – and there is already much critical material available that reads, in particular, his poetry in these terms[17] – this book is primarily a study of Ormond's output as a documentary film-maker. The documentary is not a cultural form that lends itself straightforwardly to biographical interpretation. In film and television studies in particular, the limitations of such an approach are exposed by the simple fact of the enormous range of personnel involved in the creation of any single 'text'. Ormond, after all, worked as part of a film unit which included a range of talented people: camera operators, editors, sound engineers, musicians, narrators and more – all of whom contributed to the final film in a way that renders problematic the idea of a single 'auteur' at the helm. As one observer suggests,

If television is an art-form, it is a cumbersome and expensive one. If the producer is an auteur or author, he is an author who needs the active involvement of thirty or forty other people, expensive equipment, studio space and – not least – a network to transmit the end-product.[18]

This fact has led to the predominance of a set of critical approaches to the study of film and television that foreground matters of the political economy of cultural production, as well as other, wider institutional and contextual factors. The more theoretical versions of these arguments, moreover, involve a broader scepticism toward the notion of unitary centres of meaning, and contend that all creativity inevitably takes place within and across a complex web of discursive practices that belong to no single person or institution. From such a perspective, creative acts are taken to be far too complexly interwoven in networks of sociocultural and material context than can be explained by any reading that starts from the notion of a singular auteur.

That said, there are merits to an approach that at least keeps the auteur in focus, particularly in the context of television production in the 1960s and 1970s, and even more so given the nature of Ormond's work. Ormond was known to be an exacting director: writing every word of commentary of his films, lining up every shot, sitting with the editor, selecting the music. One of the aims of this book, then, is to explore the extent to which it is possible to combine an 'auteurial' with an 'institutional' reading of television films, or at least to keep both in view.[19] Patrick Russell and James Piers-Taylor make a useful point on this score in their book on post-war British documentary, *Shadows of Progress: Documentary Film in Post-War Britain* (2010).

Here they tentatively defend the idea that a 'commonsensical' auteur-ist approach has much to offer critics:

> The career narratives of those who toiled in post-war documentary make for absorbing human stories. They are also revealing micro-studies in how the industry at large functioned and changed. As part of a collaborative process, the director undoubtedly did play an important role in mediating [. . .] the viewer's experience.[20]

I would, naturally, agree that Ormond's 'career narrative' is one worth examining as an 'absorbing human story'. However, I would further agree that his body of work as a film-maker should be viewed not only as a case study of the ways in which BBC Wales functioned as an institution, but also, as we shall see, of the ways in which the documentary functioned as a cultural form within a broadly national context. Moreover, it is necessary to modify Russell and Piers-Taylor's final point here to say that the auteur-director of television documentaries at this time played not only an 'important' but, further, an absolutely central orchestrating role in the production of programmes. Ormond was engaged in television at a time when director-producers were afforded an exceptionally high status. In his 1966 book *Factual Television*, Norman Swallow, a key producer and commentator during Ormond's era, tellingly termed such films 'personal documentaries'. The kind of 'personal documentary' that Swallow describes is 'very much the individual work of its producer',[21] and significantly, Ormond is one of the film-makers Swallow names in this connection, along-side other influential figures such as Denis Mitchell, Ken Russell and Philip Donnellan, all of whom made names for themselves during the expansion of documentary production at the BBC in the late 1950s and 1960s. In a Welsh context, we should add to this list names such as Selwyn Roderick, Aled Vaughan, Derek Trimby and Brian Turvey. It was this common understanding of the 'personal' creative potential of the individual that afforded film-makers the space, time and resources to pursue their work. By the same token, the freedom that Ormond was afforded to explore his creative vision in his work at BBC Wales – as well as the later limitations placed upon it – reveal much about the broader cultural, political and institutional contexts of that time.

This book therefore has three related aims. The first is to provide a reading of Ormond's oeuvre on its own terms, as a body of creative film-making which, read in correspondence with his poetry, exemplifies an astonishingly 'personal' poetic-filmic sensibility. The second is to use this as a means to historicise his work, to situate it within the wider social, cultural and institutional territory of Wales and Britain in this period, which necessarily means keeping in mind the fact that these were films made for a publicly-funded broadcasting institution with wide audiences. The third aim is to take Ormond's work in the television documentary film to be a revealing case study of the ways in which this cultural form engaged with its inescapable sociocultural, political and institutional contexts. It will argue that the documentary films Ormond produced at BBC Wales from the late 1950s to the 1980s constitute fascinating embodiments of – and contributions to – the sociocultural codes and preoccupations of Welsh society in those decades.

This approach is informed by an analytical model common in Media Studies, one that distinguishes three main facets of media production: broadly, 'context', 'text' and 'consumption'. A useful figuration of this is Peter Dahlgren's idea of the televisual 'prism'. Dahlgren suggests that these three aspects can be viewed as sides of a prism: 'television is simultaneously an industry, set of audio-visual texts, and a sociocultural experience'.[22] It is an 'industry' in the sense that it is subject to the political-economic contexts of ownership and government policy. It is a 'set of audio-visual texts' insofar as its output exists on the plane of cultural signification; we might also refer to this as the 'representational' aspect of television, that which Dahlgren describes as 'what the media portray, how topics are presented, the modes of discourse at work, and the character of debates and discussion'.[23] Finally television is a 'sociocultural experience' in the sense that it is viewed by audiences living within material historical circumstances. Television is inevitably subject to the cultural and ideological forces generated by those circumstances. This model is, of course, necessarily a simplification; in reality each facet interacts with the other in complex ways. This is acknowledged in the very metaphor of the 'prism', which, as Dahlgren argues,

> implies the difficulties of seeing all the sides at the same time. As we turn our attention to one side of the prism, the others vanish from our view [. . .]. Television cannot be reduced to any one or even two of these angles, but instead remains a composite and complex configuration.[24]

Given my convictions about the merits of Ormond's work, much of the focus of this book will necessarily be on the 'representational' aspects of these films, on their shape as cultural artefacts. But I will also be keeping in view each of these other important facets.[25] To do this, it is necessary here to map out something of the contextual landscape in order to provide orientation for the more detailed explorations that follow.

BROADCASTING AND A WELSH PUBLIC SPHERE

In his groundbreaking history of BBC broadcasting in Wales, John Davies asserts that Wales is a nation in which 'to a greater extent than perhaps any other country in Europe, broadcasting has played a central role [. . .] in the development of the concept of a national community'.[26] Here Davies applies to Wales an argument that theorists of modern nations now assume to be a truism: that technologies of communication are central to the creation and continuation of national communities. Benedict Anderson's *Imagined Communities* (1983) is perhaps the most well known in this respect. There Anderson pointed to the invention of the printing press as the generator of the nation as we now understand it. This technology contributed to the emergence of the modern nation state by unifying the disparate dialects and world-views of vast territories, making it possible for 'rapidly growing numbers of people to think about themselves, and to relate themselves to others' whom they would never encounter or meet.[27] Anderson's book became one of the cornerstones for thinking about the relationships between technologies of communication and national communities. Since then, however, important theoretical developments have allowed for more nuanced examinations of the role of media in the creation of nations. Tim Edensor, for instance, has built on Anderson's emphasis on the ways in which nations are not fixed, 'once and for all' entities, but created and recreated through a vast array of cultural activities. Edensor stresses that national communities as imagined are diffuse, contested, dialogic: 'found in the constellations of a huge cultural matrix of images, ideas, spaces, things, discourses, and practices', television included.[28] In a similar vein, Chris Barker has noted that notions of 'national community' frequently rest upon fixed notions of 'nationality' or 'national identity', which are, in contemporary theoretical parlance, now understood to be highly complex and contested. 'Identities', to quote Barker, are 'social and cultural [. . .] all the way down', and do not 'exist outside of cultural representations and acculturization'.[29] While 'identity' is, as a concept, indispensable to cultural analysis, its somewhat nebulous, relational existence makes it difficult to employ in examinations of political-economic structures and, in our case, broadcasting institutions.[30] For this reason, many commentators adopt Jurgen Habermas's notion of the 'public sphere' as a means of conceptualising the social domain within which the effects of the media upon national communities are felt.

In *The Structural Transformation of the Public Sphere* (1962, translated into English in 1989),[31] Habermas traced the emergence of the public sphere back to the communicative space that developed in the interstice between the state and the market in the eighteenth and nineteenth centuries. It was here, Habermas argued, that an emergent bourgeoisie began to formulate its public ideas and ideals. This was a space that had opened up gradually as the result of a variety of factors: widened political participation, public meeting places that were (in theory) freely accessible to all members of society (such as coffee houses in Britain and salons in France), and, importantly, the emergence of cheap and widely available print media (newspapers, journals, pamphlets and so on). Habermas saw the public sphere as a prerequisite for liberal democracy; it was the sphere of communication within which people who had previously been mere 'subjects' of feudal and autocratic states could discuss issues of common political concern and become 'citizens' of modern nation states. The public sphere is therefore an indispensable concept in the study of the relationships between media and societies, offering as it does a way of designating, amongst a vast range of possibilities, one precise area of social life within which the mass media can be seen to exert its effects: that area of life in which people comprehend themselves as 'citizens' of wider political communities. In modern societies, where the membership of traditional spheres of civic interaction (churches, trade unions, community centres, libraries and so on) have diminished, the mass media, as Peter Dahlgren argues, 'become the chief institutions of the public sphere'.[32]

However, discussions of the relationships between media institutions and the public sphere are complicated in the context of Wales. By Habermas's logic, the public sphere is the space within which people recognise themselves as citizens of nations, yet his argument assumes the precondition of an autonomous nation state with its own political institutions and firmly defined boundaries.[33] Wales, for much of its history, and certainly during the period with which this book is concerned, was, by most definitions, not a nation at all. It certainly did not have a 'state' of its own to speak of. Following the Act of Union of 1536, Wales existed under the jurisdiction of the nation of England, and for most of this period its own national institutions, where they did exist, were annexed to those of the English state. With the roll-out of radio broadcasting on a wide scale in the 1920s, there was an immediate rush, in Monroe E. Price's terms, of 'nation-based gatekeeper[s]' to 'maintain control of broadcasting [...] within national boundaries'.[34] Given the power of the British state over these matters, Wales's capacity to use broadcasting to articulate any sense of its own distinctive public sphere was, from the start, severely compromised. As David Morley has observed,

> The imagined community is [. . .] usually constructed in the language of some particular ethnos, membership of which then effectively becomes a prerequisite for the enjoyment of a political citizenship within the nation-state. On this argument, the Englishness of the public sphere in the UK is its most crucial characteristic.[35]

Numerous studies have examined the extent to which a narrow definition of 'Britishness' dominated broadcasting in Britain from its outset. Most of these follow the lines of Paddy Scannell and David Cardiff's observation that the driving ideological tenor of British broadcasting developed under the influence of the BBC's first Director General, John Reith. Reith's famous paternalist edict is now well known: broadcasting should 'inform, educate and entertain'. Crucially, this paternalism was to play out in a particular national key. As Scannell and Cardiff note, Reith's approach was to stress

> the importance of one general policy and one set of standards for the whole country [. . .] The regime of control was to replace informality by a studied formality; to replace local variety and differences by a standardized conception of culture and manners; to replace audience participation by a more distanced, authoritative and prescriptive approach to broadcasting.[36]

Reith was a Scotsman, yet the 'country' in question was of course 'Britain'.

Wales was therefore left in a conditional position by a media complex dominated by a politically and economically powerful neighbour, and that neighbour's own articulation of nationhood. Add to this the predicament of Wales's own unresolvedly 'plural', 'bilateral', even tripartite character,[37] and any examination of the media in this small nation becomes decidedly complicated. Clearly, then, while Habermas's notion of the public sphere is a useful one, we need to employ it with a degree of caution, and perhaps use it, in Barlow, O'Malley and Mitchell's terms, not as a definition of a reality but as a '"yardstick" against which judgements can be made about an existing system of public communications'.[38] The examination of Welsh broadcasting requires us to avoid simplistically 'internalist' approaches to the media and their effects,[39] and to keep in mind at all times the wider contexts of which it is a part.

'IF YOU ARE CALLED BBC WALES YOU HAVE GOT TO HAVE WELSH THINGS TO BROADCAST ABOUT'

It is for the above reasons John Davies argues that in any discussion of the BBC in Wales, 'the activities of the Corporation as a whole and the central role of London must loom large'.[40] While this is clearly true – and not only of BBC broadcasting, but also of many other spheres of Welsh life – I argue that it is possible to frame the discussion in a less London-centric way. It is Wales's distinctiveness, combined with the compromised power and influence of its national institutions, which makes the examination of its media capabilities so important. This book contends that broadcasting, and in particular the BBC, has been a profoundly important facet of the articulation of Wales and 'Welshness', and was particularly so in the second half of the twentieth century. Whatever the power of the image of 'Britishness' by which it generally operates, the developments that took place at the BBC in those years were fundamental to Wales's cultural and political development. For better or worse, and whether it intended to or not (often, as we shall see, it did not), the BBC equipped key figures in Wales with the means to develop a public sphere appropriate to its development as a national community.

However, it should be emphasised that this occurred in an excruciatingly piecemeal way. For much of the twentieth century, debates on broadcasting in Wales were often expressed, like most other areas of public life, in the form of grievances against policy makers in London.[41] Perhaps for good reason: while radio broadcasting had begun in Wales in 1923, the BBC did not afford Wales the precarious status of National Region until 1937 (though this was renamed

the Welsh Home Service when normal service resumed in 1945).
And although a public Welsh Advisory Committee was set up to
report on the BBC's activities in Wales in 1947 (replaced in 1952 by
the Broadcasting Council for Wales), it was not until 1964 that a
BBC Wales proper was established, with its own headquarters opening in Llandaff, Cardiff in 1967. Nevertheless, in an era in which
Welsh institutions were few and far between, these developments were
crucial focal points for discussion within, as well as key aspects of, an
emergent Welsh public sphere.

Eventually, the increased provision in Wales began to affect the
language in which Wales was described at an institutional level. This
can be seen in the Broadcasting Council for Wales's annual reports
from the late 1950s onwards. Around this time, an important discursive transition took place in the discussion of broadcasting, one
that shifted from an emphasis on Wales and Welshness in *relation* to
Britain and Britishness towards one that focused on the particularities
of Wales's own *internal* relations. The report of 1959–60, for instance,
smacks of a frustrated nation sulkily seeking further provision from
its controlling neighbour:

> The people of Wales as a national group with its own language, traditions,
> and institutions are justly entitled to a separate, distinct, and adequate
> provision of television programmes – a bilingual service which would
> in Wales be additional to what is provided for the United Kingdom as
> a whole.[42]

Yet even as late as 1965, the question of the role of regional and
national broadcasting was still an open one. This led Hywel Davies,
then Head of Programming for BBC Wales, to visit BBC headquarters in London to stake a claim for Welsh cultural distinctiveness:

> [R]egional centres must be more than studios of convenience. They should
> bear the names of Broadcasting House and Television Centre with the
> same awareness and pride as their great counterparts in London. [. . .] A
> focal point, a centre, is better when it is near; and London, in this sense,
> can be too distant and alien a metropolis. This nearness, this ready avail-
> ability, nurtures and develops the regional sense of identity.[43]

The recourse to the careful phraseology of the 'regional' is telling –
this was an era in which to talk to the BBC in London of the Welsh
'nation' was still unthinkable. Yet Davies's argument is pertinent.

He persistently returns to the importance of a devolved BBC that is attentive to the needs of the communities it serves: 'The fundamental obligations of a region, in short, are deeper towards its community than towards its central organisation. So the regional centre must proclaim its existence'.[44] The developments that took place thereafter enabled the reports of the late 1960s to speak proudly of a BBC Wales existing on its own terms, of a service that could 'fairly [. . .] reflect the many different and sometimes contradictory facets of the society'.[45] And in the following year: '[BBC Wales] has tried hard to display a lively interest in present-day Wales and to reflect as many as possible of the varied facets of the country's life.'[46] The civic terminology of 'society' was a far remove from terms such as 'region' or 'principality' favoured in earlier reports, and signalled the broader shifts of perspective taking place in Welsh public life.

The years in which Ormond was most active as a documentary film-maker were therefore ones of profound change at the BBC, as well as in Welsh society in general. Cardiff received capital city status in 1955, and the Ddraig Goch became the official flag of Wales in 1959. Saunders Lewis delivered his influential speech 'Tynged Yr Iaith' ('Fate of the Language') on BBC radio in 1962, and instantly galvanised a Welsh-language movement into action: the result was the formation of Cymdeithas yr Iaith Gymraeg (the Welsh Language Society) which campaigned successfully for greater Welsh-language provision in Welsh public life. These were also the years of the 'Second Flowering' of anglophone Welsh poetry and the rise of English-language Welsh nationalism.[47] Gradually, these cultural shifts were mirrored by developments at a political-institutional level. The formation of the Welsh Office in 1964 was pivotal, in the sense that, as John Davies has argued, it 'strengthened the concept of the territorial unity of Wales and created the need for other organizations reflecting that unity'.[48] The establishment of the Councils for the Arts (1967), for Sport (1972) and for Consumers (1975), as well as the Welsh TUC (1973), were direct responses to the Welsh Office. Such developments set in motion a sequence of events that led to a referendum on devolution in 1979, and although the result was an resounding 'No',[49] the very fact that devolution was on the agenda demonstrated that Wales was now being imagined as a national-political entity in its own right. It is worth quoting Kenneth O. Morgan at length to get a sense of how much things had changed by the end of the 1970s:

Welsh life had been reinvigorated through the rise of nationalism and the debate on devolution [. . .] No longer did Welsh [. . .] issues attract the patronizing indifference that they had so often done prior to 1964. The teaching of Welsh in schools had made steady progress. The government had given its approval to a new Welsh-language television channel, scheduled for 1982. Radio and television programmes in both languages emphasized national themes. The most unexpected of bodies now proclaimed their Welshness [. . .] The debate on Welshness and the future of Welsh government was a passionate one in the late 1970s. It was clearly destined to continue [. . .] in years to come.[50]

The activities of BBC Wales in this period should therefore be interpreted both as a means of reflecting these broad changes in Welsh cultural and political life, and as an important facet of them. Indeed, John Davies has suggested that these developments were in no small part 'media-driven, for all-Wales institutions came into existence in part because BBC Wales was there to report their activities'.[51] Patrick Hannan described it in pithier terms: '[i]f you are called BBC Wales you have got to have Welsh things to broadcast about'.[52]

DOCUMENTARY AT THE BBC WALES FILM UNIT

BBC Wales's capacity to reflect upon and invigorate Welsh public life in these years was greatly improved after it was equipped with the technical resources to create films of its own, though this did not come easily. The BBC's concessions to Britain's regional and national diversity were, as we have seen, slow to emerge, and when things did begin to speed up in the 1950s, this arguably had more to do with the threat of competition from regional commercial television than any specific commitment to regional or national diversity. Conscious that commercial television was to be not only more populist (and therefore more popular), but also, given its model of regional franchising, more recognisably pluralist, the BBC mooted the idea of expanding the capacity for programme origination in its regions in late 1954. Until this time, television footage had been obtained via the use of temperamental Outside Broadcast units, which were designed solely for live transmission, and which consisted largely of clapped-out equipment handed down from London. Ormond later wrote that this was a time when 'one of the chief requirements for working in television in Wales was ingenuity enough to get around obstacles clearly designed to prevent one getting any kind of picture on the air'.[53] The Welsh television studio at this time consisted of a disused chapel and vestry on Stacey Road in Roath, Cardiff. Ormond continued: 'one felt like the little East Ender who said, "if we had a swing we could have a swing in the park, if we had a park".'[54] Accordingly, the output of programmes produced in Wales was initially at a bare minimum. In the last quarter of 1954 the BBC in Wales broadcast a monthly average of 1 hour 52 minutes in English and 1 hour 10 minutes in Welsh.[55] But with competition from commercial television looming, the development of regional film units that could produce their own programmes became a priority.[56] In 1957, BBC Wales was equipped with its own Film Unit.

There was at first considerable debate about the kinds of programming that should be prioritised by this unit, given the scarce resources available. In the absence of a clearly defined policy, what soon emerged were two different ideas about whether the unit should focus on regional 'opt-out' or national 'network' programmes. BBC Headquarters in London naturally preferred regional and national units to prioritise the latter, even making judgements about the allocation of equipment based on the extent to which these units were 'satisfactorily carr[ying] out' their contributions to major network programmes such as *Panorama* and *Tonight*.[57] Yet at the same time, the regions were keen to take advantage of their newly acquired resources in order to produce programmes of their own. This was noted in a BBC HQ memo of 1959:

> as regional television resources have grown, the regions themselves have tended, perhaps understandably, to regard their opt out programmes as being almost the most important things they do and, therefore, to suppose that the order of priority in the use of those resources is opt out first and network second. I think this tendency is particularly marked in the two national regions, i.e. Wales and Scotland.[58]

The kinds of programming made available as Wales acquired more autonomy at this time demonstrate the fact that television was being grasped with both hands by producers. Sport was naturally an important area,[59] but drama too was a vehicle for national self-expression.[60] Most importantly, a focus on Welsh news and current affairs was now possible. This role was fulfilled with the daily Welsh-language *Heddiw* and the English-language *Wales Today*, from 1961 and 1962 respectively. These daily programmes filled roughly half of BBC Wales television's allocated twelve hours per week (seven in Welsh and five in English) after 1964.[61] Soon after, the weekly *Week In Week Out* was introduced, which was to 'give regular treatment in English to the industrial, social and political issues of the day'.[62] Such programmes invited audiences to view Wales's borders as newly political and civic, as well as historical and cultural, in a way that would not have been addressed in such detail from London.

However, if one of the central, guiding functions of national television is that of contributing to the national public sphere, the documentary form in which Ormond worked was arguably one of BBC Wales's most effective formats. John Corner sums up the observations of many commentators when he calls the documentary form 'one of [television's] defining modes'.[63] It is no coincidence that the documentary as a film form developed under John Grierson at precisely the time that John Reith was formulating his guiding plan and purpose for BBC broadcasting in the 1920s, or that the documentary became a key format on television when the medium became widely available in the 1950s. As Corner notes, the development of the documentary as an idea in the 1920s was, as with radio, 'interwoven with the development of citizenship in modern society and with the cause of social democratic reform'.[64] Grierson, a high-minded graduate of Moral Philosophy at the University of Glasgow, had seen in the nascent documentary form the potential for a new tool of democratic citizenship.[65] He set about formulating the aesthetic *form* as well as, crucially, the social democratic *function* that he felt the documentary film should adopt at this time of immense social change. In the decades that followed, Grierson built a career promoting the idea of national documentary production units, firstly in Britain, establishing what was famously to become known as the British Documentary Film Movement, then across the Commonwealth: in Canada in the late 1930s, and, after the war, in Australia, New Zealand and South Africa. Grierson's remarks on the uses of documentary in not only a 'civic' context but, further, a distinctly 'national' one exemplify his conception of its potential as a tool of social cohesion. In Canada – a nation criss-crossed with cultural and linguistic differences – Grierson zealously presented the notion that 'the most important federal media were those which imaginatively brought alive one part of the country to another, and dramatised relationships as distinct from differences'.[66] In the Canadian context, Grierson was concerned with utilising the documentary's capacity to 'make [Canada] more of a nation and less of an appendage to anyone – and articulate its own particular destiny better than it has managed to do before'.[67]

There was to be a long wait before documentary film-making could be utilised with any serious application in Wales. As in the realm of broadcasting, Wales's ability to speak to itself on its own terms was compromised by a context in which London, to return to Davies's phrase, 'loom[ed] large'. Before the age of television, it was largely through the lens of film-makers within the British Documentary Movement of the 1930s, 1940s and early 1950s that Wales was viewed in documentary films.[68] And, while there are documentaries of this period that view Wales and its people with sensitivity and intelligence – films such as *Today We Live* (1937, directed by Ruby Grierson and Ralph Bond), *Eastern Valley* (1937, directed by Paul Rotha and Donald Alexander), *Wales: Green Mountain Black Mountain* (1942, directed by John Eldridge), *Silent Village* (1943, directed by Humphrey Jennings) and *David* (1951, directed by Paul Dickson)[69] – their number is small, and, generally speaking, they were representations produced by film units based in London that constructed Wales in terms of its contribution to a wider British workforce. Indeed, if we accept that, like broadcasting, the documentary form was utilised as a tool of the national public sphere in these years, the nation in focus in these films was, undoubtedly, 'Britain'. This was certainly still the case in the late 1950s, when key left-wing film-makers and thinkers, such as Karel Reisz and Lindsay Anderson, were theorising the documentary film as a tool of British national cohesion. As Anderson wrote in 1957: 'Our aim is first to look at Britain, with honesty and with affection. To relish its eccentricities; attack its abuses; love its people. To use the cinema to express our allegiances, our rejections and our aspirations. This is our commitment.'[70] While laudable, such a commitment to the nation of Britain arguably meant that British documentary could not fully respond to the particular eccentricities, abuses, allegiances, rejections and aspirations of Wales. It was not until the advent of television production in Wales, in particular at the BBC and the ITV franchise Television Wales and West (TWW, later HTV), that the documentary form was utilised in a way that could respond to Wales's particular circumstances.

CLAIMING THE REAL

A further, perhaps more theoretical way to explore the power of the documentary in a national context is to consider its particular relationship with social reality. Every documentary is supported on some level by the assumption that film is a medium of documentation, or – to borrow the title of Brian Winston's important book – an act of 'claiming the real'.[71] This is often attributed to what film theorist André Bazin called the 'ontology of the photographic image', that is, the conception of the photographic or film camera as a purely objective instrument of representation. Bazin argued that the film camera was an technology that could overcome 'those piled-up preconceptions, that spiritual dust and grime'[72] that muddies the lens of other forms of representation, like writing, painting or sculpture. Bill Nichols suggests that the supposed trustworthiness of the documentary image contributed greatly to its effectiveness as a tool of public communication. As he writes:

> The subjective dynamics of social engagement in documentary revolve around our confrontation with a representation of the historical world. What we see and hear ostensibly reaches beyond the frame into the world we, too, occupy. The subjectivity John Grierson exhorted the documentarist to support was one of informed citizenship [. . .]. Other subjectivities are also possible [. . .], but all function as modes of engagement with representations of the historical world that can be readily extended beyond the moment of viewing into the social praxis itself.[73]

This is a key point: at a fundamental level, the documentary form is predicated on an assumed relationship between the viewer and what is represented on screen; that is, that both inhabit the same social reality. This makes the documentary a powerful tool of social integration: not only does it interpellate viewers into an assumed social relationship with what is represented on screen, but it also goes some way to produce and make real that which it represents. As a means of contributing to a nation like Wales – one which, in the twentieth century, lacked the instruments of self-determination – the documentary is evidently a potent format. Its *raison d'être* is to inform viewers of the social reality they inhabit, and it does so by constructing and reinforcing images and ideas of that reality: narratives of history, culture and society: the very stuff of nations.

The 'reality' impulse of the documentary form does make it vulnerable to certain kinds of criticism. Many critics point to its inherently dishonest nature, viewing it as perhaps an even more audacious construction of 'reality' than fiction. The latter, even in its more realistic modes, at least does not explicitly claim to be 'real'. A central strand of critical commentary on the documentary therefore views the form, as Corner notes, as 'nothing more than a sham – a fraud – which needs exposing'.[74] However, the approach I take is somewhat less antagonistic. While such commentators are right to be critical of the ways in which dominant social discourses are structured and disseminated, I want to suggest that it is the very act of 'claiming the real' that is precisely what makes the documentary form a fascinating and valuable historical resource. Here I agree with Peter Dahlgren's comments, which, while focusing on television as a medium, can be usefully applied to the documentary film:

> The point is we understand the phenomenon of television – like the public sphere with which it overlaps – as intricately interwoven into mutual reciprocity with an array of other political, economic and sociocultural fields. It is via such interplay that television [. . .] is made possible by, and makes possible, these other fields.[75]

Given that the documentary film on television is a directly and unapologetically referential cultural form that not only draws from dominant social discourses, but also inscribes them – is 'intricately interwoven into' them – it follows that these films are indispensable textual resources for those interested in the social and cultural history of Wales. I argue that the very existence of Ormond's body of films is a major resource for cultural scholarship in Wales, as well as film scholarship more generally, especially given that extant television films from this important period in television and film history are few and far between.[76]

The deeply symbolic nature of the ways in which documentaries – like all other forms of cultural signification – communicate to their audiences renders them extremely complex in their articulation of social meaning. As I have been emphasising, public spheres – of whatever inflection – are complex entities, always in dialogic tension with one another and with themselves, and often firmly at odds. This is especially the case in a 'multinational' polity such as Britain, which is uneasily constituted by a number of distinct regional and national communities, each with their own, often competing, attitudes and orientations. BBC Wales's situation – like that of any other of the BBC's 'regions' or 'national regions' – is in no way straightforward; indeed the term 'national region' alone signals BBC Wales's contradictory position within an overriding institution whose central priority is, by definition, the civic health of a unified British nation. Moreover, many of Ormond's films were broadcast on the British network wavelength, and reached homes all over Britain. This fact further complicates any conception of these films as straightforwardly or essentially 'Welsh'. In the chapters that follow, I will prioritise one facet of the televisual 'prism' in order to examine the ways in which these tensions play out textually in Ormond's films. These are films that sometimes gloss over matters of national difference, sometimes overstate it, and sometimes ignore it. Nevertheless, they are, I suggest, complexly encoded by the sociocultural and political circumstances that constituted the national public sphere(s) within which the BBC and BBC Wales were operating at this time, circumstances to which these documentary films in turn, and in equally complex ways, contributed. If they are 'Welsh' films, they are so in the sense that they made it possible for audiences to view Wales not as a region or, in Grierson's terms, an 'appendage', but as a given, an assumption, there on TV – whatever the discordances, contradictions and complexities.

That said, it is not the aim of this study to analyse Ormond's rich body of films in a way that reduces them to a set of bland civic-informational documents. Ormond was an inspired film-maker, and while it is important to read his work through the prism of their institutional, cultural and historical contexts, I want also to keep in focus Ormond's unique approach to the documentary form. Whatever the limiting pressures of working within an institution such as the BBC, Ormond consistently made the best use of the resources available to him, and his personal style – his sophisticated poeticism, his ironic playfulness, his generosity, his humanity, his craftsman-like attention to detail – is discernible in all the films he produced. This has contributed to the structure and focus of this book, which, I hope, attends to the multifaceted nature of Ormond's work.

Chapter 2 outlines in detail Ormond's own personal philosophical and creative vision, and the ways this informed the correspondence between his work in verse and on film. It examines his intellectual trajectory out of working-class, Nonconformist Dunvant, into a secular, specifically post-Nonconformist Swansea. There, as a student at the University College, under the guidance of the Wittgensteinian philosopher Rush Rhees, Ormond developed a profound (and, arguably, profoundly modernist) sense of doubt about the spiritual certainties that had guided his youth. I argue, alongside other critics, such as M. Wynn Thomas and Tony Brown,[77] that this manifested itself, in his poetry and some of his other writings, as an acute anxiety about the nature and notion of an absolute truth beyond the confines of human language. However, with particular focus on his ekphrastic poems, I suggest that this was not inevitably a source of despair. Rather, in poems that are imbued with a deep reverence for the skilled craftsmanship he believed to be crucial to all great art, Ormond channelled this anxiety into an alternative epistemology, one centred upon the redemptive qualities of art itself. His ekphrastic poems seek to immerse themselves in the epistemological worlds of their artist subjects in order to demonstrate to the reader the multiplicity of perspectives available to humanity. Pursuing this line of enquiry, the chapter shifts the focus on to Ormond's creative approach to documentary film-making. There I examine the ways in which Ormond's vision carried over into his conception of film as a creative medium, and further the sense in which this was, in fact, a philosophy that was extremely well suited to the demands of the post-war documentary film at the BBC. Indeed the documentary as a film form had, since its earliest conception under thinkers like John Grierson, carried within it a creative duality, one that emphasised the poetic possibilities of film montage along with – and as a core principle of – the impulse of public information. I argue that this made Ormond, who had at *Picture Post* learned the skills of a journalistic form of 'vertical montage' – of matching words with images – a candidate ideally suited to the demands of the form as it emerged on television. With this in mind, I embark on a primarily formalist analysis of a film that I feel best demonstrates the range of possibilities inherent in a film form that operates on a spectrum spanning the poetic and the expositional.

From here, chapters 3, 4 and 5 are organised in accordance with three broad national discursive categories. In this, they match the trio of categories that John Davies discovered in his examination of the development of Welsh radio programming in the post-war years. There he observed that radio feature programmes fell into three broad categories: 'Welsh history and topography, cultural developments in Wales and investigations into issues of current concern'.[78] This seems to have been the broad pattern in which Ormond's documentary films were conceived. The following chapters will thus examine respectively Ormond's 'culture documentaries', his 'history documentaries', and finally those that concern themselves with, broadly, 'issues of current concern' – the dominant theme of which, in Ormond's films, appears to have been the diversity of the Welsh people and the ethnic make-up of Wales in the 1960s and 1970s. That said, these themes are rarely mutually exclusive. As we will see, variegated threads of themes and ideas are woven through all of these films.

Chapter 3 is an examination of Ormond's treatment of Welsh culture on screen. Given Ormond's own status as an anglophone Welsh poet in this era, and indeed given, as outlined in chapter 2, the ekphrastic, intertextual nature of all of his creative work, this necessarily entails an interpretation of Ormond's own idiosyncratic approach to these films about fellow artists. However, as these films are also inescapably institutional texts, I combine this with an analysis of the ways in which Ormond's own ekphrastic approach to film-making was part of an attempt to mediate or, in Peter Lord's term, 'activate'[79] Welsh culture within a Welsh discursive context. This brings into view not only the struggles inherent in Wales's status as a minority nation existing under the umbrella of an overarching British nation state, but also the struggles internal to Wales, specifically the differing strategies of cultural 'activation' that marked Welsh cultural thought in the 1960s and 1970s. To this end, I split Ormond's cultural documentaries into two categories: visual art, and poetry. These two traditions developed along somewhat different lines in these years, though, as I suggest, there is nevertheless a good degree of equivalence in the ways in which they were activated at BBC Wales.

Chapter 4 charts Ormond's contribution to history programming on Welsh television. These documentaries were produced at a formative time in the history of Welsh historiography, and here I examine the ways in which such programming contributed to the important process of, like culture, 'activating' these developments within the Welsh public sphere. The activation and recirculation of historical narratives is a necessary function of any society, but is, as I emphasise, particularly pertinent in the context of a minority nation like Wales. As Bella Dicks has written, '[h]istory [. . .] is a central arena within which claims about the meaning of "Welshness" can be publicly aired, debated and contested'.[80] BBC Wales was thus a crucial way of 'airing' Welsh history, and, as I show, the documentary film was, and is, an important vehicle for doing so. However, the development of Welsh historiography in these years was dependent not only upon the establishment of the means of recirculating an accepted set of historical narratives, but also on negotiating and constructing those narratives – often for the first time – and frequently on contested ground. While on one hand a means of communicating historiographical ideas and debates, Ormond's history documentaries are also important primary sources of the ways in which broadcasting in Wales has been required to negotiate deep and often irreconcilable ideological divides.

Finally, chapter 5 centres on the representation of ethnicity on Welsh television, specifically on Ormond's films as examples of the ways in which Welsh television interacts with 'other' ethnicities within and outside the borders of Wales. Ormond's films were produced in line with broader trends in humanist journalism and mainstream broadcasting in the post-war years. These were trends that resulted in increasingly wider portions of society represented in the media, and were themselves the product of developments in an increasingly diverse British society. I suggest that, in the context of Welsh broadcasting, these developments opened up a space within which Ormond was able to produce films that, while often questionably relativising and even excluding ethnic minorities from symbolic participation in civic Wales, nevertheless constituted a means of defining the borders of a Welsh public sphere.

Welsh film and TV producer Wil Aaron noted in an essay published in the late 1970s that, owing to a variety of (mostly financial) constraints, the flame of Welsh film in the decades after the 1950s was held virtually singlehandedly by television. It was television that screened some of the best work in the medium, and that fostered some of the most accomplished directors in Wales at that time. Ormond was undoubtedly one of these, but others, such as his colleagues at BBC Wales, as well as those working for independent television – Jack Howells, Terry de Lacey and Aled Vaughan, for example – also deserve further attention. Aaron goes on to suggest that the dominance of television in that era was both a boon and a bane to younger film-makers seeking to enter the industry in the late 1970s. 'Whichever way we turn', said Aaron, 'television has usually been there before us, explored all the avenues, sign-posted the cul-de-sacs and floodlit the main roads.'[81] Thankfully, film-making in Wales has marked out new territory in the decades since Aaron wrote that piece. But the fact remains that in leaving those decades behind, the lights on those older roads are dimming, the maps fading. At the risk of belabouring the metaphor, I view this book as part of the effort to relight those lamps, to retrace those maps. I do so with the conviction that these areas of exploration in Welsh television film-making constituted prominent contours on the complex cultural and social landscape of Wales in this era. These films should thus be viewed not only as products of a single creative mind, or as mere manifestations of an institutional agenda, but in a broader sense as contributions to what Raymond Williams described as the 'distinguishing shapes' that 'give us our senses of our lives'.[82]

2

'ORMOND, YOU'RE A POET!': POETRY AND THE PERSONAL DOCUMENTARY

In 1970, roughly halfway through his career as a film-maker, Ormond produced a series at BBC Wales called *Private View*. This consisted of short films on figures associated with the arts in Wales, from writers like Leslie Norris and Dannie Abse, to visual artists such as Kyffin Williams. Given its theme, the series had rich visual potential, and some of the films are stylistically appealing – the episode on Leslie Norris contains lyrical shots of the area around the writer's home in west Sussex. Yet one of the episodes is, in terms of style, decidedly uninspiring. In fact, the film can be described as conspicuously shoddy in its production values; running for around fifteen minutes, it consists of an interview taking place in what appears to be a sparsely furnished and untidy BBC office – probably Ormond's own, if the photograph of Alun Lewis pinned to the wall is anything to go by.[1] Ormond asks a few questions; the interviewee answers them. It could be overlooked as entirely unremarkable archive fodder were the person being interviewed not John Grierson, and were he and Ormond not discussing the importance of the creative impulse within the documentary film form.

What becomes clear is that this film's stylistic plainness is calculated to amplify the stridency of Grierson's pronouncements. The Scotsman is characteristically pontificating on these matters, arguing forcefully for the importance of the creative, aesthetic dimension in documentary film-making: 'you must never forget the poet. You must never forget the poetic processes, because there is no revelation, finally, without a gesture to the poetic nature of revelation.'[2] Ormond was, of course, not someone who needed to be informed of this; he had been a poet since his university days, and had been producing poetic documentaries since the late 1950s. But there were, evidently, others within the industry who needed to be reminded. By the end of 1960s the culture and context of broadcasting had shifted profoundly, with the result that the BBC was being rationalised in new ways. The Reithian ethos of paternalist public service that had firmly underpinned the BBC's activities was being dismantled in response to a new consumer-driven society, and in 1968 the BBC brought in a management consultancy to streamline management and spending. One of the results was a more regimented attitude towards documentary film-making.[3] This was, naturally, anathema to film-makers like Ormond, who had spent years perfecting their craft, enjoying virtually carte blanche creative freedom. Viewed within the context of this discontent, the emphatic drabness of this interview with the 'godfather' of documentary can be interpreted as an ironic barb aimed at an increasingly philistine BBC management.

It was unlikely Ormond found it difficult to convince Grierson to speak out on behalf of this cause. He had long been an acquaintance of the outspoken Scotsman,[4] who, upon viewing his landmark 1960 film *Borrowed Pasture*, is said to have exclaimed 'Ormond, you're a poet!'[5] This was high and apt praise. Though the term 'documentary' has connotations that, given its etymological root, touch strongly upon notions of truth and fact, the evidentiary and the authentic, Ormond's work in the form is proof that the documentary film is far better understood when perceived in terms of creativity, style and the imagination. Ormond himself wrote of the form in a language that emphasised the importance of its poetic dimension:

> All true documentary has to have an element of revelation [. . .]; of a complex circumstance revealed in a simple and understandable form; of people and things in a seemingly ordinary, workaday world poetically revealed, inductive rather than deductive at heart, moving from particular observation to general, universal conclusion.[6]

Such pronouncements were not at all exceptional at the time. Grierson had as early as the 1920s defined the documentary as the 'creative treatment of actuality', and innumerable commentators and film-makers have since expounded on the 'poetic', 'revelatory' element essential to documentary film-making. In the 1970s it was perfectly possible to talk of television producers of the time as 'visual poets'. In

1975, BBC producer Norman Swallow described Ormond and others like him as being engaged in the work of projecting 'a vision of the world as personal and as intense as the creations of the most serious poet or painter, novelist or dramatist'.[7] However, what is exceptional about Ormond is the fact that he was, at the same time as a BBC film-maker, also a 'serious' poet. Read alongside each other, his work in verse and on screen reveal themselves to be closely intertwined.

POSSIBLE BUILDINGS

As a poet, Ormond is often associated with those writers who came to be known as the 'Second Flowering' of anglophone writing in Wales.[8] The term 'Second Flowering' stems from a 1967 editorial in *Poetry Wales*, in which Meic Stephens, then editor, made a distinction between an earlier grouping of Welsh writers in the English language – writers of the 1930s and 1940s such as Dylan Thomas, Alun Lewis and Lynette Roberts – broadly, those who published in Keidrych Rhys's magazine *Wales* – and the new poets of the 1960s. The earlier generation, Stephens argued, had often been required to orientate their life and work outside Wales, resulting in a poetry that was, for him, distractedly universalist in theme and form. The 'Second Flowering', however, were beneficiaries of a new situation in which Wales could support white-collar careers at quasi-national institutions such as the newly created Welsh Office, the Welsh Arts Council and, of course, BBC Wales. As Tony Conran later observed, where the earlier generation had been required to 'capture the attention of the English poetry-reading public and the London market',[9] the poets of the 1960s were blessed with a new situation: 'no one had to move to London now'.[10] Stephens's *Poetry Wales* was an important outlet for these poets, and the editor encouraged them to reorientate anglophone Welsh poetry around specifically Welsh topics: 'Welsh scenes, Welsh people, the Welsh past, life in contemporary Wales, or his [sic] own analysis of all these'.[11]

Ormond had famously been struck by a burst of inspiration in the early 1960s that 'broke the blockage that had kept [him] virtually silent for too many years'.[12] The resulting collections, *Requiem and Celebration* (1969) and *Definition of a Waterfall* (1973) coincided with developments taking place around the Second Flowering; indeed, many of the poems in both collections had appeared in *Poetry Wales* beforehand. But while he wrote many important poems about Wales, particularly about his upbringing in Dunvant, Ormond did not fit neatly into what some called the 'Anglo-Welsh' scene. His first published collection of poetry, *Indications*, a collaboration with John Bayliss and James Kirkup, had appeared much earlier, in 1943, and was, like much poetry of the 1940s, a rather pungent, Dylanesque outpouring. Ormond was indeed a friend of Thomas, as well as of other poets of the 'First Flowering', and himself published in *Wales*. Therefore, as Tony Conran has suggested, Ormond's sensibilities and affiliations are perhaps best understood to be split across the First and Second Flowerings.[13] In particular, Ormond sat uneasily with the more overtly political-national convictions of some adherents of the second phase. This is not to say he sat uneasily with these poets in the pub – he was a close friend of the outspoken nationalist poet John Tripp. Yet, as he noted in his introduction to the latter's *Selected Poems*, on the national question, the two took a 'different view of things'.[14] (Tripp's own view was that Ormond was a 'twittering optimist'.[15]) Ormond was certainly passionate about the culture of Wales, as is clear in the creative energy invested in his films about Wales and Welsh life, but he was no supporter of political nationalism. James A. Davies has usefully described Ormond as a poet of 'detached attachment'.[16] Perhaps Ormond himself explains this best:

> In what way is my work Welsh at all? [My work as a film-maker has] contributed to a broadening of my experience of my country. But when it comes to my poems I have to give a different account of myself. What I ask of my poems is that, first and foremost, it should be a good poem in the English language, that is to say my use of the English language. If there is a further element of Welshness in a poem, I know that it will look after itself.[17]

Ormond's primary concern was, then, not with the politics of culture, but with artistic craft as an expression of the human experience.

The approach to creativity that underpins Ormond's practice in both poetry and film can be traced back to a decisive time early in his artistic career. The shoots of his early artistic inclinations were encouraged by glimpses of experiences outside the Nonconformist world-view in which he had grown up in Dunvant: visits to the 'Tiv' cinema in nearby Gowerton, the Glynn Vivian Art Gallery in Swansea, fleeting brushes with a rebelliously long-haired Ceri Richards. However, it was not until Ormond's time at university that he experienced the total upheaval that provided the ground for his later development. The decisive stage came with his encounter with a certain modern articulation of philosophical doubt, provided him by Rush Rhees. Rhees was a close friend of Ludwig Wittgenstein, and the work of the German philosopher profoundly informed Rhees's own teaching and writing. Ormond later wrote that Rhees encouraged him, in Wittgenstein's mode, to question his every assumption: '[at university] my distrust of the easy – even moderately easy answer to any question grew sharper [. . .] as I caught something of Rhees's approach to ideas and the world. [. . .] Was there any final truth?'[18] For the young Ormond, whose philosophical world had until this time been bounded by Nonconformist horizons, this question was to prove disruptive, not least because the Wittgensteinian answer to it was to turn the very notion of the search for 'truth' on its head.

Wittgenstein famously contended that questions of absolute truth are, themselves, misleading to the point of fallacy. Such questions are, he argued, mere functions of language itself, which tricks us into believing the possibility of somehow perceiving true reality. Language is, rather, a web of 'grammatical fictions'[19] that misleadingly imply that fundamental truth-seeking questions – 'what is reality?' or 'what is time?' – can be meaningfully answered. 'We never arrive at fundamental propositions in the course of our investigation', wrote Wittgenstein, 'we get to the boundary of language which stops us from asking further questions. We don't get to the bottom of things, but reach a point where we can go no further, where we cannot ask further questions.'[20] This is an idea that manifests itself throughout Ormond's creative output.[21] It is articulated fairly explicitly, for example, in Ormond's poem 'Saying'. Here, the sense of imprisonment implied in Wittgenstein's thinking is sustained through a metaphor that figures language as a 'jail' in which 'we lie/ Prisoners', and in which communication with any form of enduring truth is, ultimately, futile:

> We tap on the jail's
> Waterpipes, signal through stone
> And wait for the vague answer.
>
> (*CP*, 185)

This despondency is perhaps to be expected in a poem that seems to find itself at a philosophical dead-end. If it is, in the end, possible only to 'reach a point where we can go no further', any quest for a fully meaningful grasp of 'reality' is destined to be a fruitless one, not only because of the imprisoning epistemological walls that language builds around us, but also because beyond these walls there is no comprehensible reality, no absolute truth. We can only know what the human imagination is capable of knowing, and that is, at the very most, its own boundaries – the very walls that language builds. Those who follow Wittgenstein will, then, have to be content with the partial truth that *full* truth is, finally, unknowable.

This is not to say that Wittgenstein's work is dominated by a sense of despondency, and, as any reader of the poetry will attest, neither is Ormond's. While any quest for absolute truth is destined to failure, this is not to say we are denied the ability to conjure a liberating multiplicity of creative responses and interpretations in and of the journey. While language has its limits, there are always multiple creative ways of seeing the world to explore *within* language – and across languages. Wittgenstein famously explained this with the figure of a building: 'I am not interested in constructing a building', he says, 'so much as in having a perspicuous view of the foundations of possible buildings.'[22] He was therefore dismissive of the process of perpetually reformulating and refining an ever more complex single structure of understanding, such as philosophical discourse itself. Rather, Wittgenstein looks optimistically to the imaginative possibilities of finding and utilising multiple discourses, multiple forms and structures of comprehension, in order, at least, to find solace in the possibilities of the imagination.

This is another of Wittgenstein's ideas that finds expression in Ormond's poetry. Ormond's well-known 'Definition of a Waterfall' for instance, is a gushing, triumphant testament to the imaginative possibilities engendered by the mind's attempt to grasp a multiplicity of definitions of an essentially unknowable phenomenon:

> Not stitched to air or water but to both
> A veil hangs broken in concealing truth
>
> And flies in vague exactitude, a dove
> Born diving between rivers out of love
> (*CP*, 163)

The poem continues in this way, gathering pace and accumulating conceits until the accumulation *is* the conceit, and in doing so enacts an effusive affirmation of the imagination. It does this in spite of the speaker coming up against the games that language plays, its 'grammatical fictions' ('vague exactitude') and its perpetual semantic flux (does the veil 'conceal' truth, or is its truth a 'concealing' one?). Finally, performing a climactic release from the iambic pulse of the preceding couplets, 'Definition of a Waterfall' breaks off with an affirmation unhindered by finalising punctuation:

> So that this bridegroom and his bride in white
> Parting together headlong reunite
>
> Among her trailing braids. The inconstancy
> Is reconciled to fall, falls and falls free
>
> (*CP*, 163)

The poem's acceptance and affirmation of 'inconstancy' therefore constitutes an act of faith in the unknowable. It revels in the potentialities of the imagination, finding sublime confidence in the face of what can never be fully known.

These Wittgensteinian ideas, and the new, anti-transcendent epistemology they offered, seem, paradoxically, to have constituted a compensatory philosophy for a post-Nonconformist Ormond. Terry Eagleton has noted this hidden potentiality in Wittgenstein's thought:

> Posed at the extreme edge as it is, it threatens [. . .] to leave everything exactly as it was. To affirm that because of the nature of [language] no analysis can be exhaustible, no interpretation ultimately grounded, valuably demystifies the metaphysical but is [. . .] quite compatible with talk of 'truth', 'certainty', 'determinacy' and so on.[23]

The loss of the possibility of final truth is, in practice, replaced in Wittgenstein's thought by a new affirmation of the realm of the imagination. Eagleton concludes that Wittgenstein's thought, in this sense, constitutes 'a negative metaphysic',[24] a new certainty in uncertainty. Certainly, Ormond was finding some compensation in art in a world in which, as he put it, 'there was plenty to be agnostic about'.[25] As Robert Minhinnick has noted, Ormond's philosophy was one in which 'absence of faith [. . .] itself becomes a kind of belief'.[26]

'IN PLACE OF EMPTY HEAVEN'

Ormond's outlook was undoubtedly informed by these new strains of philosophical thought. However, it is important not to fall into the trap that Frank Kermode had argued many critics of another eternally ruminative poet, Wallace Stevens, fall into. This is the trap of treating the poet 'as a philosopher who expresses his thought in such a way that commentators' duty is to extract it as best they can from the verse in which he chose to write it'.[27] While Ormond, as a poet, could be intensely ruminative, his creative convictions were very different from those of a philosopher. Ormond's primary preoccupation was with the artefact, the finished art object, rather than with philosophical rumination for its own sake.

Comparison with Stevens's poetry is useful.[28] Ormond once delivered a lecture on the American poet that reveals as much about his own views on these issues as those of his subject. 'In Place of Empty Heaven: The Poetry of Wallace Stevens' shows that Ormond viewed himself as someone close to Stevens in his creative preoccupations. This is unsurprising, given Stevens's sense of the high status of art as an essentially compensatory practice in a lacklustre and basically meaningless world. Ormond too was acutely aware that finding substantive meaning in the world was predicated on, and could only be perceived through, the crafted artefact. This meant carrying through the implications of Wittgenstein's pronouncement that philosophy should seek to identify the 'foundations of possible buildings'. According to Stevens, it is artists who should be revered as the creators of these new structures of understanding. His own quasi-religious term for the primacy of the material art object as a site of philosophical and existential compensation was the idea of art as the 'supreme fiction'.

Ormond certainly shared elements of this view. However, his own interpretation of Stevens's outlook contained an important proviso:

> Stevens is nearer the spiritual role he assigned to the poet [. . .] when he is working towards his 'supreme fiction' which will be the thing made; the fictor, the modeller as artist justifying man's belief in himself not only as the inventor and destroyer of gods but, in a finally unaccountable universe, the arbiter of what is. And the tool for all this is the imagination. The imagination makes the truth.[29]

What is striking here is the egalitarian character of Ormond's convictions. The terms upon which he feels artists should provide a new epistemology for humanity do not position the artist hierarchically, prophesying a way of seeing from above, but rather on the same level as humanity, 'justifying man's belief in himself'. In other words, the artist furnishes humanity with the objects through with which it is empowered to see for itself. An interesting line of correspondence can be drawn from here back to Ormond's upbringing in Dunvant, particularly his family's attendance at the local Welsh Congregationalist chapel, Ebenezer. As M. Wynn Thomas writes of the Congregationalists' model of organisation,

> [i]ts members, gathered together by a common impulse of faith, worshipping without benefit of priest, image or ritual, prayerfully concentrating on the reading and interpretation of Scripture, held their 'congregation' to be an 'independent', self-sufficient unit. They would owe no authority to any larger, centralised structure or body.[30]

While Ormond was certainly interested in 'image[s]', there are undoubtedly resonances of the Congregationalists' self-sufficient, anti-hierarchical approach to spirituality in his conception of the role of art. This was in sharp distinction to Stevens's elitist elevation of artists in the 'age of disbelief' to almost prophetic 'figures of importance'.[31] Ormond's dismissal of such a view as merely the 'high-minded wind of a braggadocio'[32] is telling. While Ormond was fascinated by the liberating epistemological potential of Stevens's ideas, his egalitarianism compelled him to translate them into a more down-to-earth, socialistic idiom. Hence the existence of a discourse of workmanship, of craftsmanship: 'The *tool* for all this is the imagination' (my emphasis). And elsewhere: 'poetry has a job on; and we must see what equipment Wallace Stevens has to accomplish the task'.[33]

This tendency to exalt the material, physical human craft of even the loftiest of creations in a plain-speaking idiom is consistent throughout Ormond's work. The best-known example of this is, rightly, his brilliantly bathetic 'Cathedral Builders', a poem that concerns itself with the invariably forgotten lives of those who labour to build these magnificent structures. Ormond describes the quaintly shambolic lives of men who 'climbed on sketchy ladders', '[i]nhabited sky with hammers', 'lay with their smelly wives', before getting rheumatism and '[deciding] it was time to give it up'. It is through this earthy humour that Ormond accentuates the profound seriousness of the task they perform. It is, after all, the workers alone who are able to stand aside on the day of consecration, '[cock] up a squint eye' and have the final word: "'I bloody did that!'" (*CP*, 28).

'Cathedral Builders' was written while the poet was in his forties,[34] but it is possible to see this strain of thinking even in some of Ormond's earliest professional work, as a staff writer for *Picture Post*. In a feature published in May 1947, 'A Bronze for the Academy', Ormond examined the process of transforming a clay sculpture into bronze for the Royal Academy. The article is not, as we might expect, a slavish celebration of the work of this elite institution, or, indeed, of the exalted art of sculpture, but a salute to the painstaking labour of the bronze-casters that goes on unheeded beneath the gallery floor. Large photographs of the casters at work dominate the page, along with a detailed step-by-step description of their process. Credit is given where due: the process is one 'which calls for skill and craftsmanship only acquired by years of experience in an art foundry'.[35] Moreover, 'the sculptor [. . .] is at the mercies of the metal-caster to complete his work'.[36] The article comments on the skewed values of a society that offers little or no recognition of this kind of craftsmanship, particularly in the context of a financially driven art market: '[a]fter exhibition in London, "The Lady of Peace" will go to a private garden in Kent, where she will sit in all weathers looking at her child with the same intransient smile, outcome of a skill and a tradition which time has left untouched.'[37]

This lifelong celebration of craftsmanship had earlier origins in Ormond's upbringing as the son of a village shoemaker who took painstaking pride in his craft.[38] M. Wynn Thomas has noted that the village of Dunvant, lying on the western outskirts of the south Wales coalfield, was 'less proletarianized than, say, the townships of Rhondda', meaning that '[t]he older concept of the artisan still had validity in a community that retained aspects of rural society, and which readily respected the skills involved in the industrial process'.[39] Ormond absorbed these values and greatly admired the artisanship of his father's trade, as is clear in the poem 'At his Father's Grave', in which his father's skill is revered in such terms: '[r]emember his two hands, his laugh,/ His craftsmanship. They are his epitaph' (*CP*, 103). These succinct lines are the apt finale to a poem of few words; the value of his father's craft speaks for itself. However, this is not to say that Ormond celebrated craftsmanship for its own sake. Returning to 'Cathedral Builders', while this poem's defining quality resides in its deflationary impulse, its effort to prick the pomp of the cathedral and its illustrious inhabitants with a single exclamation, it is simultaneously concerned with emphasising the symbolic significance of such a human achievement. The humour of the final exclamation is predicated on the enormous gulf between the builder's perspective and the implied – and uncontested – magnificence of the cathedral itself: what it symbolises, as well as its obvious physical impressiveness. Moreover, we should not forget that this is, after all, a poem. This is a form that carried for Ormond, as with all other arts, a significance that reached far beyond the materiality of its craftsmanship. In the post-Nonconformist world Ormond inhabited, art possessed a quasi-spiritual significance, the means through which humanity could navigate the uncertainty of existence. As Patrick McGuinness has noted, Ormond was consistently interested in the 'ways in which we fill our emptiness with art'.[40] Importantly, Ormond chose to be an artist, not a shoemaker, a builder, or even an architect, which he held hopes for at one time.[41] As M. Wynn Thomas suggests, this tension between the egalitarian celebration of material craft – the belief in 'a democratic art that was the finest expression of collective social life' – and a refined aesthetic sensibility that 'sternly [upheld] the highest artistic standards' was one that sustained Ormond's work and 'powered much of his art'.[42] It is therefore instructive to view these dual concerns as constituting the warp and woof of Ormond's concerns as an artist. It is through the interweaving of these threads that the texture of Ormond's wider poetic and filmic practice came into being.

THE 'ORGANIC MOSAIC'

Some of the productive tensions that resulted from this interweaving of discourses came to the surface in a statement Ormond made on his process of writing poetry:

[I]t starts in a sensual delight in building, out of words, shapes to be spoken. There was a time when I found the manipulation of words and cadences to be an almost completely intoxicating activity. Now the music – by which I mean the sound and rhythm – and the meaning must satisfy me as being, as far as I am able to make them so, one thing [. . .] [W]hen a poem of mine lacks a sensual texture, especially a sense of the tactile, it is far less likely to succeed.[43]

While there is here the presence of the egalitarian discourse of craftsmanship, of 'building', 'mak[ing]' and 'manipulation', that undoubtedly underpins Ormond's conception of the 'tactile' art object, there is a related emphasis on the harmonious arrangement of form and meaning that must exist to complete the finished object. This is a conception that affords the craftsmanship of the artist an axiological significance that far outweighs that of the skilled labourer. For Ormond, the success or failure of his poetry rests upon the question of whether he practises his craft well enough to offer humanity a compensatory epistemology. Ormond was therefore driven by the impulse to combine his artisanal heritage with the exalted appreciation of culture that he acquired at university. While revealing the mutual reciprocity of an egalitarian conception of craftsmanship and the higher epistemological service he felt art could offer humanity, his remarks here therefore also signal a further aspect of the ways in which he felt art could offer this service. As his deployment of the language of music and the visual arts implies – 'music', 'rhythm', 'shape', 'texture' – Ormond's deep concern with the epistemological possibilities of art gave rise to an interest in what has been termed 'ekphrasis' or, in other words, the relationships between various artistic media.

Ormond was an artist working across more than one medium. The themes and formal strategies he adopted in both poetry and film frequently overlapped and informed one another. There is evidence of ekphrasis and ekphrastic thinking everywhere in Ormond's creative output. In his posthumously published book with Gregynog Press, *Cathedral Builders and Other Poems* (1991), for instance, many of the poems are accompanied with his own small pen and ink sketches.[44] He once said, 'I believe a book of poems is like an exhibition of pictures, you put in things which hang together and bounce off one another even if they are separated in time.'[45] Ekphrasis was at the heart of much of his work as an artist, offering him an approach to creativity that allowed him to make productive his Wittgensteinian sense of doubt. Commentators generally agree that the notion of ekphrasis is closely connected to one's conception of the nature of reality, in particular the relationship between representation and reality.[46] For Wittgenstein, the absence of a fully knowable reality resulted in a belief in the imagination and its products as the only possible points of mediation between the self and the unknowable. As Ormond's outlook had initially been problematised by the ideas of Wittgenstein and Rush Rhees, it is useful to read his own relationship to ekphrasis in Wittgensteinian terms. Besides his awareness of the limits of language, of reaching, as Wittgenstein puts it, 'a point where we can go no further, where we cannot ask further questions', Ormond also saw there was nothing to stop artists celebrating the epistemological potential of all other media – be these visual, musical, linguistic or, of course, filmic. While none of these are ever able to access an essential 'reality' – as Rush Rhees wrote, '[a] work of art shows me itself [. . .] [I]t does not show me something which might be shown in another way'[47] – poems, films, compositions, and the interactions between them nevertheless constitute the multiplicity of 'possible buildings', of possible structures of understanding.

Ormond had his own way of figuring this notion of an ungraspable world mediated and made sense of by the plethora of possible imaginative responses to it. This was his notion of the 'organic mosaic'.[48] This phrase is key to understanding Ormond's overarching conception of culture and creativity. In a conversation with the critic Richard Poole, Ormond claimed that 'from acute observation of particularities, you build up a kind of organic mosaic – if you can mix two such conceptions'.[49] Though the phrase may appear oxymoronic, taking into account Ormond's post-Nonconformist desire for a conciliatory epistemology – a 'negative metaphysic' – it seems to contain a kind of inverted logic. Ormond uses it here in relation to the creation of a single piece of art (he elsewhere referred to filmmaking as 'making [his] mosaic'[50]), but I believe the phrase can be applied in a wider sense to Ormond's conception of the ways in which the particularities of individual artworks and artistic visions can be conceived as parts of – tiles or tesserae – within a wider conceptual matrix or patchwork – each of which corresponds and contributes to a plural yet unifying, compensatory epistemology.

On one level, Ormond's concern with these matters led him to a sustained interest in other artists and artistic visions in his poetry. This manifested itself in a key theme woven throughout his work: that of 'celebration'. A significant number of Ormond's poems enact a celebration of other artists: from the early poems 'Collier',[51] based on an Evan Walters painting, 'Elegy for Alun Lewis' and 'Homage to a Folk-Singer', on the Gower folk singer Phil Tanner,[52] to the later work published after he returned to poetry in earnest in the late 1960s,

'Certain Questions for Monsieur Renoir', 'Michelangelo to Himself, 1550' and 'Memorandum to the Dissector [Ron] Berry',[53] to name only a few obvious examples. Indeed, consistent with his preoccupation with the theme of 'requiem' as well as 'celebration', Ormond had considered the idea of working on a series of 'Letters to the Dead',[54] whose recipients would have been artists such as Louis MacNeice, Vernon Watkins, Dylan Thomas, Gwyn Thomas and B. S. Johnson, among others. All of these can be considered as in some sense 'interartistic' in their celebration of other artists and their work. But the important additional dimension to such work is Ormond's consistent effort not only to reference other artists but to 'celebrate', in the more generative sense of incorporating the formal and thematic characteristics of their work into his own.

One way to conceive this is to draw a distinction between 'interartistic' and 'ekphrastic' works of art. Where 'interartistic' works of art are concerned with the epistemological possibilities of other forms artistic representation, 'ekphrasis' does also, but goes further and attempts, in one critic's terms, the 'verbalization, quotation, or dramatization of real or fictitious texts composed in another sign system'.[55] One of the better-known examples of Ormond's works of ekphrasis is his 'Certain Questions for Monsieur Renoir', an exposition of *La Parisienne*, the great impressionist work that hangs in the National Museum of Wales in Cardiff. The poem vividly conveys the rich depth of colour explored in Renoir's famous painting with its own verbal exploration of the palette of linguistic connotation:

> The dress of La Parisienne
> (Humanly on the verge of the ceramic),
> Blue of Delft, dream summary of blues,
> Centre-piece of a fateful exhibition;
> [. . .]
> Ultramarine, deep-water blue?
> Part of a pain and darkness never felt?
> Assyrian crystal? Clouded blue malachite?
> *Blue of a blue dawn trusting light.*
>
> (*CP*, 202)

'Certain Questions for Monsieur Renoir' is not an attempt to find a poetic vocabulary in order merely to describe the artist's vision, or even the poet's aesthetic response to it. Like 'Definitions of a Waterfall', the aim is not to lock its subject into a refined, final verbal definition, but to revel in its endless imaginative possibilities. Ormond matches Renoir's flaunting of a beguiling multitude of shades of blue by revelling in the linguistic play of the infinite potential linguistic connotations of the colour. The poem flirts with a plethora of discourses, none of which is afforded final authority: artistic ('centre-piece of a fateful exhibition'), historical ('Blue on a Roman bead'), geological ('malachite'), chemical ('mercury's blue ointment'). In doing so it enacts an ekphrastic performance of the painting in a way that confirms the combined validity of all ways of seeing. It celebrates the vast interconnectedness of human discourses that inform one another in constituting the 'organic mosaic'.

Numerous commentators have registered this. Dannie Abse argues that Ormond should be understood as a 'portraitist'.[56] M. Wynn Thomas has stated that Ormond the film-maker 'unfailingly places himself at the service of each artist's vision'.[57] Moreover, in a similar but more critical vein, David Berry suggests that Ormond is occasionally 'too deferential'.[58] All of these comments are perceptive, recognising as they do something of the ekphrastic nature of Ormond's work in poetry and on film.[59] But I argue that there is a further significance to this key tendency in Ormond's work. The impulse behind all these 'deferential' works of 'portraiture' is not only to explore the imaginative possibilities of other ways of seeing. While on one level it is precisely this: the performance of a philosophical ideal, the notion of art as a compensatory epistemology in an unknowable world. But there is a further element at play. All these ekphrastic works in poetry and on film can be viewed as related efforts to place a wider philosophy in the frame: to construct an 'organic mosaic' that displays to readers and viewers the compensatory gifts bestowed by art. As one critic suggests, the 'inclination to match the visual with the verbal' in ekphrastic art 'has something in common with the first impulse of art criticism to describe its object. The division between the rhetoric of art criticism and the poetry of ekphrasis is only a matter of degree.' In this respect, Ormond's works of 'celebration' can be understood to embody a Reithian impulse to share, to educate, to inform.[60] This clearly corresponds with the creative impulse central to the documentary form, as described by John Grierson in his interview with Ormond: 'you must never forget the poet. You must never forget the poetic processes, because there is no revelation, finally, without a gesture to the poetic nature of revelation.'

PERSONAL DOCUMENTARY

Despite Grierson's pronouncement on these matters, the creative, poetic element of documentary film-making has often been overlooked. John Corner has highlighted what he views as the problem of media critics overlooking the formal and creative aspects of documentary films – those aspects that fall broadly within what he terms the 'category of the aesthetic' – in favour of sociological, political and audience-centred approaches. As he puts it:

> [d]etailed attention to the 'art properties' of television has been seen to waste investigative time that might more valuably be spent on questions of institution, practice, thematic content and consumption, on the framing political and cultural economies and processes within which programmes are produced and circulated.[61]

Of course, this tendency can also partly be attributed to the fact that, as Corner concedes, 'a good deal of non-fictional television is not particularly interested in offering itself as an aesthetic experience anyway'. Nevertheless, there are innumerable documentary films and television programmes that do take the form of 'overt textual display and performance' and that therefore 'reward repeat viewings in a way that finally has little to do with the extractable knowledge they convey'.[62] Corner has elsewhere written usefully on this score:

> [A] 'good' documentary must always, by definition, have the primary aim of directing its viewers down its *referential* axis towards 'real world' concerns. Yet [. . .] there is an *aesthetic* axis too – a documentary 'poetics'. This does not merely comprise a set of presentational skills; it is centrally implicated in the production of the referential.[63]

It is useful to view the documentary film as a form that keeps in balance two distinct poles or axes: the 'referential' – i.e. the real-world issues to which it refers – and the 'aesthetic' – the creative formal strategies it employs in conveying that information.

On the aesthetic axis, the documentary as a cultural form has a long history of emphasis on poeticism and experimentation. So much so that the experiments with the new technology of the film camera that took place outside of the burgeoning feature film industry in the first few decades of the twentieth century have prompted some critics to adopt the less loaded term 'non-fiction film'.[64] The work of film-makers in Europe, in particular, was driven by the creative impulses of modernism, and can be viewed as part of the wider cultural search for new forms and means of artistic expression and understanding that define that movement. Occasionally, the crossovers were quite real; the celebrated surrealist film *Un Chien Andalou* (1929), for instance, was a collaboration between Spanish film-maker Luis Bunuel and Salvador Dalí.[65] In general this was a time of broad intellectual and creative exchange across the arts that resulted in an essentially imaginative, experimental approach to 'non-fiction' film-making. Nevertheless, by the 1930s this aesthetic axis was beginning to be balanced against a more clearly defined social purpose – in Corner's terms, 'real world' concerns. It was of course John Grierson who almost singlehand-edly gave shape to the nebulous non-fiction film in Britain, but as we have seen, his conception of the form always contained within it a poetic dimension. This was largely a result of his admiration of the pioneering film-makers of the 1910s and 1920s, Sergei Eisenstein and Dziga Vertov in the Soviet Union, and Robert Flaherty in the United States. Grierson's arguments in favour of a creative approach to public information film-making were to have long-lasting effects at the film units formed in the 1930s and 1940s at the Empire Marketing Board, the General Post Office and the Ministry of Information (now grouped as the British Documentary Movement), and his work pro-vided the conditions in which film-makers such as Basil Wright, Alberto Cavalcanti, Len Lye and Humphrey Jennings could explore the creative possibilities of the documentary form.[66] Their legacy was continued in the post-war years in commercial film companies,[67] in the work of Karel Reisz and Lindsay Anderson within 'Free Cinema' and, of course, in the burgeoning medium of television.

The era of television film-making in which Ormond was active can be characterised as one heavily informed by the Griersonian definition of the documentary. While there would later emerge in cinema and television several other key 'modes' of documentary film-making, particularly under the influence of *cinéma-vérité*, this was still an era in which the key mode was one which kept in bal-ance two key elements: the 'referential' and the 'aesthetic'. As Jamie Sexton notes, despite the changes that were to come with the advent of new lightweight cameras and sound equipment, there was in the early days of television a sense among documentary producers that 'the improvisational nature of event capture and shaky camera work' was a 'form of amateurism [. . .] rather than an attempt to institute a new form of televisual aesthetics'. The mode that emerged was closer to a Griersonian idea that documentary film-making should be a 'merging of social reportage *and* creative expression' (my emphasis).[68] And although, as we shall see in Ormond's work, different films would balance these two modes in different ways, the dominant form was one that accommodated both. At that time, it was deemed to be the auteurial producer-director who had overall control over these. Indeed, Norman Swallow's definition of the 'personal documentary' was one which is

> very much the individual work of its producer and/or director and which, through its imaginative handling of reality, expresses his own attitude not only to the programme's immediate subject-matter but to the whole of the world in which he lives. It is in programmes of this sort that factual television has come closest to making works of art.[69]

As Swallow attests, 'personal documentaries' were 'created to a large extent by one man in isolation, forged and modified minute by minute, depending entirely on his own skill in extracting what is finest and most relevant from the corner of life which he has chosen'.[70] Tellingly, Ormond recalled being 'blessed by non-interference'[71] during the 1960s.[72]

A HEIGHTENED SENSE OF SEEING AND LOOKING AND GAZING

Ormond was practising documentary film-making on television at a time when it was possible to refer to the practice in just these terms: as not only an informational tool but also a form of poetry, an art. What is perhaps surprising is that he was trusted to do so given that, at the time of his employment at BBC Wales, his film-making experience was precisely zero. Ormond had not received the kind of practical apprenticeship in documentary film-making of others of his era. For instance, two of his contemporaries, the Welsh documentary-makers Paul Dickson and Jack Howells,[73] started their careers within the British Documentary Movement. Dickson received initial training as a cameraman in the Army Kinematograph Corps, and went on soon after to work under two of the biggest names in documentary film production: first, Basil Wright at the Crown Film Unit, and later Paul Rotha at his independent company, World Wide Pictures.[74] From there Dickson went on to produce a variety of films under commercial sponsorship, including some of the first adverts on commercial television in Britain.[75] Jack Howells's early career followed a similar trajectory. Beginning his film-making career in the 1940s under another stalwart of the documentary movement, Donald Alexander, at the left-wing production company DATA (Documentary and Technicians Alliance) Film Productions,[76] Howells later moved on to work as a newsreel editor for British Pathé and, in the early 1950s, set up his own production company, Jack Howells Productions.[77]

Ormond had, however, gained a different kind of apprenticeship in the realm of print journalism. The years he spent at *Picture Post* shortly after leaving university were to be profoundly informative.[78] As we have seen, Ormond had early on acquired a taste and a talent for the visual; while at Swansea Grammar School, he would at lunchtimes hurry down the road to the Glynn Vivian Art Gallery, and later at university would sneak off from lectures to take drawing lessons at Swansea School of Art.[79] He claimed later in life that he possessed 'a heightened sense of seeing and looking and gazing'.[80] These visual sensibilities certainly contributed to his skills as a film-maker. As he noted himself: 'I suppose, no I know that the keen visual examination of the world and my response to that observation intensified year after year in all the time I was making documentaries.'[81] Yet it was during his years at *Picture Post* that he developed skills that he later transferred to the art of film production. In particular, his time as a writer there allowed him to experiment with the technique that Sergei Eisenstein famously called 'vertical montage': that is, the synchronic juxtaposition of sound and image. As Eisenstein explained, in sound film '[t]he search for correspondence [between the aural and the visual] must proceed from the intention of matching both picture and music to the general, complex 'imagery' produced by the whole'.[82] For print journalists like Ormond, this juxtaposition was the relationship between printed word and image; but the principle certainly still applied. In M. Wynn Thomas's words, this was the art of 'mak[ing] words complement images, rather than repeating or competing with them'. Thomas continues: '[at *Picture Post*] he learned to write arresting but not patronizing captions; he learned to think like a camera'.[83] As Ormond himself confirmed, these were crucial skills for the documentary film-maker:

Writers on *Picture Post* were not only responsible for the words which accompanied a picture story, but to a large extent for the photographs too. Now I was being paid to observe and to write about what I saw, and to think in terms of pictures. All this was to be important to my future as a documentary film-maker.[84]

Examining some of his work at the magazine, it becomes clear that Ormond was already beginning to learn something of the art of vertical montage. In an article on the Gower folk singer Phil Tanner, for instance, Ormond seems determined to break free from the silent motionlessness of the printed page in order to create a new unity through the juxtaposition of image and text. The text evokes a moving filmic scene, rather than merely describing the accompanying pictures. A photo of the singer is accompanied by a caption, written in the present tense, which serves to bring the image to life: 'Phil Tanner settles himself back into his chair, and his hands close upon the stick between his knees. Once more, he raises his chin, chooses his key and strikes out his first word.'[85] Ormond even provides the reader with a musical score and lyrics to one of Tanner's favourite renditions ('Fair Phoebe and the Dark-Eyed Sailor') to accompany this, again augmenting this sense of filmic vertical montage by insisting readers hear the scene as well as see it.[86] Later, these valuable skills would be further honed during his work as a writer of verse accompaniments to the *News Chronicle*'s 'Saturday Picture'.[87] There Ormond created poetic unity from the juxtaposition of word and image; as Thomas argues, 'when, occasionally, a picture would really reverberate through his imagination, the result was not resourcefully pliant verse but compelling poetry'.[88]

Although Ormond admitted that the skills he had learned in print journalism came to be an important influence in his later work as a documentary maker, he maintained that he viewed his creative life as a poet and his professional life as a journalist quite separately. This may seem surprising, especially given the creative freedom he was evidently afforded at *Picture Post*, as well as the fact that his work there directly informed at least one poem.[89] Yet Ormond felt so strongly about the distinction between his 'work' as a poet and his 'job' as a journalist that in 1949 he abruptly left his position at *Picture Post* on the basis that it was interfering with his true calling. As he later wrote, '[b]efore joining *Picture Post* I had resolved that if my job interfered with my work (that was to say, being a poet), I would leave my job.'[90]

Unfortunately, the position at the *South Wales Evening Post* that followed his move from London did not improve matters:

> I went back to Swansea to work as a sub-editor on the evening newspaper there, thinking that a job that occupied me from 8:30 a.m. to 4:30 p.m. would leave me the evenings free to work in. It did not turn out that way. There came a point when I'd write a line of a poem and automatically start counting the number of letters in the line, as though it were a headline of the kind I'd been writing all day, as though it had to fit across eight or nine columns.[91]

He did find a way of passing the time on such monotonous tasks by testing the night-editor's patience. Geraint Talfan Davies recalls Ormond telling him of a time he constructed a three-line headline: 'Swansea Man / Weds Swansea Woman / In Swansea'.[92] But it was not until he took up a post at the BBC in Wales that he seems to have struck a compromise between his creative and professional lives.

Ormond's decision to stay with the BBC for the duration of his career after 1955 seems to be an indication that his role as a documentary film-maker satisfied many of his creative impulses. He noted this himself: 'In [my work as a film-maker] a number of things I was committed to could come together: my social concerns, my involvement with the graphic [. . .], my writing and my love of music.'[93] Nevertheless, Ormond remained uneasy about the conception of the relationship between his poetry and his work in film. While he admitted that there were 'definitely cases where observation and visual experience, things vividly seen, have started me off on poems', he firmly denied any suggestion that he saw his poems 'in a cinematic way'.[94] For instance, he once discussed the fact that his poem 'Ancient Monuments' came as a result of scouting a location for a film and coming across a cromlech in a field of barley',[95] yet the poem itself displays a revealing reluctance to make explicit reference to his day job: '*Looking for something else*, I came once/ To a cromlech in a field of barley' (emphasis added).[96] This unwillingness even to name the work of film-making in his poetry is a significant omission; it seems to say something about the perceived axiological clash between the two creative worlds within which he was working, and his desire to maintain a separation between the two. This ambivalence is quite consistent in his remarks about his film-making. Later in life there seemed to be a touch of resentment in his acceptance of the fact that the laboriousness of film-making (his 'job') absorbed so much of his creative energy (his 'work' as a poet): 'I know that my work as a film-maker obsessed me', he confessed in the passages quoted earlier, before going on to note that had he not put so much 'imaginative effort' into film he might 'have more poems'.[97]

A SORT OF WELCOME TO SPRING

Despite this reluctance to admit any overlap between his two creative endeavours, there are undoubtedly correspondences between his poetry and his film-making. If Ormond did not view his poems in a cinematic way, he certainly saw his films in a poetic way. To illustrate this, it seems appropriate to work from the beginning, with the very first film Ormond produced under the banner of the new Welsh Film Unit, *A Sort of Welcome to Spring* (1959).[98] This short film – barely fifteen minutes in length – is one of the most freely 'poetic' in Ormond's oeuvre. To borrow Bill Nichols's definition of the 'poetic documentary', the film does not attempt to expound an argument, but rather 'emphasizes visual associations, tonal or rhythmic qualities, descriptive passages, and formal organization'.[99] As the phrasing of its title implies, *A Sort of Welcome to Spring* plays with association and indefiniteness. It juxtaposes silent filmed material from the real world with classical music and a verse narration to create a poetic expression around its theme. It is worth noting that 'spring' was also the theme of one of the first films produced at the National Film Board of Canada, the prestigious Canadian government-sponsored film department set up by John Grierson in 1939.[100] We could perhaps speculate that the theme of 'spring', with its connotations of fruition, flowering, birth, was deemed appropriate for two national film units embarking on their first films. Spring is, after all, the ideal season to film a community at its most vibrant and scenic, and there is certainly a hint of local pride in *A Sort of Welcome to Spring*'s joyful evocation of a spring day in Cardiff. The city had recently, in 1955, been named capital of Wales, and in 1958 had hosted the Festival of Wales. In this sense, the film can be viewed as a descendant of the experimental European 'city symphonies' of Walter Ruttmann, Joris Ivens, Alberto Cavalcanti and others in the 1920s.

It is, however, debatable whether such a joyful paean to the new capital was a long-held plan for Ormond. More likely, the film was a product of a new producer improvising with little guidance and a tiny budget; David Berry has noted that the film had a total budget of just four hundred pounds.[101] Nevertheless the Film Unit had at that time recently been equipped with a new Arriflex silent 16mm camera.[102] It is likely then, that *A Sort of Welcome to Spring* was the product of Ormond and cameraman Bill Greenhalgh experimenting with this new piece of equipment. This would certainly explain the film's loose, improvisational feel. Indeed, according to Norman Swallow, the haphazard nature of television production in these early years resulted in a culture of improvisation and spontaneous creativity that in many ways enhanced the producer's freedom to create more 'personal', 'poetic' films.[103] Despite a somewhat unpolished finish, *A Sort of Welcome to Spring* is an aesthetic success, and offers us a useful insight into the ways in which Ormond was able to find the space at the BBC in Wales to create self-consciously 'poetic' works. Many of the techniques developed in this early film would find expression throughout his work.

The film plays off a verse commentary on the theme of spring – read by Welsh actor Meredith Edwards[104] – with a range of disparate yet connected springtime images and scenes. Ducks and swans frolic in a lake; a young couple hold hands in a park; a man sells daffodils to passers-by; a spring shower rains down on shoppers on Cardiff High Street. In contrast to the 'expository' documentary mode, whose aim is, as Nichols notes, to inform viewers within an 'argumentative logic',[105] here Ormond generates new poetic resonances out of the juxtaposition of sounds, words and images. He achieves this in a number of ways. In one scene a group of children slide, swing and play in a playground, and the otherwise mannered verse narration complements the images by switching register to a variation on the well-known bedtime nursery rhyme, 'Matthew, Mark, Luke and John':

> Matthew, Mark, Luke and John,
> Bless the seat that I slide on,
> Patch my trousers, one two three,
> Winter's in the cupboard and can't see me.

Sometimes music alone works with images to similarly pleasing, complementary effect; later in the same scene the rise and fall of a child on a swing is accompanied by the rise and fall of a musical phrase. Even when its use is not so overtly referential, music is, as it would be throughout Ormond's oeuvre, carefully chosen to augment the mood.

There are, moreover, instances in which Ormond finds a visual correlative for a spoken idea. 'With every hour of the sun the slow sap rises': here images of shadows cast by plants and flowers upon the ground nicely capture the notion. Occasionally, playful conceits are generated from oblique juxtapositions of word and image; a cut from footage of a raft of ducks swimming in a pond to rubber ducks floating in a baby's bath is accompanied by narration that archly states, 'some other ducks swim where the water's warmer'.[106] Later we see shots of a statue of a young boy frolicking in a fountain,[107] over which Edwards intones: 'heedless of chills, one [little boy] stands and thinks it cute,/ brazen and smiling in his birthday suit,/ to catch the spray from fountains as they rise/ towards his fixed and never-seeing eyes'.

These are splendid examples of the principle of vertical montage. But the film can further be understood to enact Ormond's own poetic philosophy in a way that allows us to view it as a personal documentary. The verse narration certainly bespeaks Ormond's poetic philosophy:

> Ageless proportion, ageless incantation
> Patterns and lines at once permanence, impermanence,
> A world of abstract shapes and opening lips
> The silent forms unravelling to sing
> Relentless multiplicities of spring.

This is not the throwaway greeting-card verse we might expect, but thoughtfully considered poetry. There are thematic and sonic echoes of these lines in Ormond's poem 'Finding a Fossil': 'Graftings so fused in chance/ Among cold starts that dance/ Gestures of permanence' (CP, 141). Immediately recognisable is Ormond's favourite theme of 'relentless multiplicity', the Wittgensteinian notion of the infinite ways of comprehending an ultimately elusive 'true' reality. Here reality is not total or final, but the sum of a plurality of, often, contradictory parts, an 'organic mosaic': 'Patterns and lines at once permanence, impermanence'. This sense of unending 'multiplicity' is further embodied phonetically through variations upon similar sound patterns: 'ageless *proportion*, ageless *incantation*'; '*permanence, impermanence* [. . .] *opening lips*'. This is suggestive poetry, then, even without the accompanying visual images. However, the poem should be read in its context as a piece of film narration. While Edwards reads these lines, the film cuts between extreme close-up shots of a whole variety of dewy, freshly trembling plants and flowers. The verse pleasingly complements the images, but on another level it ingeniously hints at its own situatedness within the film that houses it. 'Silent forms unravelling to sing/ relentless multiplicities of spring' could be viewed as a description of the very principle of film montage and, more specifically, of this very film.[108]

A Sort of Welcome to Spring is a film that enacts the very principle of 'multiplicity'. It attempts to capture the infinite variousness and elusiveness of existence through the 'unravelling' of 'silent forms', and its juxtaposition of disparate but connected images and scenes of spring becomes, in effect, an 'organic mosaic', an artistic embodiment of meaning in an otherwise meaningless world. The film thus clearly aspires to a higher significance than mere 'documentary' or mere 'television'. In its poetic ambitiousness, A Sort of Welcome to Spring is closer to the ideal of art as a compensatory force to which Ormond aspired in his poetry. Towards the end of the film, the verse narration reveals itself to have been expressed in the first-person:

> From all the springs that I've seen come and go,
> I'd say that when the praise of spring is sung,
> Chiefly I'd put the pleasure that I know
> From watching young things grow.

The film takes the form of a personal lyric poem, or perhaps more accurately a lyric film-poem. A Sort of Welcome to Spring is one of the purest, most 'poetic' films in Ormond's oeuvre. Viewers appear to have responded well: the BBC's Audience Research Report noted that the majority of its research group felt that 'the skilful and imaginative blending of verse, music and film had resulted in a programme which had been "as refreshing as a breath of spring"'.[109] The film possesses no explicit educative or informational purpose beyond promoting the existence of the BBC's new Welsh Film Unit, whose name is scrawled on to a brick wall in chalk at the end of the credits, and indeed is the last thing we see. More broadly, the film perhaps inaugurates a new age of BBC television in Wales.

A MAN WHO NEVER WAS?

A Sort of Welcome to Spring is proof of a fascinating yet short-lived period of considerable creative freedom in television production not only in Wales, but also in the wider realm of British television production, a time when 'personal' documentary makers could leave their distinct mark on programmes, and employ the medium in the service of a set of higher aesthetic ideals. The period was short-lived because, while this intensely creative strand of documentary informed many of Ormond's films throughout the 1960s, there was a noticeable shift in emphasis from the early 1970s that leaves its mark on some of Ormond's later films. Under considerable financial constraints following the massive expansion of output in the 1960s,[110] the BBC had appealed to an already uneasy Wilson government for a rise in the licence-fee levy three times in as many years, so, 'as part of a show of its earnest intentions to exert greater financial discipline',[111] in 1968 it employed the management consultant McKinsey and Co. to help reorganise management and balance the books. The result was far more stringent financial discipline and a total reorganisation of management, which in turn percolated into the context in which producers like Ormond were operating. As Georgina Born notes, 'individual ideas were integrated into a prediction of the bulk programming requirements for each channel; and a management system to monitor costs and operate the planning'.[112] Producers were, perhaps understandably, disgruntled. In interviews conducted for his 1977 book *The BBC: Public Institution and Private World*, Tom Burns noticed a considerable shift in attitude amongst BBC producers and personnel between 1963 and 1973. By the early 1970s there was a 'more widespread, more specific, and more intense disgruntlement displayed with superiors and with what was called "the management"'[113] than ten years previously. Perhaps most tellingly, Burns also noted 'a change in mood, in style, conveyed in the use of "working for the BBC" as against "working in the BBC"'.[114]

Among documentary producers, this mood was no doubt exacerbated by the publication of an internal BBC document, *Principles and Practice in Documentary Programmes* (1972). The document sought a formulation and formalisation of the television documentary format, the 'equivalent to a newspaper's style book'.[115] This did not sit well with creative minds accustomed not only to free rein over their approach to programmes, but also working with an evolving, unformulaic film form. As Richard Collins notes, the document in fact 'uneasily manages the contradiction'[116] between the documentary's referential and aesthetic aspects. *Principles and Practice in Documentary Programmes* accepted that idea of documentary as a 'creative work, open to subjective enjoyment, and [. . .] conceived for interpretation on different levels'.[117] Yet at the same time it severely, even belligerently, limited producers' capacity to exercise their individual voice: 'If the producer [is] [. . .] intent on expressing his views, he should leave the BBC and make his name in some other field. Perhaps one day he will be invited back in his own right to express his views as a contributor.'[118] The document represented a substantial shift in values at the BBC, one that impinged heavily upon the creative freedoms of producers like Ormond.

Ormond seems to be responding to these new, more restrictive, practices in television production when, in his film interview with John Grierson, he abruptly ends the programme with one of Grierson's characteristically bold declarations, an endorsement from the doyen of documentary that seems to function as a defiant message from Ormond to his superiors: 'There is no revelation, finally, without having to depend on creative men of [a] particular quality, and the sooner television, and particularly the BBC, looks into the future of its visual poets, the better.' The film then boldly fades to black. Evidently those superiors did not pay much heed to such warnings. By 1975 Norman Swallow was looking back nostalgically at a 'golden age' in television documentary production – an age he views as the decade between 1955 and 1965.[119] Similarly Ormond, writing near the end of his life, surveyed gloomily the development (or demise) of the form as he knew it: 'sometimes looking back, as I do now, from where most of television broadcasting stands today, I have a feeling of having been a man who never was.'[120]

Yet Ormond was at the height of his career during an exciting era in which television film-makers enjoyed considerable prestige and creative freedom. The two poles across which documentary films function – the 'poetic' and the 'informational' – are always in productive correspondence with one another in Ormond's films. In the chapters that follow, I will trace the diverse ways in which Ormond combined his personal poetic sensibilities with a creative approach to documentary film-making. As we will see, Ormond used the freedoms afforded him at BBC Wales to express his own creative vision within that institution's mandate to inform, educate and entertain a national public. In doing so, he made a profound contribution to the way Wales viewed and imagined itself in these years.

SCREENING CULTURE

A Sort of Welcome to Spring marked the beginning of a prolific career as a film-maker. The film's playful, unhurried tone, its unabashed lyricism in spite of its rough edges, is an apt first effort for a film-maker who strove throughout his career to use whatever resources were available to explore the creative potentialities of the documentary form, and to incorporate his own poetic vision into this work. However, a film like *A Sort of Welcome to Spring*, one without a clearly defined theme or informational purpose, was the exception to the norm in television. While Ormond was fortunate in beginning his career at a time when that medium was still in its infancy, when its practices and conventions were still fluid, unfixed, and open to experimentation, this was still very much a medium with a message. At that time, this message was still firmly fixed within the high-minded framework of public information and education formulated by the BBC's first Director General, John Reith. It is for this reason that many of the films for which Ormond is best known are documentaries that inform and educate the viewing public on the fruits of culture.

John Reith had taken his cue from Matthew Arnold when, in the 1920s, he envisioned broadcasting as a technology of social cohesion. Sharing with the public 'the best that has been thought and said in the world',[1] he imagined that broadcasting would raise the intellectual and moral standards of society. In Krishan Kumar's terms, Reith conveived the BBC as a 'cultural church' designed to spread the message of cultural enlightenment to the British public.[2] As a result, one of the major features of BBC broadcasting was, from the outset, the celebration and dissemination of approved forms of high culture. Classical music, philosophy, poetry and drama were all standard fare on the radio waves. And while this came under considerable pressure in a post-war era of increasingly populist consumerism – an era in which the distinction between 'high' and 'popular' was becoming increasingly hard to define – the ideal that persisted at the heart of the BBC was the notion that British society should be guided by the shining light of the 'best' culture. When, after the war, Director General William Haley split the BBCs radio service in three, introducing the Light Programme – the corporation's first major concession to popular taste – he did so in the hope that the new tripartite model of radio would 'rais[e] public taste'.[3] The smatterings of classical music on the Light Programme would serve 'to lead listeners on to the Home Service' and the Home Service would 'lead on' to the lofty Third Programme.[4] This policy of cultural enrichment and uplift persisted strongly in the formative early years of television. In its contribution to the important 1962 Pilkington Report – the first government commission on broadcasting following the explosion of television in the late 1950s[5] – the BBC argued that 'it [was] an important part of their responsibility to 'give a lead' to public taste, in literature and the arts and elsewhere'.[6]

Senior figures at the BBC framed their efforts in cultural edification as part of the corporation's role of serving the 'public interest'. Yet this notion of the 'public', was, as Thomas Hajkowski has suggested, from the earliest days, 'intimately bound to the idea of the nation, and rooted in its history of projecting and preserving national culture'.[7] The project of building and maintaining national communities has always involved the creation of what Tim Edensor terms a 'nationally codified body of knowledge which foreground[s] "high" culture' in order to cement the disparate constituencies of the national public.[8] Therefore, a key function of the policy of edifying the public was the task of colouring of the public sphere in a distinctively British hue. Yet the BBC's 'Britishness' raised an obvious challenge for figures at the BBC in Wales. How could producers in Wales construct a vision of the Welsh nation within an organisation that had historically, as Paddy Scannell has argued, 'presumed the unity of the culture and identity of the UK' in a way that 'glossed over its many disunities'?[9]

Welsh radio broadcasting has a long and rich history of promoting Welsh culture on the radio waves. This began with extensive annual coverage of the Eisteddfod from 1925, and after the BBC's policy of strict centralisation was relaxed somewhat around 1930, producers such as Cyril Wood and Dafydd Gruffydd began a long tradition of promoting radio drama that enriched Welsh consciousness in both languages, as well as providing (often much needed) employment for Welsh writers like Emlyn Williams, Saunders Lewis and, later, Gwenlyn Parry, Emyr Humphreys, Elaine Morgan and Alun Richards. Music, too, was heavily supported by the BBC in Wales; the BBC Welsh National Orchestra was deemed a priority early on, and provided work for musicians and a vehicle for Welsh composers like Daniel Jones, Alun Hoddinott and William Mathias. And though, for obvious reasons, visual art was more difficult to promote on radio, there was nevertheless a tradition of discussion programmes on this topic.[10] Nevertheless, the impact of the BBC's concessions to 'national regions' in television in the late 1950s was enormous. Television was at the time a new and incomparably powerful means of projecting a vision of national culture to wide audiences. The challenge by the time Ormond began his work as a film-maker at BBC Wales was not, then, how to secure the resources necessary to produce films about Wales. The more interesting, and culturally productive, challenge was how to present the very idea of Welsh culture on television in a way that would frame it within the context of, and yet in distinction to, British culture.

Peter Lord's work on the idea of national culture is useful here. Lord has argued that culture is fundamental to the creation of national communities. As he writes, 'the denial of the aesthetics of the one is the denial of the politics of the other'.[11] However, the creation of a cultural tradition defined in national terms is always complicated by the fact that culture is never neutrally exhibited and viewed by audiences; rather, it is 'activated' into dominant 'intellectual structures':

A tradition is a concept, not a collection of material. It is an intellectual structure into which [. . .] images are fitted. It is this structure, or simply this story, which activates the images in a culture. Without being activated in this way, by recognition and incorporation in a tradition, to all intents and purposes the images do not exist.[12]

Whatever the success of securing the capacity to produce films about Welsh culture made possible by the new Film Unit, there was, at the time Ormond was working, no accepted definition of a Welsh cultural 'tradition' with its own definitions and parameters to draw upon. Such a tradition requires, in the first instance, a set of institutions geared to its support. Yet as Lord argues, such institutions in Wales – like the BBC itself – were frequently guided by orientations other than the support for a distinctive Welsh public sphere.[13] This resulted in a situation in which the discourse on a cohesive Welsh cultural tradition was, where it existed at all, 'conducted in a fragmentary way in exhibition catalogues, newspaper articles and correspondence'.[14]

This lack of institutional coherence was further compounded by the ever-present condition of Wales's persistent cultural and linguistic 'internal difference', a result of the fractured, uneven nature of the nation's historical development.[15] Ormond's response to this challenge was to use the documentary form to creatively celebrate a disparate range of artists in a way that, in effect 'activated' them within a cohesive 'Welsh' culture. Fortunately for Ormond, he had in this cause the support of three important figures at the BBC in Wales, the three Davieses: Alun Oldfield-Davies, Hywel Davies and Aneirin Talfan Davies. All three held senior posts at the BBC in Wales in the decades after the Second World War, and each was passionate in their support for culture as a means of promoting a sense of nationhood. Aneirin Talfan Davies in particular has been credited as being integral to the project of overcoming the divisions in Welsh cultural consciousness at that time. Sarah Rhian Reynolds has described him as a 'cultural broker' whose 'work was permeated by a holistic vision' of Wales.[16] In this respect, Talfan Davies's work was no different from Reith's in London: as John Davies notes, 'the Reithian ideal that broadcasting should elevate public taste and buttress public morality [. . .] certainly held sway in Wales'.[17] Yet the crucial difference was that figures like the three Davieses were working to mould the BBC in Wales in the shape of a Welsh nation. It is in precisely this task of cultural brokerage, of shaping a discursive space for the diverse – and sometimes competing – range of cultural voices in Wales, that Ormond was involved in his documentaries. A central feature of this effort was Ormond's own creative vision and the way he implemented this on film.

Ormond was not alone in the production of such documentaries in this era. It was in these films that many of the most influential television directors of this period were able to exercise their creative capacities, partly because films on art and artists were an obvious format for creative film-makers. In such films, the formal possibilities of television could be tested out on topics in which creativity and innovation is paramount. At a time when the conventions of some television genres were at risk of becoming unimaginatively fixed in the service of staid public information, sport, and generic drama, this was one of the few areas in which the license to experiment was, as Laura Mulvey argues, 'more likely to be granted'.[18] There were some areas of experiment; the new commercialism initiated by ITV sparked a newly irreverent approach to some BBC programming, such as the short-lived *That Was The Week That Was* (1962–3), *Top of the Pops* (1964–2006), and *Monty Python's Flying Circus* (1969–74). Yet in matters of high culture, the Reithian mindset stood firm against these new trends, with the BBC producing the high-budget *Civilisation* (1969), a 'blockbuster' series, presented by Sir Kenneth Clark, which sought to display the fruits of two millennia of Western civilisation on the screen within a firmly Arnoldian framework.[19]

Most historians of this era point to Ken Russell as the exemplar of the culture documentary.[20] Another influential early figure was the producer John Read, who, in conjunction with the Arts Council of Great Britain and the British Council, produced in the 1950s a series of documentaries on esteemed English artists such as Henry Moore, Stanley Spencer and L. S. Lowry. John Wyver argues that it was Read who 'defined the forms of the filmed profile' on television, and that it is this form of 'filmed profile' that has persisted as the dominant form ever since.[21] Read himself possessed an Arnoldian view of culture, and viewed the documentary as a means of providing cultural sustenance to an ailing society. In one essay outlining his purpose, Read portentously argued that 'today [. . .] apathy and ignorance interact to produce a degree of unrest and frustration that constitutes a grave illness, sapping vitality from the democratic organ'.[22] The success of the genre that he developed, as well as its prevailing ethos, was picked up later in esteemed BBC arts series such as *Monitor* (1958–65) – famously presented by Welshman Huw Wheldon[23] – and its ITV equivalent *Tempo* (1961–7), as well as innumerable stand-alone films from the late 1950s onwards. The novelist Angus Wilson, in a book about *Tempo*, described the sensibilities of this kind of film-making as being in sharp distinction to the usual televisual fare: 'in probing and presenting the creative imagination at work [. . .] the television producer seems to come nearest to producing something original of his own, a work of art.'[24] It is easy to imagine Ormond nodding in assent to such a statement. Indeed, he deserves to be viewed as a pioneer of this era, one who celebrated the arts on screen in innovative ways, while drawing imaginatively on his own poetic philosophy.

This chapter views Ormond's culture documentaries in a way that attends to their twin, related modes: as both important vehicles for the discussion and definition of culture within the Welsh public sphere, and distinctive examples of a form of experimental documentary film-making that are themselves important contributions to the cultural history of Wales. To do this, it is necessary to separate the films into the two cultural forms with which they principally concern themselves: visual art and literature. These two forms developed along separate lines in Wales, and, despite certain exceptions such as Brenda Chamberlain and David Jones, who excelled in both forms, each pulled in different directions, with often different and differing institutional and cultural coordinates. The result has been what Peter Lord terms a 'mis-match' between the 'visual culture and the complex of understandings which inform the established elements of national tradition through literature'.[25] As we will see, it is precisely such kinds of mis-match that Ormond was creatively equipped to negotiate in his work.

HORIZONS HUNG IN AIR; *LAND AGAINST THE LIGHT*

Ormond's first film in this mode was *Horizons Hung in Air* (1966), a profile of the enormously popular Anglesey-born landscape painter Kyffin Williams. Williams's iconic paintings of the landscapes and farmlands of Snowdonia and Anglesey have made him one of the defining artists of Wales, and true to Ormond's poetics, the film employs the documentary form ekphrastically to corroborate and convey Williams's vision. The narration takes particular aim at the fashionable London-centric metropolitan art scene: 'Kyffin Williams's attachment to the Welsh mountains goes further than merely wanting to paint them', says Ormond (who himself narrates this film). 'Perhaps they represent to him a certain country Welsh disdain for urban success.' Williams, interviewed on screen, himself confirms his contempt for the 'vulgarization' of the London art world, despite at this time living in Chelsea. His distaste is further expressed through the visual construction of London in the film: contrary to the ubiquitous trope of 'Swinging London' and the trendy stirrings of postmodernism appearing elsewhere at this time,[26] the London evoked in *Horizons Hung in Air* is the hub of a tawdry modernity. The film's opening sequence seeks to establish the city's bewildering superficiality; the viewer is immediately disorientated by an opening shot in which two clashing directions of visual movement drive at each other within the frame: heavy city traffic speeds towards us in a rapid zoom shot. We cut sharply to an obliquely framed shot of London traffic lights which seem to be failing in their signal to 'STOP': the sound of cars roars on; pedestrians bustle past; next, we cut to a shot that seems to struggle confusedly to navigate its way across the city: a long zoom into the iconic London Underground sign is intermittently obscured by the relentless traffic.[27] The unnerving confusion of this place is emphasised by fast cuts and abrupt, discordant music. The camera pans sharply across clustered urban back gardens, and it soon becomes clear that we are heading towards Kyffin Williams's place of residence, Bolton Studios in Chelsea. The message here is that finding this place is no easy task in such an endless urban sprawl. Inside, though, the studio is a haven of quiet, a place where we can find politely refined conversation with a sophisticated Welsh artist. Williams's world is presented in agreeable contrast to the fast-paced life of London. Soon we are transported to Snowdonia, following the artist out on one of his hikes, looking for inspiration. In these scenes the camerawork is smoother, more evenly paced and fluid, the soundtrack soothing. Extended pans follow the long ridges of the mountains; low-angled stills capture the grandeur of their cloud-capped peaks. Yet a later return to London, in which Williams describes his intense dislike of the fashionable metropolitan art market, again returns to a more erratic visual mode; strange works of modern sculptural art are framed obliquely, with a shaky, hand-held camera shifting in and out of focus, emphasising the distance – philosophical as well as geographical – between this world and the artist's true home in Wales.

Horizons Hung in Air stylistically corroborates Williams's aversion to metropolitan trends in a way comparable to Ormond's ekphrastic poetry. Williams himself makes a telling reference to Ormond as a kind of portraitist in his autobiography, *A Wider Sky* (1991). Remembering the process of making *Horizons Hung in Air*, he notes that he had 'complete confidence in [Ormond's] judgement, I allowed him to use me much as a model allows a painter the freedom to interpret in whatever way he or she desires'.[28] Ormond's second film on Williams, *Land Against the Light* (1978), though broadcast fourteen years after *Horizons Hung in Air*, works in a similar way. The film can be viewed as a sequel to the earlier film: the narration starts by telling us that 'it's been five years and more now since the painter Kyffin Williams decided to get out of London and move back once and for all to his native Anglesey'. It utilises the far higher quality of cameras and film stock in use at BBC Wales by the late 1970s (the film is shot widescreen and in full colour), and replicates the rare eye condition which affected Williams's vision and informed much of his work, whereby the pupils fail to dilate in bright light. *Land Against the Light* films Snowdonia against the glare of the sun, which achieves the startling effect of sun flare streaking across the screen.[29] Ormond later informed film historian David Berry of his intentions: 'When [Williams] set up his easel like as not he'd be painting in the sun and not with the usual flat effect. Accordingly, I nearly always shot my film against the sun.'[30]

These two films are quintessential examples of Ormond's mode. They exemplify Ormond's skill as an ekphrastic documentary film-maker and the ways in which he employed this as a means of projecting a cultured vision of Wales and its arts on screen. Central to this is the way the films construct images of the Welsh landscape. Tim Edensor is one of many observers who note that images of 'national geographies' are powerful symbols of national identity, providing national communities with a defined, if imagined, space within which their nation resides.[31] Edensor perceptively suggests that national landscapes provide 'a common-sense spatial matrix which draws people and places together in spectacular and banal ways':[32] 'spectacular' in the sense that landscapes are sublime visual symbols with the power to connect vast national communities, yet 'banal' in the sense that these become readily absorbed into the common-sense symbolic vocabulary of everyday national life in ways that disguise their political significance. Landscape art has, historically, been the principal means of constructing such visions of the national geography, and in Wales, Kyffin Williams was one of the chief imaginers of the Welsh symbolic landscape. Peter Lord describes him as one of 'the most extensively collected of all Welsh painters in the twentieth century', and his legacy endures. However, as Lord argues, Williams's vision of Wales was, like all imagined geographies, a highly selective one that emblematised a Wales defined by particular aspects of its physical and social landscape, in particular, the 'affirmation of the romantic myth of the landscape and y Werin Gymreig'.[33] Lord traces Williams's vision to the Romantic landscape writers and artists of the eighteenth century and their patrons, such as Sir William Gilpin, Paul Sandby and his patron Sir Watkins Williams Wynn, and Moses Griffiths and his patron Thomas Pennant. Lord argues these figures imaged Wales as a politically ineffectual, quasi-mythical space, a vision that was, in the nineteenth century, appropriated by Welsh Liberal intellectuals as a means of projecting the image of a 'racial' Wales that excluded its industrial working class.[34]

The effectiveness of Ormond's mode lies in its light touch with these matters. In both films, Williams is positioned as the inspired imaginer of this particular vision of Wales. Both were transmitted from the Welsh television masts as 'BBC Wales opt-outs', meaning they would have been screened to working-class south Walians who might never have ventured to Snowdonia, and would likely not have agreed that north Wales was the symbolic heartland of the nation. However, true to Ormond's bathetic poetics, there is everywhere a sense of humour and irony in the films' presentation of Williams. The film elides the 'banal' and the 'spectacular', normalising Williams's importance in the construction of landscape in Wales's cultural imagination, while maintaining a down-to-earth humour and irony about such matters. This is partly the result of Williams's own charismatic on-screen presence, and his ability to switch effortlessly between plummily sophisticated expositions of his artistic mode and humorous impersonations of his Anglesey neighbours. In the second film, Williams stands outside his new house on the shore of the Menai Strait, recounting a conversation he had with a new neighbour who told him he would 'have to get himself a woman'. 'But what if we don't get on?' Williams asked. 'Well,' she said, 'if you don't get on, duw, it's a great place to drown the bugger!'

PIANO WITH MANY STRINGS

Ormond's ability to unobtrusively position an artist as 'Welsh' is similarly at work in his second film about visual art, *Piano with Many Strings: The Art of Ceri Richards* (1969). Ormond had been acquainted with Richards since that early encounter at Ebenezer chapel in their home village of Dunvant. Interestingly, Richards's work had its own ekphrastic tendencies, often absorbing the energies of other arts and artists, as in his series of paintings inspired by Dylan Thomas's poem 'The force that through the green fuse'. Richards's biographer Mel Gooding notes that the poem 'unleashed a complex of images, expressive visual metaphors for [Richards's] own vision of the universe of living forms and of the dynamic natural processes which generate their distinctive and recurrent

configurations'.[35] Richards's interpretations of Thomas went on
to generate further configurations in Ormond's work. The poem
'Salmon', for instance, is dedicated 'first for, and now in memory of,
Ceri Richards',[36] and itself swims in the waters of Richards's vision
of organic generation and regeneration, finding in the migration
of salmon a potent metaphor for the dynamism of life's natural
forces, and for artistic expression. Its short, vigorous lines pulsate
irrepressibly down the page, as it searches instinctively for a language
to match the dynamic proto-sexual energy of Richards's visual work
on the same theme:

> [. . .] Sea-hazards done,
> They ache towards the one world
> From which their secret
> Sprang, perpetuate
>
> More than themselves, the ritual
> Claim of the river, pointed
> Towards rut, tracing
> Their passion out.
>
> (*CP*, 165)

In this sense, the poem's very artistic genesis reincarnates something
of the generative life energy that provides all these works with their
inspiration. Its concluding appeal to Buddha brilliantly enacts this
self-perpetuating desire for never-fulfilled satisfaction by ending in
inquisitive suspense:

> Why does this fasting fish
> So haunt me? Gautama, was it this
> You saw from river-bank
> At Uruvela? Was this
> Your glimpse
> Of holy law?
>
> (*CP*, 167)

Piano with Many Strings profiles Richards in a way that does not
shy away from that artist's often highly conceptual work. While missing some of the light-touch humour of his films on Kyffin Williams,
it nevertheless positions Richards as Welsh in an accessible way.
Ormond had attempted this some years earlier in a radio programme

he had written for the Welsh Home Service in 1954, *Rest and Unrest: The Art of Ceri Richards*; there he made use of his favoured layman's idiom of craftsmanship: 'the artist [. . .] feels the need to hammer out for himself a language [. . .] to communicate what he wants to say.'[37] Similarly, *Piano with Many Strings* begins with a perspective on Richards that emphasises the basics of his craft. It opens with images of Richards's finely sketched portraits of his family – demonstrating that whatever his tendency to experiment fancily with high forms, at heart Richards possessed the abilities of the true draughtsman: 'when he chooses to', Ormond narrates, 'Ceri Richards can draw like an old master.' The film explains the developments in artistic practice that led Richards's work to evolve under the influence of non-figurative movements, particularly impressionism and expressionism, under the influence of Wassily Kandinsky (from whose essay 'On the Spiritual in Art' the programme derives its title, and Ormond's narration quotes at length). The film itself is a fine artwork, with splendid sequences that showcase Richards's series *Interior with Music* and 'The force that through the green fuse', in which the cuts and camerawork eloquently follow the cues of music and verse.[38]

The overall effect is to evoke the sense of Richards as an artist in tune and on a par with the wider tradition of twentieth-century European art. Richards received numerous accolades in the 1960s: a CBE in 1960 was followed by major retrospectives in London's Whitechapel Gallery in the same year and the Venice Biennale in 1962–3, as well as a Gold Medal for best foreign painter at the International Exhibition of Contemporary Art in Delhi in 1968.[39] Indeed, Richards's fame on the international stage partly explains the context in which this film was made. This was one of four films Ormond produced in the run-up to the Investiture of the Prince of Wales in July 1969, declaiming the fruits of Welsh history and culture to television audiences. Unlike many of Ormond's films, which were screened as BBC Wales opt-outs, the four were screened on the BBC2 national network in the weeks leading up to the ceremony.[40] John S. Ellis suggests that they were part of the BBC's effort to enrol Britain, 'like Prince Charles' – who famously spent a term in Aberystwyth University – on 'an intensive course in Welshness'.[41] What is notable about *Piano with Many Strings* is that despite this context, the film resists the pressure to position Richards as a 'British' artist. As Eric Rowan has noted, by the 1960s Richards was frequently lauded in 'British' terms: 'Of all Welsh artists it is his name that occurs most

frequently in the histories and catalogues of the period [. . .] representing Britain rather than Wales.'[42] Yet *Piano with Many Strings*
strongly emphasises the rootedness of Richards's vision. One extended
sequence explores Richards's wartime *Tinplate* series (commissioned
by the Ministry of Information to document industrial workers on
the home front), undertaken at the Gowerton tinplate works where
Richards's father had worked. Footage of the interior of the works
is followed by a montage of sound recordings set against images of
Richards's paintings. The effect is to corroborate the connection
between Richards's art and the industrial process it was depicting.
This is followed by another striking sequence in which a montage
of the artist's sketches and paintings of his father, Thomas Coslett
Richards, is accompanied by a sonorous recording of the man reading a Welsh-language poem. The sequence – one of the few extended,
untranslated instances of the Welsh language in Ormond's oeuvre
– transitions smoothly into a scene in which Richards's sister Esther
plays the middle movement of Beethoven's *Sonata Pathétique* on her
piano, indicating a connection between Welsh-language poetry and
the wider European tradition. The film concludes with a sequence
celebrating Richards's *La cathédrale engloutie* series, accompanied
by recordings of Richards playing the Debussy prelude that inspired
them. The film emphasises the place of the Welsh landscape in
Richards's creative process; shots of the artist walking on a blustery
Gower coastline are followed by a scene in which he explains that
that particular piece of music 'reminded me of the coast of Gower'.
Richards, like Ormond's salmon, has come home to the place of creative conception.

A DAY ELEVEN YEARS LONG

Lauding Richards's Welsh credentials was a way of showcasing Wales'
contribution to the development of European modern art in the
1960s. However, by the early 1970s, Ormond was producing films in
a different context. The social and economic progress that had infused
post-war British art with a certain spirit of abandon was coming to
an end. Huw Jones has summarised the situation in the early 1970s:

> For the past two decades, most contemporary Welsh artists had worked in
> accordance with the principles of Modernism. This stressed the import-
> ance of form over subject-matter and the autonomy of the artist from

wider social concerns. However, the growing political division between left and right, and conflicts such as the miners' strikes, language activism, anti-nuclear protests and opposition to the Vietnam War and Apartheid in South Africa made this an increasingly untenable approach for the politicised artist in Wales.[43]

The result in Wales was a certain 'proletarianisation'[44] of art. By way of example: during the 1960s, the Director of the Welsh Committee of the Welsh Arts Council was Roger Webster, who had favoured modernist, internationalist forms over national or political particularity. Webster had once controversially claimed that Ceri Richards was 'the only Welsh artist to successfully keep pace with international aesthetic trends'.[45] However, Webster was in 1967 replaced by Aneurin Thomas, a director with a more egalitarian vision informed by the intellectuals of a re-energised British Left, such as Raymond Williams and Richard Hoggart, who themselves later worked at the Arts Council for Great Britain under the Labour Minister for the Arts, Hugh Jenkins.[46] Wales had of course been a crucible for artists with proletarian affiliations for decades; Ernest Zobole, Glyn Morgan and Charles Burton had been, since the 1940s, painting vivid scenes of industrial Welsh life. The political climate in the 1970s brought the work of these artists back into vogue, as well as that of a new wave of Welsh painters, such as Nicholas Evans and David Carpanini. Yet, despite this abundance of home-grown talent, it was, as Peter Lord notes, the 'sustained interest' in a Polish émigré in south Wales, Josef Herman, that had 'raised the public profile of the artist's view of the life of Welsh industrial communities'.[47] Herman, a Polish Jew, had settled in the Swansea valley mining village of Ystradgynlais in 1944, having fled his home country some years earlier. The small mining community would prove to be a revelation for him, and he lived and worked in the village until 1955.

By the 1970s, Ormond presumably felt that the time was right to profile one of Wales's most famous artists, and the result was *A Day Eleven Years Long* (1975). Herman was himself experiencing something of a revival at this time. He was the subject of a major retrospective at the Kelvingrove Art Gallery in Glasgow in 1975 (having earlier spent three years living in the heavily industrialised Gorbals area of Glasgow), and in the same year, Herman published his memoirs, *Related Twilights*. Ormond's film can in one sense be viewed as an ekphrastic response to this book. It adapts key passages from the

sections about Ystradgynlais: Herman's vivid descriptions of the 'low
hills like sleeping dogs' and a 'copper-coloured sky' are set against
long, sweeping pans of the village and its surrounding landscape. A
key sequence visualises the epiphanic passage that Peter Lord suggests
became as 'familiar as [Herman's] paintings',[48] a description of a sight
he saw on his first day in Ystradgynlais:

> Unexpectedly, as though from nowhere, a group of miners stepped onto
> the bridge. For a split second their heads appeared against the full body
> of the sun, as against a yellow disc – the whole image was not unlike an
> icon depicting the saints with their haloes. With the light around them,
> the silhouettes of the miners were almost black. With rapid steps they
> crossed the bridge and like frightened cats tore themselves away from
> one another, each going his own way. The magnificence of this scene
> overwhelmed me.[49]

Here the film captures Herman's excitement on that important day: a
low-angle shot looks up at a figure walking across a bridge (likely the
very bridge that Herman describes), silhouetted by the disc of the sun
behind; Herman's 'split-second' memory is replicated by a series of
sharply cut still frames of the figure at the moment at which it crosses
the sun behind.[50] Though *A Day Eleven Years Long* does go on to
explore other influences on Herman's work and his ideas about art,
the film's presentation of the artist suggests that it was this Welsh village that gave rise to a key phase in his artistic development. Ormond,
narrating over scenic shots of this now picturesque village, cleared
of its tips, suggests that '[i]t was almost as if [. . .] Ystradgynlais had
somehow been invented to heal the artist's wounds'. There is a plaintive quality to the film that matches the mood of many of Herman's
paintings, and is emphasised, as in many of Ormond's films, through
an emotive soundtrack. Images of Herman's paintings of the village
are intercut with shots of the same locations; set against Herman's
bold yet subdued palette, the sequences throw into relief the village's
now quiet, understated splendour. The film concludes by returning
to that epiphanic moment on the bridge, a moment so powerful that
Herman never painted it. Ormond asks him why 'that site which so
moved him on that first day never get on to canvas'; Herman responds
that if it was ever to get painted, 'then I will call this picture the sum-
mary of my life's work'. Ystradgynlais is thus constructed as the locus
of Herman's genius.

SUTHERLAND IN WALES

Ormond's final film on visual art, and the final full-length culture documentary of his career, *Sutherland in Wales* (1977), profiles another artist who found artistic sustenance in Wales. Graham Sutherland was someone with whom Ormond had a close affinity and indeed friendship; Ormond delivered a moving address at the artist's memorial service, and had earlier written an ekphrastic poem, 'Landscape in Dyfed', that, like his film, presented a vision, or as he called it, 'account' of the artist's mode. The poem bears reading alongside *Sutherland in Wales*. As Ormond stated, it 'sprang from a view of the work he had given to Wales; it is an account of his Pembrokeshire, some of his metaphors for reality'.[51] 'Landscape in Dyfed' brilliantly translates the visual effects of Sutherland's paintings into poetry:

> Because the sea grasped cleanly here, and there
> Coaxed too unsurely until clenched strata
> Resisted, an indecision of lanes resolves
> This land into gestures of beckoning
> Towards what is here and beyond, and both at hand.

(CP, 222)

These lines find a linguistic homology for Sutherland's characteristically elaborate visual patterns: consisting of a single, complexly interlocking sentence that draws on the lexicon of geology, its consonantal emphases generate a phonetic dissonance that replicates the harsh visual geometries of rock formations: 'there/ Coaxed too unsurely until clenched strata/ Resisted'. It shares Sutherland's concern with the hidden significance of geological phenomena, or, as Peter Lord has put it, 'the primitive forces which [Sutherland] came to perceive beneath all landscape'.[52] Here the natural world takes on a meaning and a life of its own: the sea 'grasp[s]', the land 'beckon[s]'; aeons are revealed within a single image.

Interestingly, the second stanza of 'Landscape in Dyfed' appears to move outside this frame of reference to provide an exterior view – a shot, almost – that pictures Sutherland as a film camera might. Though Ormond denied ever seeing poems in a 'cinematic way',[53] this poem appears to go on to perform an explanatory documentary function that corresponds with his film about the artist. Addressing Sutherland in the second person, the poem views the artist against the backdrop of the almost spiritual grandeur of natural form, which is itself viewed through the artists' imaginative vision: 'here are rock cathedrals which can be/ As small as your span' (*CP*, 222), 'rock cathedrals' being a reference to Sutherland's well-known painting *Cathedral (Study of Rocks)* (1974–6). However, the verse is able to capture a reality deeper than that of the camera:

Walk where you will, below is an estuary.
In advance to a fleeting brightness you traverse
So many shoals of the dead who have drowned
In stone, so many hibernations
Of souls, you could be in phantom country.

(*CP*, 222)

Sutherland in Wales similarly follows the artist on one of his hikes, and while Ormond's cameraman does not quite capture the 'shoals of the dead who have drowned/ In stone', he does very effectively augment, through impressive landscape photography, Sutherland's reading of a letter he had written in the 1940s explaining his affinity for the landscape.[54] Like *A Day Eleven Years Long*, the film brings to the screen the precise locations to which Sutherland refers in his writings in a way that extols their geographical rootedness.

Sutherland's paintings have been critiqued by some as more an extension of the English Romantic tradition than as an exploration of a distinctively Welsh social and geographical milieu. Peter Lord has noted that Sutherland's extensive work in Pembrokeshire is 'devoid of the human culture of the place'.[55] It is certainly difficult to argue that Sutherland's intensely imagined, elaborate and often surreal visual extrapolations of natural forms and scenes engage with a Welsh milieu in any overtly social, political or historical sense. However, Sutherland, despite this imaginative detachment, did off the canvas view Wales as more than an unpeopled area of natural beauty. In 1976 he gifted a large number of his works – some old, some specially created – to Picton Castle in Pembrokeshire. In his foreword to the book that accompanied the opening of the Graham Sutherland Gallery, the artist stated that he wished to 'make a gift [. . .] for the benefit of Pembrokeshire and the nation' with the view that it was 'high time that there should be some move towards decentralization'.[56] There had, indeed, been some move towards the 'decentralization' of the arts from London around this time, moves that were in large part a result of the Welsh Arts Council, which helped finance exhibition spaces such as Aberystwyth Arts Centre, Newport Museum and Gallery, and Chapter Arts Centre in Cardiff in the early 1970s, and opened its own gallery, Oriel, in Cardiff in 1974.[57] The 'decentralization' that Sutherland speaks of was high on the agenda in Wales at that time, and his gift of a substantial number of drawings and paintings to a gallery in west Wales was a generous and significant contribution to this process. Ormond's film is arguably a further extension of this process of 'decentralization'; in fact, it celebrates the new gallery with footage of the opening, and contains an extended sequence showcasing the new space and its contents. The narration gratefully acknowledges Sutherland's gift 'to the Picton Castle foundation, and to Wales'.

Accordingly, the occasionally over-reverent *Sutherland in Wales* celebrates the artist's work as a response to – and product of – the astonishing natural beauty of the Pembrokeshire coastline. The film's opening sequence alludes to the enduring existence of a Dyfed of magic and ancient legends, referring to the fact that the county of Pembrokeshire had recently (in 1974) reverted to its ancient name of Dyfed (itself part of the process of devolution occurring at a local administrative level in Wales at that time). 'In Welsh legend', says the narrator (Meredith Edwards), 'Dyfed was a region of magic, enchantment and apparitions.' Slow dissolves between shots of the magnificent beauty of the Dyfed coastline, accompanied by a sprightly yet haunting Celtic melody, evoke a sense of the ancient history of this landscape. From this vision of an ancient Welsh land, the film shifts into an evocation of the singular obsession with natural form that constituted Sutherland's neo-Romantic vision: sweeping shots survey the scenic Pembrokeshire coastline before cutting to minute natural features and formations – rocky outcrops, beach puddles reflecting the sky – as though adopting Sutherland's acute eye for natural detail. Crucially, Sutherland himself emphasises the sense in which this landscape gave rise to his artistic vision: shot on location, he proclaims: 'I think I can say that it was in this triangle of land that I first began to learn my trade as a painter.' Later, Sutherland explains in detail the locations and landmarks that inspired particular paintings and themes, which are corroborated through further location shots. The film relies heavily on Sutherland's own expositions of his work, and the pace is tempered by Sutherland's carefully measured speech. The overall effect is to imaginatively interweave Sutherland's work with the symbolic geography of this corner of Wales.

UNDER A BRIGHT HEAVEN

Visual art lends itself well to film-making for obvious reasons. It provides the film-maker with something to put on screen – the film camera can explore the details and textures of a particular artwork, and bring to life the implications of mood and movement contained in a painting or sculpture. Ormond was adept at exploring the multifarious possibilities of this, and collaborated with colleagues in creating impressive montages that combined narration, music and imagery in a way that generated something genuinely new from the works he was profiling. Moreover, the work of artists like Kyffin Williams, Ceri Richards and Graham Sutherland was apposite to his purposes of, in Peter Lord's terms, 'activating' art to Welsh television audiences. Whatever their international influences, these artists' particular concern with physical and natural themes and forms enabled Ormond to counterpoint their work with imagery of the locations that inspired them, and in doing so, to interweave them with the imagined national landscape.

Films about writers, however, pose a different kind of challenge. Literature is the art of written language, and even where rich in imagery, this rarely lends itself straightforwardly to filmic precis. In this sense, any attempt to 'film' a piece of writing is from the outset an implicitly interpretive, ekphrastic endeavour. Moreover, Ormond's films about Welsh writers in the English language posed an additional challenge. While these films were produced in the late 1960s, a time when a new generation of anglophone Welsh poets were finding voice, three of Ormond's four full-length films were profiles of Welsh writers better associated with the 'First Flowering' of anglophone Welsh poetry: Vernon Watkins, Dylan Thomas and Alun Lewis. In the 1960s, many poets of the 'Second Flowering' were steering themselves away from this earlier generation in order to find ways to express the distinctively 'Welsh' aspects of their experience, and tended to view the earlier poets as 'universalist', even un-Welsh in preoccupation and form. Ormond was of a more conciliatory position – coming of age in the 1940s, he was well acquainted with poets of both generations. While his most substantial work was published alongside the Second Flowering poetry of the 1960s, and shared its earthier, plain-speaking registers, it was thematically closer to the first generation in its universalist, humanist concerns. His films can, in part, be viewed as an effort to use the medium of film to reclaim and reframe these earlier poets in Welsh terms.

Given the challenges of producing a television film about poetry, Ormond set himself a tricky task with his first film about a Welsh poet. *Under a Bright Heaven: A Portrait of Vernon Watkins* (1966) is a profile of a poet of famously ungrounded preoccupations. While Watkins was, by the 1960s, a 'Faber poet' of some standing, and one of those being considered to succeed John Masefield as Poet Laureate,[58] he was at the same time writing steadfastly against the grain of 1960s poetic fashionability, remaining (neo-)romantically obsessed with, as Kathleen Raine notes, 'true cosmic or metaphysical apprehension'.[59] Watkins viewed himself as a transcendental Romantic artist, one whose 'strength', as his 'Rewards of the Fountain' insists, is found outside the vicissitudes of the present, in a place not easy to take a film crew: the 'sepulchre/ Where time is overthrown'.[60] Ormond gives structure to Watkins's lofty vision by ordering the biographical elements of the film around a set of thematic dichotomies. Scenes in which Watkins plays cricket in the garden with his children set the spiritual profundity of the poet's imagination against the physicality of his body: 'his fragility of manner is deceptive', says Ormond, narrating, as Watkins bowls overarm to his son, 'His friends know him to be about as fragile in fact as a concrete wall.' Similarly, the hurried monotony of Watkins's day job as a bank clerk in Swansea is contrasted with the deliberating imaginative labour of his work as a poet. Watkins reads 'Rewards of the Fountain', a poem that expresses his defiance in the face of life's material rewards – 'Let the world offer what it will,/ Its bargains I refuse. Those it rewards are greedy still./ I serve a stricter muse'.[61] Meanwhile, a close-up of a pair of hands flickers rapidly through a wad of banknotes; next, the hands hastily arrange a pile of strewn coins.[62] These fast-paced images then segue into an entirely different setting. Watkins sits at his desk at home, pondering a pile of manuscripts, and the quiet intensity of the scene is conveyed through the careful manipulation of *mise en scène*. The poet is shot against a pitch-black backdrop, dimly lit from the front in a way that illuminates him in ghostly silhouette; only the leaves of his drafts and one side of his face with its shock of white hair are visible. The effect is startling.

These scenes accessibly establish a sense of the deeper dichotomies that drive Watkins's art. But they serve also to connect his poetry with the context of his everyday life in Wales, and the landscape in which he lives. As Ormond states in the film's narration: 'The coastline of Gower is like a whetstone on which Watkins sharpens the blade of his ideas.' The film opens with a magnificent shot of Watkins strolling on Three Cliffs Bay, and there are extended readings of poems such as 'The Feather' and 'Music of Colours – White Blossom', accompanied by spectacular images that visualise their imaginative topography. Shots of the 'Blinding white' of snow on the Gower cliffs confirm the latter poem's vision of waves that seem 'grey' and 'dull'; images of 'Buds in April, on the waiting branch,/ Starrily opening'[63] are enhanced rather than diminished by the monochrome film stock. Watkins once stated that 'I marvel at the beauty of the landscape, but I never think of it as a theme for poetry until I read metaphysical symbols behind what I see.'[64] The film pursues this idea through its dichotomies of the physical and the imaginative, building to a stellar crescendo in which a reading of 'Bread and the Stars' is explored through an ambitious (and not a little high-flown) sequence of grand images of the cosmos accompanied by the Venus movement from Holtz's *The Planets*. *Under a Bright Heaven* ends with the poet speaking candidly in close-up to the camera:

> What one wants of a poem is that it should be ancient and fresh at the same time. A poem should create the illusion – if it is an illusion – that it has always existed, and that it was only waiting for the poet to write it down.

The film's closing tone of cosmic grandeur is given an almost clairvoyant poignancy when viewed in the light of Watkins's sudden death on a tennis court in Seattle barely a year after it was screened.

A BRONZE MASK

Ormond's penchant for elegiac themes and moods is further demonstrated in his next film, *A Bronze Mask*, subtitled *A Film in Elegy for Dylan Thomas*. This was not Ormond's first film about Dylan Thomas; his earlier *Return Journey* (1964) was a dramatisation of Thomas's famous radio programme about a return to Swansea after the Blitz, screened as a BBC Wales opt-out on 27 October 1964 – what would have been the poet's fiftieth birthday. Neither was it his last; *I Sing to you Strangers* (1982) was a profile that relied mainly on interviews with friends of the poet. But *A Bronze Mask* was the first film profile of Thomas's work, and the way in which it contextualises the poet in Wales is partly explained by the context of its production.

Like *Piano with Many Strings*, *A Bronze Mask* was produced for and aired on the BBC2 Network in the run up to the Investiture of the Prince of Wales in 1969.[65] The film focuses on the placement of one of David Slivka's bronze death masks of Thomas in the art collection of the National Museum of Wales.[66] The film is perhaps best viewed as an accompaniment to this exhibit, as well as a guided tour through the museum's collection.

While the film follows Ormond's other culture documentaries in using scenic shots of Laugharne to frame Thomas's work against the backdrop of the Welsh landscape, the main focus of the film is the celebration of Thomas as an important contribution to the Western cultural canon. *A Bronze Mask* achieves this via a form of filmic curation, juxtaposing recordings of Thomas reading some of his own best-known poems with shots of the exalted works on display elsewhere in the museum. The lovers with 'their arms/ Round the griefs of the ages' are symbolised by Auguste Rodin's sculpture *The Kiss*; the cynical commentary on the universal futility of war in 'The hand that signed the paper' is read against footage of the museum's Roman war collection; elsewhere Thomas's work is discussed with visual reference to the museum's collection of French impressionists, such as Renoir and Monet. August company, then; indeed the film is a sort of 'best of' Dylan Thomas, a show-reel of his great works on all the grand human themes: art ('In my craft or sullen art'), war ('The hand that signed the paper'), religion ('There was a saviour'), the innocence of childhood ('Fern Hill'), death ('And death shall have no dominion'). The effect is to corroborate Thomas's place among the greats of European civilisation. Crucially, while the museum is certainly presented as a repository of greatness, the film does not evoke it as a place inaccessible to or detached from the public. *A Bronze Mask* is structured around a school visit to the museum – children chatter loudly through the museum doors and poke inappropriately at statues; later, two men discuss the exhibitions using sign language. The first sound we hear in the film is the whistling of a museum security guard; the implication is that we have been invited in behind the scenes. In this sense the film is a reply and antidote to Kenneth Clark's *Civilisation*, the impressive but stuffily mannered series that had screened earlier that year. While Ormond's film does not quite aim for the iconoclasm of John Berger's 1972 *Ways of Seeing* – which famously opened with a shot of Berger carving into a painting with a Stanley knife – *A Bronze Mask* is playfully irreverent, lauding

Thomas's place in the National Museum's exalted collection while celebrating the museum as an open, accessible public space.

THE FRAGILE UNIVERSE

Ormond was evidently busy in the year leading up to the Investiture. The other documentary showcasing a Welsh writer ahead of the event was the more sombre *The Fragile Universe: A Portrait of Alun Lewis* (1969). Lewis's suspicious death near the front line against the Japanese Army in Burma in March 1944 brought an outpouring of tributes, elegies and obituaries from literary luminaries in Wales and England, one of which was penned by a young John Ormond and published in the magazine *Wales* in summer 1944. Critical consensus has since settled on an interpretation of Lewis as a writer of conflicted allegiances, 'divided sensibilities'.[67] For some he possessed all the best qualities of the south Walian bard: hailing from the village of Cwmaman in the Cynon valley, Lewis was intensely sensitive to Wales's historical and linguistic culture. Poet Harri Webb described Lewis as a 'lost leader' who 'undoubtedly belonged by inheritance and personality' to south Wales.[68] This was a perception confirmed by stories of Lewis's solidarity with the lower ranks of his battalion, the South Wales Borderers (Lewis, an educated ex-schoolmaster, was a second lieutenant), as well as by remarks in his letters home that he 'regret[ted] his lack of Welsh very deeply' and that he would determine when he returned home to learn the language and to 'always tackle [his] writing through Welsh life and ways of thought'.[69] Recent scholarship has shown that Lewis's sense of Welshness was far from straightforward, and, as Gareth Evans has shown, informed his 'cultural interaction' with India in complex and often contradictory ways.[70] Yet, as a sensitive observer of the universal significances of the quiet, unheralded moments of war, he found a firm place in the canon of British war poetry, achieving a 'cultural eminence' that, as Alan Vaughan Jones argues, 'had less to do with his vision of Wales than with his function as a writer who satisfied the craving for a 'war poet' during the 1939–45 conflict [. . .] and an embodiment of the 'noble' qualities of such men – patriotism, courage and self-sacrifice'.[71] Given the context of the Investiture, it is, unsurprisingly, this facet of Lewis's work that is emphasised in Ormond's film.

This is not to say that the film presents Lewis in any simplistic sense as an archetypal British soldier. *The Fragile Universe* paints a portrait of an emotionally complex and sensitive character through interviews with his mother Gwladys (with whom, in her own words, he had a 'very special and close relationship'[72]), his widow Gweno, his friends and fellow-soldiers, as well as through interspersed scenes in which an actor (Henley Thomas),[73] dressed in army uniform and shot in gloomy light, reads Lewis's poems and letters, conveying a sense of this brooding, tormented figure.[74] Something of the contrast between the stiff-upper-lipped culture of the British military and Lewis's almost grotesque unsuitability for it is hinted at through two starkly contrasting accents: the film's sharply cut-glass commentary (Arthur Phillips), and Henley Thomas's softly Welsh-tinged, plaintive readings of the poetry. Some of the more evocative comments in the film come from an interview with Lord Chalfont (Alun Gwynne Jones), who served alongside Lewis.[75] 'There was about him this strange quality of depth, which in those days, in that particular atmosphere, was a rare quality.' Yet while Lewis was, as Lord Chalfont notes, 'intensely vulnerable' to the life of the soldier, the film asserts that he was no less courageous than the other men. Rather, he was driven, as is implied through further remarks from Lord Chalfont, by the deeper sensitivities of the poet: 'almost everything frightened him, and it was that that made him determined to behave in [an] outwardly courageous way.' Indeed, the emphasis in *The Fragile Universe*, as its title implies, is on the extent to which Lewis's poetic sensibilities, the 'cast of his disposition as a writer', as the narrator states, afforded him a deeper insight into the nature of his experiences of war: a more profound understanding of the worlds he was encountering in India and Burma ('Where others had seen the outward symbols and ceremonies of Buddhism, he had glimpsed the very heart of the Buddhist faith') that led to a deliquescence of the 'fragile universe of [his] self' and towards a subjectivity that was at once dispersed and unified, yet wholly appropriate to the visionary war poet.

Some have traced Lewis's sense of difference and internal conflict to his cultural background. Dai Smith, for example, interprets Lewis's attraction to this peculiarly dispersed sense of self as a symptom of a deeper national-historical disjointedness – one that resulted in the intense anomic malaise that eventually 'exhausted him'[76] but might, under different circumstances, have benefited Wales. Similarly, Ormond's own 1944 elegy to Lewis presents the poet as a proud son of Wales:

Through many requiems, and gentle summers
and autumns, when the seeds
of secret love burn and are lost in Wales, his grave will wait for snow
that in our winter valleys covers the tilted fields
where as a boy he learned to be a poet.[77]

(Section III, lines 1–6)

The mode is that of the communal bard mourning the loss of a national voice now buried in a distant land. Here Wales is 'ours', a communal land of familiar landscapes where life is lived and shared through all seasons, and where Lewis lies in spirit, if not body.[78] While *The Fragile Universe* does cover Lewis's early days in Cwmaman, the film emphasises Lewis's writing in India and Burma as symptomatic, not of his Welshness, but of a profoundly universal, Romantic, perhaps Keatsian, self-effacement, from which flowed his consummate war poetry and prose. That this was a necessary interpretation of an honourable British war poet at the time of the Investiture is strongly confirmed by the film's gloss of the controversial circumstances of Lewis's death early in the morning of 5 March 1944. The single bullet wound in Lewis's right temple had, in official reports, been explained as the consequence of freak accident with a loaded revolver, with the Battalion Roll of Honour listing Lewis under the heading 'Died from Battle Accidents'.[79] This was famously dubious given Lewis's well-known propensity for depressive moods, particularly in the morning,[80] and indeed as Pikoulis notes, among the Borderers it was 'universally assumed that Alun had killed himself'.[81] Yet Lord Chalfont, one of Lewis's closest friends at the time, offers only a sketch of the events that unfolded on that morning, and the film concludes with the sense of confusion that surrounded his death immediately after the event: '[a] message [came] through from the company to say that there had been some firing during the night, and that lieutenant Lewis had been shot'. The film offers no further clarification on the matter, leaving Lewis's death ambiguously open to the interpretation that he had died in battle.

PRIEST AND POET

If *The Fragile Universe* accommodates the mood of the Investiture by presenting Alun Lewis as a British war poet for BBC network audiences, the subject of his next film was perhaps trickier to showcase

in such terms. Nevertheless, *R. S. Thomas: Priest and Poet*, broadcast to a network BBC2 audience on Easter Sunday 1972, is a film
quite clearly produced with a British audience in mind. In fact,
R. S. Thomas was by this time not unfamiliar with working with the
BBC. The poet had been a presence on the airwaves for many years,
having written lectures in both Welsh and English for radio, besides
his radio verse drama, *The Minister* (1953).[82] Roland Mathias has
suggested that it was the coverage received by Thomas's 1952 volume
An Acre of Land on the BBC's prestigious culture programme *The
Critics* (broadcast on the Third Programme) that, twenty years earlier, brought the poet into the English literary spotlight. The three
critics on that programme deemed it 'the best volume of poetry they
had read in 1952',[83] and the result was the almost immediate selling
out of all Thomas's work in print,[84] followed by the commissioning
of *The Minister* and shortly afterwards the publication of a selected
collection, *Song at the Year's Turning* (1955), introduced by the doyen
of English poetry at that time, John Betjeman.

Given Thomas's considerable renown by this time, it seems
appropriate that Ormond should produce a film profile of him at
BBC Wales, and appropriate, too, that this profile should not dwell
on some of Thomas's more piquant views on Welsh nationhood. The
year 1972 perhaps seemed an appropriate time to profile the milder
side of the priest-poet; readers had by this time been waiting four
years for a new collection from Thomas, and it was this year's *H'm*
that is often referred to as the one that marked the poet's shift into
the poetry of 'spiritual search'[85] in his later years. Thomas had a few
years earlier moved to a post as vicar of Aberdaron, that 'romantic
sea-lashed spot on the remote tip of the Llŷn Peninsula', and it was
here that, as Tony Brown and M. Wynn Thomas suggest, Thomas
'largely abandoned political poetry [. . .] and dedicated himself, under
the influence of the ancient rocks of the region, to meditation on
the eternal'.[86] *H'm* contains little of the biting cynicism ('Holding
our caps out/ Beside a framed view/ We never painted, counting/
The few casual cowries/ With which we are fobbed off'[87]) or visceral
frustration ('Where can I go, then, from the smell/ Of decay, from
the putrefying of a dead/ Nation?'[88]) of 1968's *Not That He Bought
Flowers*. This is not to say that Thomas had, by any stretch of the
imagination, abandoned his commitment to Welsh nationhood. If his
poetry was finding its emphases in the spiritual, his public appear-
ances were no less outspoken on national matters than earlier in

life. There is an illuminating contrast between the representation of
Thomas in *Priest and Poet* and that of the poet's own remarkable
autobiographical lecture, 'Y Llwybrau Gynt' (translated by Sandra
Anstey as 'The Paths Gone By'), delivered in Welsh on BBC radio
in the same year. 'Y Llwybrau Gynt' charts the development of a
self-described 'proper little bourgeois, brought up delicately'[89] into
the prophetic spokesman of an ethno-linguistic national culture. For
Brown and Thomas, it was the lifelong effort to gain imaginative
access to that culture that 'hurt R. S. Thomas into verse'.[90] It is this
effort, and particularly the centrality of the Welsh language to it,
that the poet describes in the lecture: 'I set about learning Welsh to
get back to the real Wales of my imagination.'[91] This was a concern
at the core of Thomas's imaginative vision, and one to which he
would continue to return as a public figure in Wales from the mid-
1970s.[92] His important lecture at the 1976 National Eisteddfod at
Cardigan, 'Abercuawg', further elaborated on the ideas established in
'Y Llwybrau Gynt', particularly the political importance of striving
for an imagined nation, an aesthetic vision that emblematises a social
ideal, however ostensibly unreal.

Thomas's prominence among an English literary readership, contrasted with his stature within the Welsh nationalist movement in
the 1970s, means Ormond's film should be viewed at the interface
between what Ned Thomas had recognised as 'disparate "English"
and "Welsh" perspectives' on R. S. Thomas that '[drew] on different
aspects of his work'.[93] Despite the political furies that were driving
much of Thomas's thinking at this time, *Priest and Poet* does not offer
an explicit description of his politics, and BBC2 viewers who were
not aware of them would not have learned much about them from
the film. Ormond instead focuses on some of the connections – and
contradictions – between Thomas's spiritual and artistic vocations. He
elicits some tantalisingly candid remarks on this; one notable instance
is Thomas's cool response to Ormond's astonished probing. 'You are
saying that the notion of Christ's Resurrection is a metaphor?' asks
Ormond, to which Thomas replies,

> We are not so hag-ridden today by heresy hunters as they were in the
> early centuries of the church. There's no doubt that we commit a lot
> more important heresies probably than by saying that the Resurrection
> and Incarnation are metaphors. My work as a poet has to deal with the
> presentation of imaginative truth. Christianity also seems to me to be

a presentation of imaginative truth. So that there is [. . .] no necessary conflict between these two things at all.

The film goes on to afford Thomas the time to explain his complex, self-confessedly 'Coleridgean' conception of the imaginative relationship between language and 'ultimate reality'.

On the surface, then, *R. S. Thomas: Priest and Poet* is an examination of some of the features of Thomas's Christian poetics for BBC2 audiences on Easter Sunday. However, there is something about the film's mood that hints at more than this. The carefully considered visual vocabulary, the measured pacing of both in-frame movement and the diachronic shot, and the deliberation with which Thomas recites his poems over scenic images of the landscape of the Llŷn Peninsula, all complement the poet's measured, deceptively simple verse.[94] And though the film perhaps occasionally borders on the 'Lord Privy Seal' effect in its visual strategy (Thomas's readings of poems such as 'Kneeling', 'The Moor' and 'The River' are accompanied by footage of, respectively, a church interior, the expansive Welsh moors, and Thomas surveying a brook), it does powerfully evoke a sense of a poet firmly in his place. The first words we hear in the film are Welsh, as the poet quietly welcomes his congregation to church – 'Bore da, bore da' – a touch that would have been striking to predominantly anglophone BBC2 audiences. Interestingly, in 'Abercuawg', Thomas lauded the medium of film as one with the capacity to bring to life a sense of imaginative reality, to 'show flowers and the leaves quivering in the breeze, and not still to the point of lifelessness as on a postcard'.[95] In the same lecture, he pronounced that

[Man] will never see Abercuawg. But through striving to see it, through longing for it, through refusing to accept that it belongs to the past and has fallen into oblivion; through refusing to accept some second-hand substitute, he will succeed in preserving it as an eternal possibility.[96]

If Thomas's poetic mode captured glimpses of an imaginative reality that brought the nation to life as an 'eternal possibility', Ormond's film also tentatively gestures in this direction.

This chapter has examined the best of Ormond's work in this genre, though it should be said he did produce many other films about artists and writers. Not all of these were directly connected to Wales; neither do they all share the same attentiveness to compositional and technical detail. He directed two programmes for an interview series,

My Time Again, with Harry Secombe and Richard Burton, in 1966. His series *Private View* (1970), while interviewing figures such as John Grierson and Robert Graves, also consisted mainly of talking-head interviews. *Fortissimo Jones*, a profile of the Swansea-born composer Daniel Jones, produced in time for the latter's sixty-fifth birthday in 1977, is a personal study of the composer's life and work that similarly adopted the interview format. In the same year, Ormond produced a documentary on the history of his earlier employer, *Picture Post* magazine, *The Life and Death of Picture Post* (1977). Ormond's acquaintance with editor Tom Hopkinson enabled him to glean fascinating interviews with him and other important figures, including Stefan Lorant and proprietor Sir Edward Hulton. The film paints a nuanced picture of the magazine's rise and fall.

Ormond once wrote about the experience of his initial interview for the role of documentary producer at the BBC. He recalled that one of the questioners, 'not having much idea of what kind of question he should be asking, suggested that the beautiful scenery of Wales would make for a good documentary'. Ormond's response was that 'such material was a bonus, but [. . .] true documentary would have people and concern for people at the heart of it'.[97] Ormond's best profiles of Welsh artists and writers certainly meet this tenet, and translate sophisticated and often personal readings of artists and their work into compelling, accessible films. Ormond, an artist himself, and frequently a friend of those he profiled, was well positioned to do this. But his films at the same time make more of Welsh landscape than a mere visual 'bonus'. His film-making displays an enduring interest in the *place* of culture, and invariably foregrounds the locations and environments that give rise to different forms of cultural expression. Tellingly, his final work as a producer for BBC Wales was *Poems in their Place*, a series of ten-minute films profiling poets in their locales. His talent lay in his lightness of touch with such matters. Crafting informative television films from often complex subjects, he worked in a hybrid form that was both popular and high-flown. In this way his films negotiate tricky terrain, and locate his subjects in a Welsh context without the need to essentialise or overstate a defining 'Welshness'. His films perform the role of 'cultural broker', using an 'organic mosaic' approach to bridge cultural and geographical divides and celebrate the broad multiplicity of cultural forms to which the place we call Wales has given rise. In doing so, they constitute an important contribution to that culture.

4

BROKERING HISTORY

In 1990, Gomer published *Wales in Vision*, a collection of essays looking back at the history of Welsh television from its inception. The year marked the end of a decade or so of considerable advances in Welsh broadcasting. The year 1982 had seen the advent of S4C (Sianel Pedwar Cymru, 'Channel Four Wales'), a dedicated Welsh-language television channel, after considerable political wrangling,[1] as well as the rise of dedicated Welsh radio stations in both Welsh and English: BBC Radio Cymru had begun broadcasting in 1977, BBC Radio Wales in 1978. The book was commissioned to mark twenty-five years since the establishment of BBC Wales proper in 1964, but despite being an anniversary undertaking, most of the contributions were clear-eyed rather than nostalgic or blandly celebratory. It opened with an essay by Ormond, 'Beginnings', in which he recalled the early days of television production in Wales: 'There was no Cardiff studio, no news cameras, no film, no (as the saying goes) nothing.'[2] Elsewhere, Dai Smith reflected on what had been accomplished since those meagre beginnings. Writing as a historian, he lauded BBC Wales's efforts to bring Welsh history into public consciousness:

> the production line of broad-based programmes on the history of Wales should not be seen as the duty of Television being done but rather a signal that the nature of historical experience and of its method of enquiry has begun to enter the general consciousness of Wales. I would like to think that the presence of the Past in our daily lives has been underscored by the efforts of all those who had made films on our history.[3]

Yet Smith ended with a note of caution, warning that television in Wales, if it was to avoid becoming a mere 'dazzled blink for a nation', ought to pursue the 'steady, and long-term, Janus vision that comes from historical understanding'.[4] The seriousness and cautiousness of the tone of much of *Wales in Vision* is perhaps a sign of the perceived magnitude and, at the same time, precariousness of what had been achieved. Each of the contributors had worked with or within the BBC in Wales, had been accustomed to its fraught relationship with BBC headquarters – not to say its own internal disputes – and knew that in this particular context, its accomplishments, and indeed the very opportunity to look back and reflect on them, were not to be taken for granted.

In a way, Smith's endorsement of the role of history on television may seem an unusual move for an historian. Television necessarily simplifies complex, contradictory themes, with the result that the perception among many academic historians is that, as Simon Schama has suggested, 'the subtlety of history is too elusive, too fine and slippery to be caught in television's big, hammy fist'.[5] Smith, however, was writing at the end of a decade of considerable successes in Welsh television documentary, with the production of two acclaimed series: HTV and Channel 4's joint production, *The Dragon Has Two Tongues* (1985),[6] as well as Smith's own iconoclastic series for BBC Wales, *Wales! Wales?* (1984).[7] As their titles suggest, both series displayed a marked reflexivity about the forces that shape not only historical development, but also the writing, or in this case, televising of it. Both Smith and the historian behind *The Dragon Has Two Tongues*, Gwyn Alf Williams, were informed by the radical revisionist approaches to history that had taken place since the early 1960s, emblematised by E. H. Carr's influential book *What is History?* (1961). There Carr had stressed the importance of examining the ideological assumptions that condition historical enquiry, no matter how ostensibly 'factual' its evidence: 'The belief in a hard core of historical facts existing objectively and independently of the interpretation of the historian is a preposterous fallacy'.[8] The writing of history, argued Carr, invariably 'reflects our own position in time'.[9] One significant result of this was the formation, in the 1970s, of new associations of historians with explicit ideological agendas, such as the History Workshop Movement and, in Wales, the Welsh Labour History Society. These 'history from below' approaches sought primarily to expose and combat dominant, primarily Liberal historical narratives by rewriting history from the perspective of those who had traditionally been marginalised and excluded by it.

This generation of historians knew that writing history was a hard-won right. They also knew that the writing and dissemination of it were powerful political tools, and critical to historical development. As Raphael Samuel, one of the founders of the History Workshop Movement, argued in his later work, *Theatres of Memory* (1994), these historians were interested not only in the kinds of history being written and taught, but, simultaneously, in the related issue of the means through which dominant historical narratives were becoming hegemonic, and the effects they were having upon society. Historians, Samuel argued, should focus their attention on all those arenas, or 'theatres of memory', in which discourses relating to the past play out – in his words, the 'ensemble of activities and practices in which ideas of history are embedded or a dialectic of past-present relations is rehearsed'.[10] Given the capacity of television to reach audiences of millions, some commentators began to view the medium as one that was performing a basic yet powerful social function, as 'bard',[11] 'chronicler'[12] or 'large-scale cultural ritual'.[13] From this perspective, television is not something to be scorned as a simplifier of historical narratives, but a part of the process of historical development itself. The production cooperative that produced *The Dragon Has Two Tongues* self-referentially signalled this in its very name: Teliesyn.[14]

If television is both shaped by and forms of part of the ongoing dialectic through which 'past–present relations [are] rehearsed', then it follows that television documentaries are themselves valuable historical sources. One way to view this is through the lens of what Gary Edgerton describes as television's 'presentism'. Edgerton notes that television necessarily functions within a certain set of formal requirements that impact upon the ways in which history can reasonably be treated in the medium. Television, until very recently, with the advent of the Internet and on-demand viewing, was predominantly broadcast simultaneously to vast audiences. In this sense, television is quintessentially a medium of the present, a medium of 'immediacy'. In order to attract and retain the enormous audiences demanded by advertising and/or the justification of a licence fee, it must respond to a correspondingly enormous number of social pressures. In particular, it has to appeal to the immediate tastes, cultural assumptions and ideological requirements of the society to which it broadcasts. Proof of this can be seen in the kind of programmes that preceded Ormond's own history documentaries at the BBC. As television historian Robert Dillon notes, there was an exponential rise of factual history programmes on British television in the years after 1945.[15] Programmes such as *Germany Under Control* (1946) and *The Heart of an Empire* (1946) 'offer[ed] reassurance that a bitter enemy has been tamed and that London is still functioning as the capital city of the world'.[16] Ormond, however, producing films on Welsh history for, primarily, Welsh audiences, was responding to rather different circumstances.

PLURAL EXPERIENCE

The BBC in Wales had been utilising its position as a national broadcaster to produce programmes on matters of Welsh history long before the Second World War.[17] However, the major precedents for Ormond's Welsh history programmes were heard on radio in Wales in the 1950s, with series such as *The Making of Modern Wales (1815– 1914)* (1955) and, across two series broadcast during the winters of 1958–60, *Wales Through the Ages*.[18] These were important efforts to educate audiences on major new developments taking place in Welsh history. A central driver of this, as Kenneth O. Morgan notes, was the expansion of university education in Britain from the late 1950s to the 1970s, of which one major benefactor was the University of Wales. This had provided the basis for a major re-examination of the Welsh past. As Morgan notes, '[e]xpansion meant progress [. . .] [What] flourished mightily in the sixties and seventies, was a sense of Welshness and a serious concern with Welsh issues.'[19] Nevertheless, Welsh history was at that time characterised by a conflict between two opposing interpretations of historical development. One of these had roots in Welsh Liberalism, which had found political voice in the late nineteenth century, and reached its zenith in the landslide General Election of 1906, when every seat in Wales was Liberal. The Welsh Liberals of this era had built new national institutions – the University of Wales (1893), the National Library of Wales (1907), the National Museum (1907) and the Welsh Department of the Board of Education (1907) – designed to embody the Welsh Liberal view of history. As Huw Pryce notes, Welsh Liberal intellectuals knew that only a focus on the Welsh past could give 'legitimacy to claims that modern Wales was a nation reborn'.[20] They therefore set out on a project of writing a history of and for themselves. The most notable examples were O. M. Edwards's books *Hanes Cymru* and *Wales* (1895 and 1901, alongside his many periodicals of the 1890s), John Rhys and

David Brynmor-Jones's *The Welsh People* (1900), Owen Rhoscomyl's (Robert Scourfield Mills) *Flame-bearers of Welsh History* (1905) and J. E. Lloyd's *History of Wales* (1911). These were the products of a Welsh-speaking Nonconformist bourgeoisie whose conception of the nation was built around the mythology of the respectable rural *gwerin*, a people that was, in Gwyn Alf Williams's terms, 'cultivated, educated, often self-educated, responsible, self-disciplined, [. . .] Welsh-speaking, Nonconformist, imbued with the more social virtues of Dissent, bred on the Bible and good practice'.[21] These were the histories that, as Gwyn Alf Williams went on to explain in the 1980s, were 'to shape the outlook of whole sectors of Welsh life' in the twentieth century – the BBC included.[22]

However, while Liberalism was reaching its peak, a new industrial society was developing in south Wales, sucking the population out of rural Wales. In contrast to the *gwerin*'s spirituality and temperance, the urbanised working-class south was anglicised, increasingly godless, and frequently drunk. In 1851, 135,000 were employed in agriculture; by 1901, this figure was 92,000; in contrast, mining in 1851 employed 65,000, and by 1921 the figure was 278,000.[23] This expansion of working-class life was accompanied by a rise in working-class politics that, throughout the course of the twentieth century, changed the political colour of Wales. In 1922, just sixteen years after the Liberal landslide of 1906, Labour held half of Wales's constituencies; by 1966 it held thirty-two of the thirty-six seats. Twentieth-century Wales, then, was, in one of Dai Smith's oft-repeated phrases, not 'singular' but 'plural',[24] and its two main elements were, largely, politically irreconcilable. As Morgan notes, with the 1950s and 1960s the years in which Labour was at the height of its power and influence in Wales, 'those teaching the history of Wales [. . .] tended to be Labour',[25] and the result was a new generation of historians dedicated to the history of industrial south Wales. As Daryl Leeworthy notes, there had been many important works written in the years after the war, often by participants in the labour movement.[26] But 'the father'[27] of the movement that was to come, according to Gwyn Alf Williams, was David Williams, whose *The Rebecca Riots* (1955) set the direction of travel; Glanmor Williams followed, founding the extant *Welsh History Review* journal in 1960 and compiling the important collection of essays *Merthyr Politics: The Making of a Working Class Tradition* in 1966.[28]

This was the heated context of new historiographical renegotiation in which Ormond began producing history documentaries at the BBC.

Clearly, any effort to construct a balanced sense of a 'plural' Welsh history at that time was no easy task. As a television historian of sorts, Ormond was operating, to borrow Keith Jenkins's phrase, within a historical 'field of force' in which 'directions [were] contested'.[29] In his work at the BBC, it is useful to draw a parallel with the related aims of Wales's National Museum, which, as Rhiannon Mason notes, is, like the BBC, 'expected to play specific national roles within a wider nationally charged public sphere':

> It may be challenged in terms of what it is perceived to be saying or not saying about the nation and will be used by all sorts of different parties as a kind of 'staging ground' [. . .] for wider debates and conversations about national identities, national cultures and national histories.

Mason goes on: 'the challenge [. . .] is to balance the conflicting pressures they produce'.[30] Ormond's history documentaries reveal a similar effort to broker two competing historiographical traditions. Produced between 1961 and 1979, they span the period in which the crosswinds of those debates were at their most turbulent. The ways in which these films answered the question, to rephrase Carr, 'What is Welsh history?' not only reflected their own position in the history of Wales, but, further, contributed to the making of that history.

ONCE THERE WAS A TIME

The first, broadcast in 1961, is *Once There Was a Time*, a curious film that is part observational study, part elegy to coalmining in the Rhondda. By 1961, the culture and community of the south Wales valleys was, in tandem with the economic base on which it was predicated, in sharp decline. The 1960s was the decade in which Welsh coalmining was dismantled almost entirely, with the number of major working pits in the Rhondda dropping from twelve in 1958 to just one in 1969.[31] While these shifts in employment did not result in the serious levels of unemployment that would be seen later in the 1970s and 1980s, the 'relative affluence' of the 1960s was, in John Davies's words, the 'result of development, some distance away, in newer industrial areas, where the values of Welsh working-class culture were not paramount'.[32] The result was that the traditional working-class communities of the Rhondda were undeniably atrophying. Aneurin Bevan had died in 1960, an event that tolled the end of an era, and streets that were once 'stuffed with people [in a] never-ending civic parade'[33] were by this time showing 'a more tranquil, anodyne appearance'.[34] Filmed on the cusp of these changes, when the remnants of a once vibrant culture were visibly fading, *Once There Was a Time* attempts to capture that Rhondda.

The film revels in the familiar iconography of south Wales: the chapel, the pub, the spotlessly respectable front parlours, the workmen's library,[35] the steep streets of endlessly terraced houses that all led to the pithead frame.[36] However, Ormond does not resort to easy nostalgia. The film is structured around the theme of learning, expressed through a series of discussions between two impressively erudite working-class veterans, William Thomas, an atheist Marxist, and Teify Jones, a Christian scholar. The two men sit on a bench and converse eloquently (though a little desultorily) on a range of topics: Shakespeare, Hume, the Bible, the Great War, time itself. In this sense, the film is a celebration of the fiercely intellectual life of south Wales; the south Wales of communally funded libraries and institutes, and of miners' scholarships to Oxford and London. There are heavy overtones of the vision of 'the valleys' contained in Paul Dickson's film for the 1951 Festival of Britain, *David*. *David* was filmed in the Amman valley, a predominantly Welsh-speaking area on the western edge of the south Wales coalfield, and different in character from the English-speaking valleys of the eastern coalfield, but its depiction of miner-poet D. R. Griffiths (the brother of Labour politician Jim Griffiths) as its cultivated protagonist is similarly designed to emblematise the most admirable qualities of south Wales life. *Once There Was a Time*, however, reaches beyond such nostalgia in its attempt to capture something of the complexly dialectic spirit of that culture.[37] Though quietly observational in tone and mood, the film touches upon an historical fault-line that reaches back to the disputes over workers' education in the 1900s. This split, as Richard Lewis has noted, was between the Workers' Educational Association and the National Council of Labour Colleges, each of which represented two separate political traditions: the former 'collaborated with the state system of education' whereas the latter 'stressed its independence of the state and the class interests it represented'.[38] *Once There Was a Time* portrays a sense of these competing political forces through the figures of its two protagonists. Teify endorses the Lib-Lab view: 'isn't education and culture the main goal in life?', whereas William is sceptical of learning for its own sake, viewing the

Liberal education reforms of the late nineteenth century as a product of employers 'looking for clerks and people to count the other people's pay [. . .] not for my benefit but for their own'. He proudly recalls arranging classes on industrial history, walking down from Blaencwm to Treherbert 'carrying coal in a fish-sack to light the fire in the room we had'.

While the film certainly celebrates this culture of political difference and learned debate, its purpose is not to keep the fire of such debates burning into the 1960s. Rather, it enshrines the men's dialogue and the wider culture it represents as an admirable but now passing sociocultural moment. William and Teify are filmed entering the workmen's institute, and continue their conversation there, but appear to be the only men still using it for this purpose. Their rambling discussions on communism, socialism and philosophical rationalism are playfully but nevertheless firmly undermined when intercut with footage of younger men indulging in more frivolous pursuits: cards, dominos, pints.[39] A short dramatised scene sees a member choosing a book from the institute library, and from the wide-ranging material available – Neville Chamberlain's *The Struggle for Peace*, Edward Hallett Abend's *Japan Unmasked* and Lancelot Hogben's *Science for the Citizen* are three of the books shot in close-up – he chooses a work of romance. The librarian disapproves: '"The old boys years ago, they wouldn't look at such rubbish as this!" "Well, Bryn, those other ones are too high for me."' This is the pattern of the film as a whole, a vision of a once vigorous culture now aged and ailing: the streets are empty, as are the chapel pews, leaving the elderly choir to sing to themselves. Faces once young in photographs on a parlour mantelpiece are now old and weary. True to Ormond's poetics, the film is as much a 'requiem' as a 'celebration', a paean and elegy to what 'once there was'.[40] In this sense, the film taps the same vein of melancholic historical-poetic energy that ex-miner and poet Robert Morgan discovers in his own poem reflecting on miners' libraries:

> Their history is now a spiritual concession
>
> Recorded in new books on the same shelves
> That once bordered their besmirched lives.[41]

Morgan's poem even draws upon the leitmotif of Ormond's film, the 'aged ones, who remain, recite/ Their stories on park benches'.

However, *Once There Was a Time* ends with a firmer sense of finality: William and Teify's bench, at the film's close, is empty.

If the film elegises the final days of the south Wales coalfield, it far from signals the final days of a wider national community. Rather, its elegiac poeticism lends itself to the uses of televisual history in the formation of a national public sphere. *Once There Was a Time* aims at this sense of the elegiac not only in content, but also in its formal construction and its sense of the poetic, personal documentary. In contrast to the expositional, expert-led factual history documentaries developed on television in the later 1960s and 1970s – the kind Ormond himself would go on to produce – *Once There Was a Time* is self-consciously associational and fluid in form. These are qualities that Norman Swallow, writing in the BBC's *The Listener* magazine in 1976, suggested are ideal for history-telling:

> [Television] is a poor communicator of ideas, but a splendid transmitter of history's sense of place and time and mood. Its cameras can go almost anywhere; to any historical site, any evocative landscape, any museum, any fine example of art or architecture. By the combination of the available visual images and an imaginative sound-track it can, arguably, convey a truer sense of the past than any book, any lecture, or any public exhibition.[42]

Once There Was a Time illustrates Swallow's point in the way it chooses association over explanation, mood over argument: it builds its 'sense of place and time and mood' through the careful accumulation of sounds and images. There is no scripted commentary, only the voices of our two protagonists interspersed with disconcertingly mysterious musical arrangements. The camerawork follows no expositional logic, but rather acts as ghostly observer of this now ageing community, quietly surveying the scene with undulated panning shots down the mountainside and dolly shots that glide through the streets – indeed the conceit is that we stumble upon the two interlocutors as if by accident. The film perhaps embodies the role of poet-chronicler of a passing historical moment.

Once There Was a Time of course observes a *present* community in decline (and perhaps somewhat prematurely, given that there were still 106,000 miners in Wales in 1960), but through its emphasis on the passing of the past – encapsulated in a title that reaches towards the parlance of storybook nostalgia – it partakes in this process of historical re-examination. Interestingly, that this was not something that BBC Wales had attempted in the years while industrial south Wales was still a fully active, living community. As John Davies notes, there had been a 'resistance to the portrayal of history of the industrial areas' on radio, particularly in the 1930s, when those areas were highly politically turbulent. 'There was a belief that pre-industrial Welsh history was a less dangerous subject.'[43] The film can be viewed as part of an effort to position the more disquieting elements of industrial south Wales into a safely irretrievable past. But whether we view the film an effort to consign the Welsh industrial experience safely into history, or as a magnanimous effort to balance two competing historiographical traditions, it is certain that the film was entering the historical 'field of force' in Wales. Broadcast on St David's Day 1961, *Once There Was a Time* was clearly an attempt to bring the urban industrial working-class experience into the Welsh historiographical frame.[44] This was met with resistance from some. Robert Graham, the television critic for the *Western Mail*, asserted on the Saturday after the broadcast of *Once There Was a Time* that he 'deplored the choice of the Rhondda as St David's material'.[45] Similarly, some members of a BBC audience research group suggested that 'nothing of what these two old men said seemed to have much in common with St David's Day nor with the Rhondda Valley proper'. That said, one Welshman in the group seemed to appreciate the film, stating that 'all the abstract qualities which make up the Rhondda valley had been portrayed' and that the film 'caught the imagination and stirred the soul'.[46]

THE DESERT AND THE DREAM; Y GYMRU BELL

The year after, Ormond and a fellow producer, Nan Davies, together with a small film crew, travelled across the Atlantic to the Welsh colony, Y Wladfa, in Patagonia, Argentina.[47] Robert Graham, evidently preferring a film more in keeping with the Liberal, *gwerin* interpretation of Wales, judged Ormond's film about Patagonia to be 'first class'.[48] The colony, led by Michael D. Jones, began with the landing of the *Mimosa* on Patagonian soil in 1865, and was, as Prys Morgan suggests, a prime manifestation of the *gwerin* spirit in the nineteenth century.[49] It is therefore unsurprising that the story was revisited in the years leading up to its centenary. Alongside the decline in industrial society that had galvanised a historiographical movement in south

Wales, the simultaneous decline in Welsh-language communities was energising Welsh language and political-nationalist constituencies. The mechanisation of agriculture was at this time, in John Davies's words, '[causing] the agricultural worker, by far the largest single labour force in Wales a century earlier, to become virtually extinct'.[50] With the economic base on which the *gwerin* was based irretrievably changed, some turned back to the past to this story of perseverance and resilience in order to find a platform for the maintenance of an identity in the present. R. Bryn Williams's major history of the movement, titled *Y Wladfa*, was published in 1962, and Williams acted as adviser to Ormond's films. In that same year Saunders Lewis delivered a lecture that became pivotal for the language movement in Wales, 'Tynged yr Iaith' ('The Fate of the Language'). In that lecture Lewis held up Patagonia as an example of the importance of constructing a useable past at a time of national crisis – or rather, in line with the apocalyptic tone of the lecture, as an illustration of Wales's failure to construct such a past. Lewis deemed the colony an 'heroic experiment', arguing that '[t]o this day our want of national consciousness and our lack of the pride of nationhood prevent us from understanding the significance and heroism of the Patagonian venture'.[51]

The programmes that resulted from Ormond's trip to Patagonia were the English-language *The Desert and the Dream*, written and produced by Ormond, and the Welsh-language four-part series *Y Gymru Bell*, directed by Ormond but written and presented by Nan Davies, both broadcast in 1962.[52] Both were efforts to revive the story of Y Wladfa, but Ormond's film was also an effort to translate the story for anglophone audiences.[53] As Glyn Williams, R. Bryn Williams's son and fellow historian of the colony, wrote in 1991, 'Welsh speakers are far more familiar with this part of the nation's history than are those [. . .] who do not speak the language.'[54] The BBC's Audience Research Report on the film found that many were 'glad to have some information about this "little known story"'.[55] R. Bryn Williams later attempted to address this in a concise version of his history of the colony, *Gwladfa Patagonia: The Welsh Colony in Patagonia 1865–1965* (1965), which was, in a clear attempt to bridge the two linguistic communities, printed bilingually on opposing pages. This was a response to the fact that, as Williams noted, '[n]ot only has most of what has been written about the settlement been published in Welsh but the ideological content of what passes as the history of

Wales in Welsh and English is [. . .] often quite different'.[56] He was
perhaps referring to Ormond's two productions, which, despite being
filmed simultaneously and utilising much of the same footage, address
their shared topic very differently, as the contrasting registers of their
titles suggest. Viewed together, they emblematise a deep rift in Welsh
historiography.

In contrast to the poetic, cinematic approach Ormond adopted
in much of his work, *Y Gymru Bell* aims at a more systematic and
structured study of the colony, albeit in an informal manner.[57]
Interviews with Welsh-speaking Patagonians provide much of the
material, and this gives *Y Gymru Bell* a prevailing tone of familiarity.
As John Corner has suggested, the adoption of such a tone in some
documentary films is no accident, but a deliberate and effective representational strategy. Corner observes that television in the 1950s and
1960s saw a gradual shift away from stilted 'cinema-based styles of
exposition' towards a more populist form of 'people's television', in
which 'earlier registers of authoritative, public-service commentary
[. . .] [were] mixed with fresh attempts at exploiting the domestic, per-
sonalised and sociable dimensions of the new medium in such a way
as to provide documentary with egalitarian accents'.[58] The intention
was to develop a 'more informal relationship' between the viewer and
the representations on screen, to construct a 'bridge [. . .] between
viewer's world and subject's world'.[59] Its purpose in *Y Gymru Bell* is
to forge an active link between two threatened linguistic and sociocultural communities in order to strengthen the health of both. The
series does partly serve to inform a Welsh-language viewership of the
history of the colony, and the interviews allow for an interesting focus
on the particularity of individual recollection over the formalities of
historical generalisation, but the emphasis of the film is rather on
constructing an image of a linguistic community in the present, and
on inviting the viewer into conversation with that community. The
opening scene of the series, for instance, is an encounter between the
presenter, Nan Davies, and two Patagonian gauchos on horseback.
There is a light-hearted informality to the scene: Davies – standing
in for the viewer – greets her acquaintance who, after carefully tying
up his horse, informs her in Welsh that 'my car is in the garage'. The
scene partly points up the romantically constructed nature of the
myth of the exotic, gallant Welsh-speaking gaucho, but also emphasises the fact that we are in conversation with a recognisable and real
linguistic community.[60]

Compared with *Y Gymru Bell*'s light-hearted informality, *The Desert and the Dream* is decidedly melancholic. This can be compared with Ormond's poems on the subject, 'Instructions to Settlers' and 'Patagonian Portrait'. Both poems and the film are predicated on the same themes of desolation and lost hope. 'Instructions to Settlers' is a single, monolithic stanza, free of the colourful verbal embellishments we see elsewhere in Ormond's work – a solitary stone in a dry Welsh Patagonian graveyard, perhaps. The film ironises the settlers' misplaced hope by transposing the journey on to that of the Exodus – 'who needed to be a farmer when they were going to the land of milk and honey?'[61] – and 'Instruction to Settlers' shares its cynicism: Patagonia was a 'mistaken Canaan', no bountiful paradise but a coarse and inhospitable land where 'nothing but thorn thrives', and where 'springs bitter with brine' leave a bad taste in the mouth (*CP*, 136). 'Patagonian Portrait' paints a similarly desolate picture of the Patagonian landscape: 'League upon league of thornscrub,/ the receding pampa of dust/ where the nameless Atlantic withdrew' (*CP*, 220). Unlike these poems, the film does applaud the settlers' successes, drawing attention to the canals dug to irrigate the dry plains, and the farming cooperatives that later saved the colony from economic catastrophe. But where *Y Gymru Bell* emphasises the active, continuing efforts to sustain the economic and cultural feasibility of the colony, *The Desert and the Dream* poeticises them in a way that consigns them to the past. This was noted by the Audience Research Report on the film, with one audience member suggesting that the film left 'one a bit vague about their present day status'.[62] Indeed, each film addresses the same social issues in strikingly different ways. *The Desert and the Dream* uses of shots of a sermon at a Welsh chapel being delivered in Spanish, for instance, as evidence of the steady invasion of the Spanish language into Welsh Patagonian life, whereas *Y Gymru Bell* uses the same footage to suggest that its use is rare in Welsh chapels, claiming that Spanish preachers are only used when their Welsh equivalent is unavailable. There is a further telling distinction between the ways in which each film addresses the system of gavelkind in place at that time – a system of land tenure which required any piece of land, upon the death of its owner, to be split equally between his children. *The Desert and the Dream* uses bleak footage of barren expanses of land separated by barbed wire to make the point that gavelkind was 'beginning to loosen the hold of the Welsh settlers on the land. Every death means a division – of land, and of the original dream.' *Y Gymru*

Bell, however, stresses the way the Welsh inhabitants were seeking solutions to the problem; one interviewee claims that it is 'not too late' to solve the land problems, and indeed, the 1965 edition of the programme elaborates upon this, pointing to some farmers' decision to invest in fruit farming as a more economical use of their smaller plots. While *Y Gymru Bell* does address the real social problems that threaten the colony, its emphasis is on the pragmatism of its efforts to sustain its culture and language, rather than its decline.

This is not to suggest that *The Desert and the Dream* seeks to diminish the significance of the Patagonian colony in the Welsh national memory. The film chronicles and translates it into a mythology for the purposes of the Welsh present. Like *Y Gymru Bell*, the film presents the colony as a symptom of persecution and hardship, noting that the first emigrants had been 'victimised for their religion and political beliefs'. In fact, where Nan Davies recites the history in measured tones, *The Desert and the Dream* embarks on a melodramatic dramatisation of the situation. However, this is a strategy that ultimately asks us to understand the Welsh colony as a chapter in a history book. As 'Instruction to Settlers' suggests, Wales's claim to that barren land was a 'brief union'. *The Desert and the Dream* ends solemnly, with plaintive Spanish guitar overlaying footage of a solitary gaucho roasting meat on a small fire, a man who, heeding the advice of the poem, has clearly 'Possess[ed]/ The wilderness with [himself]'. The final shot of *The Desert and the Dream* too visualises an image from the poem: 'At noon cross-winds foregather/ To suck and subdivide/ The dust and the white sand'. Yet *Y Gymru Bell* ends on a note of optimism; an elderly Welsh Patagonian suggests that the first settlers 'planted a seed that will come to fruition again', and the film closes with a shot that follows a truck speeding down a desert road. The image, along with the cheerier flamenco music that accompanies the image, implies that life in the colony goes on.[63]

THE ANCIENT KINGDOMS

Once There Was a Time and Ormond's Patagonia films confirm BBC Wales's efforts to address two conflicting strands of Welsh historiography. Yet despite such efforts to balance these perspectives – if not to bring them closer together, then at least to place them on the same screen – the underlying forces that were driving this ideological split were, throughout the 1960s, in fact pushing them further apart. Wales was becoming unprecedentedly affluent in these years,[64] but this was predicated on substantial changes in occupation and lifestyle. An economy that had been built upon agriculture and extraction was, by the early 1970s, based increasingly upon light manufacturing and white-collar work.[65] These changes, allied to the cultural tumult of the 1960s, were placing pressure upon well-established communities and social identities, and as Martin Johnes notes, though this was affecting people across the whole of Britain at this time, in Wales the 'national element added a different dimension and vocabulary to the problem'.[66] The 1960s in Wales marked a new era in Welsh cultural, linguistic and political nationalism, with a new language movement underway after 1962, and Plaid Cymru winning its first seat in a 1966 by-election at Carmarthen. Yet this was, simultaneously, a time when the Labour party was at the height of its powers in Wales. Wales was not only questioning its relationship with itself, but also, more than ever, its relationship with the rest of Britain. It was clear that in this 'heady atmosphere',[67] as John S. Ellis puts it, Britain was in need of what Eric Hobsbawm and Terence Ranger have termed an 'invented tradition' through which the nation could be 'imagined and unified'.[68] In 1958, when these sociocultural and national shifts were beginning to be strongly felt, a Conservative government headed by Harold Macmillan arranged for a 'Festival of Wales' to take place in the freshly minted Welsh capital of Cardiff. In the same summer, the city hosted the British Empire and Commonwealth Games, and on the final day of the competition it was announced, via tape recording, that Charles, the nine-year-old son of Queen Elizabeth II, would, when 'grown up',[69] be invested as Prince of Wales. On 1 July 1969, his investiture was carried out at Caernarfon Castle. As Ellis notes, while it is often supposed that the 1969 Investiture was conceived by a Labour government 'specifically to thwart the resurgence of nationalism in Wales',[70] the idea was actually formulated by the Conservative government of the late 1950s, although the Labour administration that came to office in 1964 pursued the scheme with some relish. For a Labour government keen to appease a restive Welsh nation in the 1960s, and particularly to validate the new Welsh Office, successive Welsh Secretaries of State Cledwyn Hughes and George Thomas took it upon themselves to '[employ] the investiture as a means of demonstrating the value of the Welsh Office, of projecting and even implementing Labour's Welsh policy, and of re-establishing Labour's credentials as the

"Party of Wales"'.[71] Naturally BBC Wales, as a national broadcasting institution, was caught up in this process. Indeed, if, as Ellis
suggests, Britain, in the months leading up to the ceremony, was 'like
Prince Charles [. . .] enrolled on an intensive course in Welshness',[72]
BBC Wales was one of its senior tutors. I examined in the previous
chapter the cultural documentaries that Ormond produced for the
BBC2 network during these months, films that sought to promote
Welsh artists and writers to a wider British audience. Here I want to
focus on the history documentary that was broadcast on the BBC1
network on the morning of the Investiture, *The Ancient Kingdoms:
A View of Wales*.[73]

Though broadly chronological in structure – moving swiftly from
the prehistoric era through medieval Wales and on to agricultural,
industrial, then modern Wales – *The Ancient Kingdoms* draws heavily on the kind of poetic mode to which Ormond aspired in many of
his films of the 1960s. Visually, it is fluid and peripatetic, with con-
stantly moving shots that cut and dissolve freely between viewpoints
of locations across Wales, and it utilises a lyrical commentary, voiced
by Meredith Edwards, alongside an evocative soundtrack scored by
Daniel Jones.[74] Of particular interest in terms of its proximity to the
Investiture is the way the film attempts to bridge the rifts in Welsh
historiography. *The Ancient Kingdoms* offers up a cohesive 'view of
Wales' for a British viewership, and does this by accommodating the
historically divisive facets of Wales, in particular its two dominant
socio-economic formations, agriculture and the extractive industries,
integrating them into a seamless narrative that obviates the potential for conflict. Shots of the Rhondda valley are qualified with a
narrated soundtrack that convinces viewers of the coalfield's historical link with an older Wales: 'Here in the heyday of the Rhondda's
boom, farm labourers of the last century klondiked by the thousand
in search of higher wages'. Emphasis is placed upon Wales's contributions to the wider British nation, from the 'great slabs' of rock from
the Preseli hills that ended up in Stonehenge, to south Wales becoming in the 1960s 'the greatest steel and tin-plate centre in Britain. We
produce a quarter of Britain's steel.' The use of the collective first
person is significant in terms of the film's voice: the narrator switches
between first person singular, plural and possessive pronouns, and
even claims that he '[speaks] for most Welshmen'.

The Ancient Kingdoms is unusual in that, unlike many of his
other films, Ormond is not credited as writer but as producer, despite

the film borrowing from two of his own poems. One of these is his translation of the *Canu Heledd* englynion 'The Hall of Cynddylan', attributed to the seventh-century poet Llywarch Hen. The use of the poem appears to bear the mark of a certain mischievousness. It is transposed on to a sequence about Deheubarth's battles with Norman invaders at Dinefwr in the twelfth century, in which the film finds, in the Normans, a common enemy with the English, thereby evading the question of English–Welsh hostility. Yet the poem Ormond had translated was a moving requiem commemorating the bloody battles between the Celtic kingdom of Powys and the Anglo-Saxon Wessex. Evidently Ormond's mischievousness stretched only so far; there is no mention of the circumstances surrounding the creation of the first English Prince of Wales, Edward II, after his father Edward I's conquest of Llewellyn ap Gruffydd's brief unification of the Welsh kingdoms.

The film sounds some melancholic notes about the decline of aspects of rural Welsh life. The narrator, speaking over shots of derelict hill farms, 'can't help but mourn a whole way of life that is passing', and borrows phrases from another of Ormond's poems, 'Landscape without Figures': 'No sign of blood of battle [. . .] but a place once lived in, and now no longer lived in'. However, the thrust of *The Ancient Kingdoms* is to project a picture of an optimistic nation that is a vital and integral part of a wider British polity. Moving from those desolate scenes of rural Wales and, later, the Rhondda, *The Ancient Kingdoms* provides a vibrant vision in line with Labour's new economic plan, spelled out in its 1967 White Paper *Wales: The Way Ahead*, which 'prescribed a mixed dosage of diversifying industry, retraining the labour force, easing off the traditional heavy industry of coal while buttressing the newer [. . .] heavy industry of steel'.[75] The film aestheticises the steel industry in this optimistic idiom: low-angle shots of the high-rising new steelworks at Port Talbot are accompanied by a joyously majestic soundtrack, and the action shots of the interior of the works contain further, admittedly spectacular, images of an industry boiling with activity; steam billows from furnaces and white-hot molten metal spits and bubbles like Jackson Pollock's paint.[76] The sequence promotes a vision of a proud, culturally distinct nation, but one firmly welded to a Labour-validated British polity.

The Ancient Kingdoms concludes with another mischievous sequence: footage of the Wales–England match at the 1969 Five

Nations, though the commentary is gracious enough not to mention the score: 30–9 to Wales. This was, in fact, the game that inaugurated a new 'golden era' in Welsh rugby, during which Wales won three Grand Slams and six Triple Crowns within ten years, and it is significant that the film foretells the new significance that rugby was to take in the era of televised sport. As Martin Johnes notes, the 1970s would be the decade in which rugby, 'an important part of male popular culture in south Wales since the late nineteenth century, [would embrace] a much broader social and geographical spectrum,' and would go on in these years to become a 'genuinely national game'.[77] The film is not above wheeling out the classic 'Celtic' stereotypes that would go on to dominate British coverage of the sport,[78] appealing as it does to a Welsh Celtic mysticism when it notes that the Welsh players had become 'new folk heroes' and 'poets', while a medieval harpsichord is played over footage of Welsh skill on the field. There is an ironic air to the sequence, but such representations were not insignificant; Johnes notes that '[s]uch alleged [Celtic] national characteristics may have been grounded in a distinctly limited reality but they formed part of a very real patriotism'.[79] Of course, this was a patriotism confined to sporting and cultural pride; as the film informs British viewers (and reminds the Welsh), 'the things that satisfy our pride in being Welsh lie very often outside the story of power'.

The Ancient Kingdoms was broadcast on the BBC network to the whole of Britain at 10 a.m. on the morning of the Investiture, immediately before the coverage of the ceremony began at 10.30 a.m. It contributed to something that Daniel Dayan and Elihu Katz suggest all televised ceremonies evoke: a 'ceremonial politics' that, like the investiture itself, 'expresses the yearning for togetherness, for fusion'.[80] Though there are moments of playfulness, *The Ancient Kingdoms* broadly complements the national politics of a ceremony that, in Ellis's terms, 'asserted and celebrated the image of a unified and indivisible Welsh nation, in turn unified and indivisible with the larger British state of which it was a part'.[81] This is not to say that the film – or indeed the Investiture itself – was wholly successful in this. Wales was, despite the efforts of the BBC, sharply divided over the issue, and these were divisions that cut across the BBC itself; there were producers working at BBC Wales at that time, such Selwyn Roderick, who refused outright to work on Investiture programming.[82] Ellis suggests that the Investiture's attempt to heal some of those divisions ultimately failed:

[it] highlighted the fault lines and fissures of Welsh and British national identity. The debate over the [Investiture] reflected an antagonism between supporters and opponents where the presence of the 'Other' blocked each side from fully realising their identities as Welsh people.[83]

To viewers who had, that very morning, watched news of the sentencing of those involved in the 'Free Wales Army' movement, along with reports that two other nationalist militants had a day earlier accidently blown themselves up carrying a stockpile of gelignite, *The Ancient Kingdoms* may have seemed somewhat idealistic in its depiction of a Welsh nation altogether at ease with its neighbour.[84]

THE LAND REMEMBERS

Evidently, divisions persisted in Wales that were the product of far deeper cultural and political rifts than could be bridged by a single exercise in regal pomp and ceremony. Pressure groups such as Cymdeithas yr Iaith Gymraeg had been energised by the mood of the 1960s and scored successes that brought political nationalism on to the mainstream agenda in Wales. This translated into some political progress for Plaid Cymru, with the party securing its first seat in 1966 and then doubling its vote by 1970.[85] Yet these political successes had begun to hit a wall, and due to its narrow failures to achieve a major breakthrough in the south, Plaid Cymru became increasingly associated with the Welsh-speaking communities in the west and north,[86] communities that saw few similarities between themselves and a predominantly Britishist, anglophone south. As Ned Thomas wrote in 1971:

> As the educated Welsh-speaker looks at the new affluent working-class of south Wales he is bound to see people who have lost a culture and gained only a higher standard of living, people made particularly vulnerable to commercially fostered pseudo-values by their own rootlessness.[87]

These 'pseudo-values' were a matter of perspective; another way of viewing the situation was to see the English speakers of the south Wales conurbations finding nourishment in another sociocultural soil. Some recognised this, but saw it as their duty to enrich that majority with a cultural and historical education that could provide, perhaps, better sustenance. Thomas's *The Welsh Extremist*, for instance, argued that the 'relationship between the two language groups [was] crucial to any political situation'. His book, published in English, was partly an attempt to foster a better understanding between the two by informing the English-speaking population of the legacy of the Welsh past. There was a similar impulse behind Ormond's next history project, *The Land Remembers*, which ran across two series in 1972 and 1974.

The Land Remembers seems to have evolved into the large production that it became from a rather modest initial idea. In a column for the *Western Mail* in the year in which the second series was aired, Ormond explained that, while visiting a cromlech he needed to shoot for a film he was making some years earlier,[88] he had been inspired to write a poem about the experience; this would become the poem 'Ancient Monuments'. Ormond explains that, in the process of writing the poem, he needed to expand his vocabulary of such standing stones: 'once you've said slab and pillar and rock there aren't many words for stone around'.[89] He called upon his friend Wynn Williams, a geologist (to whom he later dedicated his poem 'Letter to a Geologist'), to inquire about such words. This led Ormond to pursue an interest in Neolithic history, and, after reading a book found in Cardiff Central Library, Alexander Thom's *Megalithic Sites in Britain* (1967) (as well as, it is likely, viewing a 1970 episode in the BBC documentary series *Chronicle* that profiled Thom and his controversial ideas[90]), he decided to embark on a television programme about these ancient sites in Wales.

Interestingly, the use of archaeological history in the early episodes of *The Land Remembers* is, in its politics, quite far from Ormond's own. Ormond often made use of archaeological terms and tropes in his poetry as a means of tapping into a universalist idiom that evaded the overt cultural and national politics of the Wales of his era. His poem 'Ancient Monuments' (which is, in fact, dedicated to Alexander Thom) is a case in point; for Ormond, the monuments convey in themselves no meaning, no message, but merely a stolid, impassive presence, '[a]loof lean markers, erect in mud' (*CP*, 175–6). There is no message of trans-historical, ethno-national allegiance with a prehistoric or Celtic ancestry. Rather, in keeping with his respect for skilled craft, Ormond quietly lauds their workmanship, 'how those men/ Handled them'. The presence of these monuments in the Welsh countryside does not even lead Ormond to revel in or idealise the beauty of their surroundings – for the speaker, the countryside is mostly a hindrance through which one must 'slog on/ Through bog bracken, bramble'. There are no idealised *gwerin* figures here, only 'A bent figure, in a hamlet/ Of three houses and a barn'. The monuments merely demarcate the edge of what we know, and the only sense of familiarity with them is one of shared bewilderment: '[w]hat they awaited we, too, still await'.

If the title *The Land Remembers* and its historiographical range – the series ends at the beginning of the industrial era – are, together, not enough to give some indication as to where its rather different priorities lie, then the political leanings of its presenter, Gwyn Williams, should. This is not the Marxist historian Gwyn Alf Williams, but Gwyn Williams, Trefenter, literary translator and poet. Though born in Port Talbot in 1904 to a mother from that town, Williams was not caught up in the Labourist politics of south Wales of the 1920s and 1930s. His father was from Trefenter, in rural mid-Wales, the place where, as he admits in the first episode of *The Land Remembers*, he felt he 'had [his] roots'. After studying at Aberystwyth, Williams headed to Oxford, where he attended meetings of the Dafydd ap Gwilym Society and discovered the politics of an emerging Plaid Cymru, and he held closely to his national consciousness throughout his life, despite a peripatetic career that spanned universities across the Near East. It was during his work as a teacher of English literature at universities in Cairo, Alexandria, Benghazi and Istanbul that he wrote translations of Welsh poetry, as well as his own poems in English, both of which are a clear indication of his political position. The self-written introduction to his *Collected Poems* (1987) begins with the bold declaration that '[t]he writing of poetry is always a social function'.[91] Williams felt the salvation of the Welsh nation lay in its cultural and historical heritage, and his own poems are preoccupied with an awareness of a connection with an organic Welsh past, and further with the potential of that past to inform and enrich an alienated, materialist present. Far from Ormond's vision of a distant, unknowable past in 'Ancient Monuments', Williams's poem 'Places in Our Spirit', for example, insists that 'these things on the mountain and coastland/ are in our blood, are our bones, our backbone,/ are our claim to being a person, belonging to a nation'.[92]

This idea is channelled through *The Land Remembers*'s treatment of the Welsh landscape. As I discussed in chapter 3, the construction of landscape in television is a powerful means of anchoring diverse themes into a national context. As Robert Dillon notes, British history programming had long employed this:

> [d]isparate landscape elements, a natural feature such as a river, great houses, churches, cathedrals, homes and public buildings act as tangible 'spots of time' in the formation of a nation-state and also as symbolic sights that fuse together the collective memory framework required to 'imagine' the concept of Britain as a nation.[93]

The same can be said of the process of imagining the concept of the nation in Welsh broadcasting; visits to Welsh sites of historical interest had been one of the pillars of Welsh television since its beginnings in the early 1950s.[94] *The Land Remembers* is as preoccupied with the visual representation of national space and landscape as it is with history itself. But where Ormond's culture documentaries tend to construct Welsh landscapes as places that inspire individual artistic sensibilities, *The Land Remembers* series does so in a Welsh Liberal idiom. This had developed within a post-Darwinian Victorian context which espoused the principle that each nation consists of a single, unique ethnic group.[95] For the Liberal intellectuals who espoused the notion of the rural *gwerin*, the Welsh landscape was key; as one Welsh commentator wrote in the first issue of a new periodical, *Welsh Review*, in 1906, 'The scenery of our land has played a large share in our sympathetic development as a race'.[96] In this period the Welsh landscape was inscribed with a significance that was not British but unique to Wales; the capstone on this was, as Peter Lord notes, O. M. Edwards's decision to place, at the top of the first page of *Hanes Cymru*, 'not [. . .] a text or a poem but [. . .] a picture of Snowdon painted by Samuel Maurice Jones'. As Lord notes, 'The picture [. . .] was intended as a metaphor for the soul of the nation whose history he would describe'.[97]

    The Land Remembers can be viewed as a televisual effort to imbue the Welsh landscape with national historical significance, and to do so in a way that rejuvenates the nation's relationship with a certain set of historical roots.[98] The series, subtitled in the first episode as *An Excursion with Gwyn Williams*, is dominated by images of rural Wales; virtually all of Williams's lengthy explanatory pieces to camera are set against the backdrop of the mid- and north-Walian landscape, and are shot in the style of the landscape painting. Granted, this is where much of Welsh history prior to the industrial era – the cut-off date of the series' interests – took place. Yet in those instances when town and city life is brought into the picture, *The Land Remembers* is quite openly hostile to it. Images of Cardiff and its City Hall, shot from the then recently constructed Capital Tower, for instance, are undermined by Williams's commentary, which presents town life as the antithesis of a 'Celtic' racial ancestry that never constructed a coherent empire:

> The story of our town life is one of coming to terms with a concept alien to our inherited culture. [. . .] Are we really the kind of people who like great centres? Certainly no great enthusiasm was shown for Cardiff as a capital. In the old Welsh society, only bondmen lived huddled together in the villages. (Series 1, episode 3)

Of course, such pronouncements did not necessarily reflect the view of Ormond or of BBC Wales in any simple or straightforward way. Statements such as this clearly stem from Williams's own world-view, and the series makes fairly clear the fact that we are hearing one man's individual perspective.[99] But the overall effect of the series is implicitly to endorse this view, and to convince viewers of its validity.

The Land Remembers makes every effort to interpellate a Welsh national viewership not only by imbuing the landscape with historical significance, but further by encouraging the audience to actively cultivate their own historical understanding of it. Williams frequently addresses the viewer directly: 'I'm sure you must have seen it [. . .]'; 'even from a motorway you can spot them [. . .]'. Related to this is the series' effort to encourage an aesthetic as well as historical appreciation of the landscape. Its visual palette, across twelve episodes, rarely veers from images of undulating, bucolic beauty, and the lilting classical compositions that accompany the images only add to the series' sense of refined aesthetic appreciation of the land. Town and city life are referred to only in passing, usually when Williams is expounding a point about pre-industrial history, and are frequently judged in superficially aesthetic terms: Port Talbot can be 'pleasant enough on a day like this, but it can be grey and dismal too'. Inhabitants of the south Wales coalfield are pitied for their lack of access to picturesque scenery: 'the coal tips were their alps, [. . .] the blast furnaces were their volcanoes'.[100] The second series ends in the early eighteenth century, a time that Williams exalts as a time of peaceful calm for the *gwerin*. It is worth quoting at length a

statement from the last episode in the series in order to get a sense
of Williams's vision:

> The happiest times for ordinary people were those which have left no
> monuments. Times when no castles or prisons were built, when there were
> no new battlefields to scar the land and enrich it with blood. When even
> the towns were static, and the countryside largely undisturbed. When
> there was much poverty but little grim want, when men didn't quarrel
> over politics or religion. Wales, at the beginning of the eighteenth century,
> was like that. But before the end of the century, new things were to come
> that are not easy to forget.

These words, accompanied by slow, picturesque panning shots of a
peaceful and verdant rural Wales, verbalise *The Land Remembers*'s
overriding visual aesthetic, its attempt to project Wales as an agricultural idyll disturbed by the anglicising, urbanising forces of industry
– ominously alluded to in the final sentence.

It should be said that the final sequence of the series, at the end
of the very last episode, does in fact shift towards a different visual
and, perhaps, different political idiom. After a discussion of some
of the prominent intellectual figures of Wales in the eighteenth century – Methodist leaders such as Griffith Jones and Daniel Rowland,
the poet William Williams Pantycelyn, the Morris brothers, founders of the Honourable Society of Cymmrodorion – Williams comes
to the Enlightenment polymath Richard Price. Price, hailing from
Llangeinor, near Bridgend, was, in addition to being a Dissenting
minister, influential in a number of fields, but he most memorably
found favour with the Founding Fathers of the United States with his
writings on liberal democracy.[101] It is this that *The Land Remembers*
interests itself in, with particular reference to his lecture written
in support of the French Revolution, 'A Discourse on the Love of
our Country' (1789). Price's lecture is appropriated by *The Land
Remembers* for a contemporary Welsh context; Williams quotes at
length Price's principles of democratic self-governance, some of which
are curiously at odds with the logic of a series that places such heavy
emphasis on the significance of the national landscape: 'by our country is meant [. . .] not the soil or the spot of earth on which we happen
to have been born, not the forests and fields, but that community of
which we are members'. Revealingly, Williams omits the second part
of Price's statement: 'or that body of companions and friends and

kindred who are associated with us under the same constitution of government, protected by the same laws, and bound together by the same civil polity'.[102] The final words of the series are again borrowed from Price, but modify their intended meaning: 'an enlightened and virtuous country must be a free country'. Price had been referring to the democratic freedoms of citizens within the British nation state, but the message that chimes here in the final moments of *The Land Remembers* is quite radical in the context of BBC television – one of political freedom for the Welsh nation. Here the visual idiom of the film shifts to accommodate this idea; as Williams iterates Price's inspiring remarks, the camera, which has, for the vast majority of the series, remained fixed to the ground, confining itself to slow pans and zooms, lifts off into a series of aerial shots that encompass not only the rural landscape but also industry, the coalfield conurbations and the ports – all of which had been omitted from the series' visual vocabulary until now. In aiming toward an endorsement of a form of civic nationalism, *The Land Remembers* thus seems to gesture toward a rapprochement between agricultural and industrial Wales.

THE COLLIERS' CRUSADE

While *The Land Remembers* was constructing a vision of Wales with political foundations in a rural Nonconformist Liberal past, in the same years, a new Welsh historiography from a rather different perspective was coming into full swing. Recently educated children of south Wales were embarking on their own careers in Welsh history, adopting the burgeoning new methodologies of 'people's history' and 'history from below'. One of the major achievements of the freshly established Welsh Labour History Society[103] was the two-year South Wales Coalfield History Project (1972–4), led by R. Merfyn Jones and Hywel Francis, which sought to collect documents and books from miners' institutes and libraries from across the coalfield in order to '[reconstruct] the history of a unique but rapidly changing community and culture'.[104] The project led to the establishment of the South Wales Miners' Library in Swansea as a repository for these valuable materials. The work being done on Welsh industrial society was in large part a political project aimed at the commemoration and implantation of the radical activities of coalfield workers into received history, activities that would otherwise be forgotten by historians consulting only the official annals of historical and political documentation. One of the most effective strategies the project adopted to this end was the use of oral history. Hywel Francis justified the approach in an essay published in 1980: 'to ignore oral evidence is tantamount to taking a decision to write off whole areas of human experience. Indeed there are human activities which can only satisfactorily be uncovered by collecting oral testimony.'[105] Oral history became a central facet of the South Wales Coalfield History Project, and its researchers recorded interviews with miners caught up in the major political events in the coalfield in the first half of the twentieth century. Important studies were undertaken that, in Francis's words, 'rely heavily'[106] on the oral history facet of the project. One of these was Francis's own doctoral dissertation on the 200 or so miners who volunteered to fight in the Spanish Civil War,[107] the research for which provided the basis of Ormond's final history series in 1979, *The Colliers' Crusade*, and, later, Francis's book *Miners Against Fascism* (1984).[108] Both use extensive oral testimonies of volunteers to the International Brigades, and in drawing on these personal testimonies, Francis's book and Ormond's series provide a unique and often intimate perspective on what has, since the first event that publicly memorialised it in 1938, become a central episode in the history and popular understanding of the south Wales coalfield.[109]

The Colliers' Crusade, drawing heavily on Francis's research,[110] was a product of the burgeoning new historiographical methodologies that greatly enhanced the capacity to write and disseminate Welsh history in this era. The series could, being a BBC production, quite conceivably have explored in more general terms the British involvement in the Spanish Civil War, given that some 2,500 volunteers from across Britain fought in Spain,[111] (as, for instance, Ken Loach did in his film *Land and Freedom* (1995)), and in time with a rise in interest in Spain following the death of General Franco in 1975 and the country's subsequent transition to democracy. But the series capitalises on these wider European historical developments in order to remember an earlier moment in Welsh history. The series is consistent with Francis's interpretation of the Welsh contribution to the war; it too downplays the influence of the Communist Party in its portrayal of a south Walian society primed by a domestic radicalism for military intervention in a foreign war that echoed its own political problems.

The first episode sees the ever-effusive (though by that time ageing) Gwyn Thomas describe a south Wales that was ignited in indignation by the almost simultaneous occurrence of the major pit disaster at Gresford in September 1934 and the Asturian miners' uprising crushed by Spanish forces led by Franco in October of the same year.[112] He recalls 'time and again in the Rhondda valley' stopping to talk to men who 'saw the logic of this. [. . .] This definitely did fix a mood in South Wales, that there was a link between what had happened [. . .] in Gresford and what was happening in the Asturias'. It is significant, too, that Ormond uses Thomas not as narrator of the series, but rather, like the miners interviewed, as a historical contributor; instead, René Cutforth steps in to read Ormond's commentary. This may seem peculiar, given Thomas's extensive experience in broadcasting and his own ties to both south Wales and Spain, but was likely in part to have been due to the fact that his deeply partisan position on the war would not have been sanctioned by the BBC. The BBC's recently published internal guidelines on documentary production, *Principles and Practice in Documentary Programmes* (1972), had been firm on the issue of political neutrality; an entire section dedicated to 'Balance and Fairness' made clear the BBC's commitment to this fact:

> [T]he producer or director of a documentary occupies a complex position. On the one hand he is the BBC; half of him cannot escape being an official delegated to supervise broadcasting policies and practices. On the other hand half of him has creative responsibilities to the programme. Since many programmes deal with matters of high controversy [. . .], should he allow his own views to dictate the nature of the programme? The classic answer is that unless he can lay his own views totally on one side, he should on no account be producing this particular programme at all.[113]

In fact, Ormond evades this problem by including Thomas as a contributor rather than narrator, a strategy that *Principles and Practice in Documentary Programmes* sanctions: in programmes 'dealing with a contentious subject on which differing opinions exists', it states, opinions should be 'carried firmly on the shoulders of the contributors'.[114] This enables the series to implicitly, and quite emphatically, endorse Thomas's political pronouncements on the war without fear of the charge of bias, and the series exploits this to powerful effect. Gwyn Thomas's characteristically bombastic pronouncements on the 'anger [that] will rise like a great lion, [. . .] [a] great tawny lion that will come and eat injustice' are underlined by picturesque images of

the plains of the Spanish Meseta and the solemnly rousing tones of
the Asturian miners' folk song, 'En el pozo María Luisa' ('In the Pit
of María Luisa'). Ormond elsewhere provides political balance by
including as one of his contributors the unlikely Welsh volunteer to
the Nationalist cause, Frank Thomas, though such sequences leave
little question as to whose side the series is on.[115]

The major strength of *The Colliers' Crusade* is the extensive use of
oral testimony. Given its interviews with some of the figures central
to the Welsh contribution to the Republican cause, men such as Will
Paynter, Jack 'Russia' Roberts and Tom Jones,[116] the series should
be viewed as both an historical document and a powerful means of
broadcasting history. The miners movingly recall the hunger, the
exhaustion and the fear of combat in a foreign land, but also tell
tales of camaraderie and laughter, all of which adds human texture
to the recounting of history. They do so in a Welsh accent and from
a Welsh perspective. One example worth quoting at some length is
Edwin Greening's recollection of the death of his friend during the
Battle of the Ebro in late 1938:

> I got my weekly *Aberdare Leader* [. . .]. I read it in the intervals of the
> bombing, then I crawled up to where Tom Howell Jones, from Aberdare,
> was in a stone crevice. I said 'Here's the *Aberdare Leader*, Tom', then I got
> back to my place straight away. An hour later, there was terrible mortaring
> of the upper ridges of the Battalion area. There was a lot of shouting,
> and they came and said, 'Quick, your mate has had it'. And I rushed up
> and there Tom Howell Jones and his mates had been killed instantly. And
> the *Leader* lay there, blood-stained in the trench.

This vignette demonstrates something of the power of oral history. Greening's matter-of-fact phrasing, pronounced in a clipped
yet unmistakeably south Walian accent, adds power to the heavily
symbolic recollection of the presence of the *Aberdare Leader* on the
battlefield.[117] Here this commonplace Welsh item – a token of local
affiliation and camaraderie between two Welsh volunteers – potently
symbolises the presence of the Welsh contingent in Spain, and its
subsequent despoliation with Welsh blood powerfully brings home the
reality of war. The testimonies here function in the same way as the
interviews with Welsh-speaking Patagonians in *Y Gymru Bell*, providing, to reiterate John Corner's suggestion, a 'bridge [. . .] between the
viewer's world and subject's world'.[118]

Ormond's history documentaries amply demonstrate the internal differences in the way Wales viewed – and views – its past. Brokering these debates and screening them to wide audiences, they both reflected and contributed to the historical process. During the 1980s a new set of socio-economic challenges would soften the acrimony between these competing interpretations of Welsh history. Martin Johnes has suggested that during these years,

> as the working class fragmented and the labour movement seemed to offer little hope, the anger began to adopt something of a national angle, especially since it was easy to see the Tories as a government imposed on Wales by the choices of an English electorate.[119]

In such a context, Welsh historians began to spend less time examining what divided them than on the ways in which the Welsh could be understood in more cohesive terms. While this had not translated into national political expression in the 1970s – the campaign for Welsh devolution had failed miserably in the 1979 referendum – by the time of the 1984–5 miners' strike, as Hywel Francis later wrote, there was a sense of 'Welsh unity and identity, overcoming language and geographical differences, which failed to materialise in 1979'.[120] In the later 1980s, St Fagans, the Museum of Welsh Folk Life, a heritage museum initially founded upon assumptions which 'patently drew on long-standing and romantic notions of the *gwerin*',[121] added to its grounds two major emblems of proletarian, south Walian life, a row of miners' cottages and a workmen's institute, and by 1995 had changed its name to the more inclusive 'Museum of Welsh Life'. Scholars wrote of 'corresponding cultures',[122] exclaimed 'vive la différence!'[123] And despite Dai Smith's assertion that Wales 'rings with the self-righteousness of those who make claims for it according to the image of the country necessary for them',[124] the title of his book – *Wales! Wales?* – at least demonstrated that the voice of the argument was shifting from one of a battle of declarations to self-reflection. Gwyn Alf Williams's *When Was Wales?* (1985) matched this tone, and was, alongside Smith's book, a significant contribution to – and token of – a process of slow but sure historiographical reconfiguration at a time of considerable crisis. Significantly, these two important texts were derived from television history series.[125] This seems to me to encapsulate the astonishing developments that took place in the Welsh public sphere in those years, and the importance of television within this process. From the situation of BBC Wales in the mid-1950s that Ormond could describe as having 'no news cameras, no film, no (as the saying goes) nothing', by the late 1980s, Wales could comfortably be said to be living in the 'presence of its past'. Ormond's work on history at BBC Wales was a substantial contribution to that process.

Popularising Ethnography

John Grierson once suggested that the function of documentary was to 'explain society to society'.[1] This phrase, persuasive in its simplicity, is characteristic of the Scotsman's aphoristic, no-nonsense style. Stemming from his intellectual roots in a lower-middle-class, Calvinist, Labourist household in Stirling, and an education under Idealist philosophers at the University of Glasgow,[2] it bespeaks an absolutist's faith in both the objectivity of 'explanation' and the cohesiveness of 'society'. Grierson was fond of such phrase-making. It was he who defined the term 'documentary' as the 'creative treatment of actuality', having watched the ethnographic films of the American Robert Flaherty, such as *Nanook of the North* (1922), which found its material in an Inuit family in northern Canada, and *Moana* (1926), whose subject is a Samoan tribe.[3] His ideas helped crystallise the ontology of the documentary around the idea that this was a form of film-making that could inform and thereby improve society. It was predicated on the notion that social phenomena can be neutrally observed, recorded and shared with audiences who passively accept the claims of the film-maker. These ideas found filmic expression at a time of immense social and political upheaval, in British Documentary Movement films such as Paul Rotha's *Shipyard* (1935) and *The Face of Britain* (1935), and Edgar Anstey's *Housing Problems* (1935). Such films, in portraying everyday life on film, connected with a burgeoning aesthetic of social observation that spanned numerous art-forms, exemplified by writers like Orwell and the Auden generation, and photographers like Brandt and Cartier-Bresson.

Starting work at *Picture Post* in 1945, Ormond cut his teeth as a journalist in an era that was pursuing this profound shift in aesthetic focus. *Picture Post* was contributing to post-war consensus politics through social observation, an approach that Stuart Hall describes as a 'democratisation of the subject', the 'desire to break through the [. . .] social-sightlessness which had kept the greater half of Britain such a well-guarded secret from the other, lesser but more powerful half'.[4] Later, for the *News Chronicle*, Ormond wrote poems to accompany photographs by, among others, Brandt and Cartier-Bresson, and though these were expressed in verse, they found their subject matter in everyday observation.[5] He joined the BBC in 1955, a time when broadcasting was beginning to acknowledge these changes. This was the year that a commercial television channel – a populist recommendation of the Beveridge Report on Broadcasting (1949) – began broadcasting. The BBC responded by relaxing the stiff Reithianism that had dominated broadcasting policy since the 1920s. Reith's preferred metaphor of the BBC had been that of a 'ship', of which 'he was the chief pilot', which, as Ien Ang notes, 'suggested a mission of leading and directing the audience in the modern world'.[6] Reith's successor after the war, William Haley, preferred the idea of the BBC as a cultural 'pyramid', and split the radio service into three, guided by the conviction that this would lead audiences from the populism of the Light Programme up to the 'best' content on the Third Programme. By 1960, when Hugh Greene took up the job, the metaphor had become one of the BBC as the 'mirror' of society. The BBC now saw its task as being that of 'representing and 'registering' society's many different voices and faces'.[7]

These changes of attitude percolated down into policy and programming. Cecil McGivern, Controller of BBC Television in the 1950s, devised, alongside Norman Swallow, the BBC's pivotal series *Special Enquiry* (1952–9), viewing it as the 'television equivalent of *Picture Post*'.[8] *Panorama* (1952–) was established along similar lines. Swallow was himself a vocal advocate of a more populist, egalitarian broadcasting style to supersede the stuffy Reithianism of the pre-war BBC. Swallow noted some years later that 'What was missing [. . .] from television documentaries before the mid-fifties was, quite simply, *people*.'[9] It was thought that the BBC's project of enriching and deepening Britain's understanding of itself could be achieved through, in John Corner's terms, the 'de-metropolitanisation'[10] of the BBC's administrative structure and its programming priorities. Swallow had insisted that *Special Enquiry* should have a 'strong regional bias', and that each edition should 'state an important national issue in local terms'.[11] The end of the 1950s had seen the investment in and development of regional sectors of the BBC on an unprecedented scale.

One of the consequences of this initiative was, as we have seen, the emergence of new regional film units, such as the one with which Ormond was connected in Cardiff. As technical resources began to improve, producers in the regions capitalised on the opportunity to embark on new forms of observational film-making. Alongside Ormond, producers such as Denis Mitchell at BBC North and Philip Donnellan at BBC Midlands were using the new technologies available to them to produce documentaries that represented the 'underprivileged and unmapped sections of British society'.[12] Mitchell's celebrated *Morning in the Streets* (1959) paints a sensitive portrait of life in a northern working-class community.[13] Hailed for 'bringing television documentary to a new level',[14] the film deliberately evades stereotype by utilising the possibilities of the 'think-tape' technique, whereby silent footage is accompanied by separately recorded, improvised sound, thereby jettisoning authoritative voice-over commentary. These techniques were also seen in the work of Philip Donnellan, who was similarly concerned with representing the lives of the unrepresented, and focused in the mid-1960s on immigrant and diaspora communities. Donnellan later described the act of producing documentaries that were able to concern themselves with the 'voices of the ignored' as 'intoxicating'.[15] Films such as *The Irishmen* (1965), a film about the marginal status of male Irish migrants 'responsible for rebuilding much of Britain's post-war infrastructure',[16] and *The Colony* (1964), an examination of the West Indian migrant community in 1960s Birmingham, also use the dialogical potential of the 'think-tape' technique to offer open-ended and unresolved, but nevertheless sensitive poetic accounts of marginalised communities. As we will see, Ormond's early film *Borrowed Pasture* (1960), about two Polish soldiers living on a farm in Carmarthenshire, undoubtedly fell into this category.

Related to this process of 'democratising' broadcasting was the fact that producers of these films were also responding to the new ethnic make-up of post-war Britain. Migrants from across war-torn Europe were welcomed in the years after 1945, and the 1948 British Nationality Act awarded the 800 million subjects of the Commonwealth full British citizen status, with the right to freely enter and settle in Britain.[17] Britain as a whole was becoming, to borrow Will Kymlicka's term, more 'polyethnic',[18] and the BBC, as the

principal instrument of the British public sphere, was obliged to register these demographic changes. This has led John Corner to suggest
that the new style of television documentary that emerged at this time
amounted to 'a form of popular ethnography'.[19] It was thought by key
producers within the BBC that the documentary was the ideal format
to perform the humanistic purpose of reflecting on these matters. In
their more fluid, associational style, such films were well equipped to
approach what were often thorny and complex social issues, and were
an antidote to more 'objective' news reports and documentaries that
'[ran] the risk of confusing people with statistics, [. . .] and [had] a
habit of [ignoring] the fact that people cannot accurately be lumped
together as though they were identical pieces of machinery'.[20] Denis
Mitchell claimed that the role of the documentary producer was to
'impl[y] his own view of life, but without editorialising and without
distorting the truth that is the lives of the people he has chosen'.[21]
Ormond wrote in similar terms about the documentary as a form
through which 'complex circumstance' could be 'revealed in a simple
and understandable form [. . .] things in a seemingly ordinary, worka-
day world poetically revealed'.[22]

However, the process of straightforward 'representation', of
'explaining society to society' through poetic film-making, is, as many
theorists since the 1960s have attested, in no way an ideologically
neutral activity. Rather, placing a 'mirror' up to society is inevitably
caught up with and structured by reflections of power. As Henrietta
Lidchi has argued, ethnography is

> not *reflective* of the essential nature of cultural difference, but classifies
> and *constitutes* this difference systematically and coherently, in accord-
> ance with a particular view of the world that emerges in a specific place,
> at a distinct historical moment and within a specific body of knowledge.[23]

To embark on a different metaphor of this process, James Clifford
notes that one of the principal functions of ethnography 'is "orientation"'.[24] It is as much an act of mapping out and describing reality
in a way that reinforces one's own position as it is about extending
the boundaries of knowledge. From this perspective, the efforts of
the BBC to represent other cultures in the years after the war can be
viewed as a contribution to a process of 'orientating' Britain within
the wider world. Moreover, given the developments in Welsh broadcasting in these years, the BBC in Wales can be seen to have embarked

upon a process of orientating Wales. This is evident in the outward-looking titles of radio programmes such as *Citizens of the World* (1955) and *Hosts of the Nations* (1955),[25] in Welsh translations of European plays (such as Max Frisch's *Biedermann und die Brandstifter* ('Y Llosgwr Tai'), Molière's *Le Misanthrope* ('Y Cybudd') and Ibsen's *Hedda Gabler*),[26] and in Broadcasting Council of Wales reports that, in a not incidental navigational idiom, proudly proclaimed that 'from Patagonia to Perth, from Bardi to Berlin, from California to New York – and all over Wales; this is an indication of the compass of features and talks programmes during the past year'.[27] This chapter will examine a group of films in terms of their treatment of cultural difference and interaction. Indeed, these concerns are signalled in the titles alone of many: *Borrowed Pasture* (1960), *From a Town in Tuscany* (1963), *Song in a Strange Land* (1964), *The Mormons* (1965). The final film is *Music in Midsummer* (1968), a film about the International Eisteddfod at Llangollen. This chapter will address the ways in which Ormond's distinct approach to film-making – the cultural and aesthetic assumptions that shape his films – intersects and interacts with the politics of representation on Welsh television.

BORROWED PASTURE

Those familiar with Ormond's work may notice that this book has so far neglected what is perhaps his best-known and most celebrated film, *Borrowed Pasture* (1960). Ormond had been asked by Head of Programming Hywel Davies to 'do something on the expatriate Polish people who had settled in Wales after the war'.[28] The resulting film, examining the lives of two Polish refugees, Eugenius Okolowicz and Vlodek Bulaj, eking out a meagre existence on a remote farm in Carmarthenshire, is a splendidly poetic piece of film-making that deserves its reputation as one of Ormond's best. With Ormond's lyrical commentary read by Richard Burton,[29] the film was shown at the Edinburgh International Film Festival and received high praise from important figures in British documentary-making at the time. Norman Swallow deemed it one of the key films in a 'golden age' of television documentary,[30] and John Grierson, after seeing the film, is said to have exclaimed, 'Ormond, you're a poet!'[31] It was particularly well received in Wales: Alun Richards has suggested that 'were it a book upon the shelf it would be much thumbed'.[32] Newspaper reviews at the time were laudatory: the usually reserved Robert Graham at the *Western Mail* deemed it a 'triumph',[33] and the *Evening Post* called it a 'fantastic story [. . .] perfection'.[34] The BBC Audience Research Report suggested that audiences were almost unanimously 'touched and humbled' by the film.[35] Ormond himself saw the film as a poetic statement. His wife Glenys later recalled that, upon suggesting to him that he might write a poem on 'the subject that had so moved him', he replied 'No, that film was the poem'.[36]

Borrowed Pasture immediately announces itself as a documentary with poetic intentions. It opens with shots that are clearly designed to strike an emotional chord and provoke an aesthetic response: extreme close-ups of two gnarled men, their sombre, hardened faces set dramatically against a black backdrop, dissolve into close-ups of hardened plant-life: nettles rustling in the wind, a rose-stem with disconcertingly sharp thorns on display; nature's own inuring against a hostile environment.[37] Burton's sonorous voice narrates, and though this provides us with explanatory information and context – itself a rarity for a film-maker who predominantly allows the visual image to speak for itself – this is overtly poetic in cadence, and matches the visual vocabulary of toilsome, toughened nature:

> This is a simple story of two men who came upon a stubborn piece of land that lay neglected for a generation. Here in despair but hoping in their hands they worked together and as best they could borrowed rough pasture from the alien ground and water, and coaxed small comfort from decrepitude.

Cue a rise in background music that quickly reaches a plangent crescendo, and the film's title, *Borrowed Pasture*, suddenly appears, scrawled obliquely across the screen in an austere white paint-effect typeface. These early moments signal the film's aesthetic intentions: its attempt to poeticise, to cinematise these men's lives. Ormond is aesthetically disciplined in this film as in much of his best poetry. He utilises only the symbolic palette of his subject in his aim to find a poetic correlative for the men's austere existence. The film restricts itself throughout to the vocabulary of scarcity and toil adopted in the opening scenes, and we never venture outside the farm's vicinity and the meagre resources it offers. A stream that runs through the land is dredged by hand and used to power a small dynamo; tiles from the pigsty are borrowed to fix the cottage roof; scaffolding is made out of the tall trees that surround the farm. Such instances of bricolage serve brilliantly to convey the men's process of 'coax[ing] small comfort from decrepitude'. Even the film's soundtrack is drawn from the world of the men themselves; BBC Wales composer Arwel Hughes based the orchestrations on Polish lullabies Ormond had picked up from another Polish farm in Pembrokeshire.[38]

While 'ethnographic' in subject, *Borrowed Pasture* is far from the kind of observational-expository format that was being developed in programmes such as *Special Enquiry* at the BBC in the same era. Rather, Ormond's hand is visible at every turn. This is clear from the film's narrative structure as well as its poeticism. The film impressionistically dramatises the men's refurbishment of the farmhouse from a dilapidated abandoned structure to a habitable homestead, and, as Ormond later noted, 'there are four fades in, four fades to black and [. . .] four movements, each representing a season'.[39] True to his professed strategy of 'moving from particular observation to general, universal conclusion', the film draws themes of wider poignancy from otherwise prosaic observations. The most central of these is that of forbearance, of enduring life in spite of time's inexorable passing. Bulaj tries to fix a tractor and finds his glasses are too weak, while Burton intones, 'You can muster a few more years of life from almost anything, given that you can see. But you begin to blunder when half-crown glasses hinder your subtle gadgetry.' The film, in its skilful poeticism, is genuinely moving. One sequence portrays Bulaj reflecting upon missing his daughter's wedding. We see him looking through photos his family have sent from Poland. 'Twelve years in Penygaer Farm', he sighs. 'It broke my heart.' The film cuts to a shot in which Bulaj forcefully slams metal milk containers on to his truck, and his sense of resentment and frustration is palpable.

On one level, *Borrowed Pasture* profoundly confirms one of David MacDougall's claims about ethnographic films, namely that in their most sensitive form they are able almost to transcend the political and to 'reiterate [. . .] the commonalities of being human'.[40] This is clearly the aim of *Borrowed Pasture*. The two men were members of the some-150,000 ex-Polish servicemen who had fought with the British Army and were thus encouraged to settle in Britain under the 1947 Polish Resettlement Act.[41] With ethnic tensions at a high at this time, the BBC began producing programmes in aid of the perceived 'refugee problem'.[42] At least one BBC Wales programme had addressed the issue before Ormond: in 1956, Dafydd Grufydd produced a film whose name betrays something of the anxieties of the time – *Strangers in Our Midst* – which, according to David Berry, 'presented the plight and life-style changes of the thousands of Poles living in Wales since the War'.[43] The power of *Borrowed Pasture* is derived from a poeticism that pushes these political tensions to the background, and encourages audiences to recognise these men's humanity on their own terms. This is hinted at in the opening lines of *Borrowed Pasture*: 'this is a simple story of two men'. The film mollifies concerns about the 'refugee problem' in Wales by accentuating the noble, *gwerin*-like simplicity of two respectable, God-fearing men forging an honest life from the land.

While the film draws intriguing parallels with Welsh folk life, the emotive force of *Borrowed Pasture* lies in a sustained dramatic tension predicated on the symbolic social exclusion of its protagonists. The film eloquently conveys the drudgery and hardship that Okolowicz and Bulaj endure in order to eke out a life from this unforgiving plot of land, and yet, as the film's title implies, this is land that is never fully theirs. As the film's commentary explains, these are men who 'struck a bargain with the land upon the land's conditions', whose 'home has meant surrender to the land. The land's demands are everything.' It is also significant that the commentary speaks for the men throughout much of the film. This would partly have been for pragmatic reasons – the men speak very little English, and seemingly no Welsh – but the device additionally confirms their disenfranchisement. Indeed, the first time we hear either of the men speak is a scene in which Okolowicz tries to teach himself English, and there his words are described by the commentary as 'strange syllables [. . .] from the student who never leaves Penygaer'. The fact that Okolowicz is attempting to learn how to ask a train conductor for information adds a further sad irony to the scene. This sense of dispossession and isolation is compounded, moreover, by the transient nature of all their dealings with the outside world: they meet once a week with a 'travelling grocer', and twice a year are visited by their 'only visitor', a Polish priest – himself an 'itinerant in a Nonconformist country'.[44] On this score, the restricted visual palette of the film – there is no footage outside the farm's boundaries – only serves to enhance the sense of isolation. Perhaps the film's most powerful depiction of this is a scene in which Bulaj attempts to send a telegram to his wife. The frustrated – and rather comic – conversation with the prim telegram operator potently conveys both Bulaj's distance from his wife and from the Welsh society that exists unheedingly outside the farm's borders:

OPERATOR: Telegrams. Telegrams?
BULAJ: Speaking seven nine one eight.
OPERATOR: Pardon?
BULAJ: Speaking seven nine one eight.
OPERATOR: Seven nine one eight where?
BULAJ: Yes.
OPERATOR: Swansea?
BULAJ: Pardon?
OPERATOR: Seven nine one eight where?
BULAJ: This is Penygaer Farm.
OPERATOR: Yes, but are you Swansea? Or Carmarthen? Or Port Talbot? Or Llanelli?
BULAJ: Yes.
[. . .]
OPERATOR: I'm very sorry, are you speaking from Carmarthen?
BULAJ: Yes! No! From Penygaer Farm.

Borrowed Pasture ends with Bulaj's eloquently broken English – 'You know, without the farm, I am nothing. And you know, the farm, it is me.' It is perhaps Bulaj's final claim on this merciless plot of land. *Borrowed Pasture* is a film that finds its poetry in measuring the distance between these men's isolated lives and an implied Welsh society of the present. While the film does not quite exclude Bulaj and Okolowicz from this society – it does, after all, offer them a space in which to reside, however compromised by isolation and hardship – it nevertheless, in its poetic observation of them, implies a Welsh society that is not theirs.

SONG IN A STRANGE LAND

With immigration and its attendant racial politics a prominent theme in British current affairs in the early 1960s (1962 had seen some of the freedom of movement encouraged by the 1948 British Nationality Act restricted by the Commonwealth Immigrants Act), Ormond would soon return to the topic. Indeed, there was an ideal location for such a film on just the other side of the city in which he lived and worked: Tiger Bay. This vibrant multi-ethnic community had been fuelling the Welsh popular imagination for close to a century, and Ormond's 1964 film *Song in a Strange Land* profiles the range of religious identities in the area. Tiger Bay, or to use its real name, Butetown, is a district close to what were the docklands of Cardiff, and was at that time renowned for being one of the few truly multicultural areas in Britain.[45] In the 1960s some eighty per cent of its inhabitants were non-white,[46] and the area was made up of people from over fifty nations.[47] The community had emerged as a result of its close proximity to the coal-exporting docks, which attracted, as Glenn Jordan and Chris Weedon write, 'a kaleidoscope of immigrants to build and service the docks, to work aboard the ships and to otherwise service the new industrial and maritime city'.[48] Seafaring labourers from all over the world would arrive on the tramp steamer freight ships that carried Welsh coal out from the docks, and while most would leave again with the ships, many would stay. Over time a community was forged.

Tiger Bay gathered considerable attention over the years, becoming the subject of a vast range of representations in popular culture and the media. Jordan and Weedon have scrutinised the variety of such representations, and make the claim that Tiger Bay consequently became a discursive construct whose wild reputation far exceeded its social reality: 'ultimately, it is impossible to separate Tiger Bay from stories about it. Tiger Bay is a textual phenomenon [. . .] as much as it is a physical and social one.'[49] Frequently, these representations have been harmfully sensational. Glenn Jordan in particular has spent considerable energy debunking those that 'combine negative portrayal[s] with a sense of exoticism, danger and mystery'.[50] He has also written of the significance of the more restrained, liberal and indeed positive images that emerged in the post-war years. In 2001 he contributed to a book that revisited a series of photographs that were printed in *Picture Post* in the 1950s, *'Down the Bay':* Picture Post, *Humanist Photography and Images of 1950s Cardiff*. Naturally, given its humanist concern with, in Jordan's words, the "universals' in human experience [. . .] that are shared across societies and cultures',[51] *Picture Post*'s portrayal of the area was far closer to Ormond's sensibilities. Indeed, the series of photographs no doubt contributed to – or were at least a part of – the shift in perception that took place in the 1950s and 1960s: from Tiger Bay as a hotbed of depravity to Tiger Bay as, in Neil Evans's terms, a 'respectable [. . .] symbol of tolerance to the world'.[52] Ormond's *Song in a Strange Land* should be understood as a part of this shift toward a more tolerant perception of Tiger Bay in 1960s Wales.

The film announces itself as a determinedly poetic documentary film in its opening minutes.[53] It opens with a slow-motion shot of a seagull gracefully gliding over the ocean, while a plaintive melody, played by a solo flautist, rises and falls with the bird's wings. The music directs our mood towards the montage of images that follow: rusting, derelict handling cranes stand at the water's edge; a slow pan shot of tidal mudflats. Small waves break and roll inland; tugboats haul a cargo liner into port; a captain stands at the bow of a ship that sails past the frame; a flag flutters on some rigging. The film refrains from offering the viewer explicit contextual information; rather a tone, a mood, is impressionistically set using images and music. This mood is one of a kind of sad transience, a sense of the passage of time (implied by the derelict cranes) and – as it slowly becomes clear from the impressionistic visual fragments that build towards a scene of the incoming of a ship – of the passage of people. This idea of the movement of people is further established by a cut to different sort of music, with the plaintive flute giving way to the rousing sound of Arabic singing. Here follows a shift to a more buoyant mood: we cut to footage of what is clearly, to any local viewer, Cardiff docklands (for anyone in doubt, the bow of a tugboat is shot displaying the name of its port), and once again the speed of editing increases to match the footage. Now we see the docks operating in full flow: cranes shifting cargo, incoming ships, the bustle of the working day. The texture of sound thickens; we hear the slosh of water against the side of the ships; cranes mechanically whir and clunk; a van chugs past. All is movement, and another kind of song is heard in the distance, this time a Greek tenor singing a hymn. Without the need for voiceover commentary or superimposed text, the film eloquently conveys its message that this is a film about the multiple religious cultures that reside in Tiger Bay. However, the manner in which it achieves this simultaneously signals the film's representational focus. Like *Borrowed Pasture*, while offering an ethnographic insight into 'other' peoples living within the borders of Wales, the film anchors these ethnicities to the docks, and links them with ideas of movement and migration rather than with stasis and integration.[54] The film's title (and the manner in which it is displayed – superimposed over a shot of the sea meeting the land's edge) further echoes the melancholic irony of this, using as it does a line from Psalm 137, the lament of the Jews in Babylonian exile: 'How shall we sing the Lord's song in a strange land?'

Following these impressionistic opening minutes, *Song in a Strange Land* shifts into a more expositional, informational format, but still within a poetic mode. It concerns itself with three men of differing ethno-religious backgrounds – A. A. Callinicos, a Greek Orthodox Catholic; Sheikh Said Hassan Ismail, the Imam of the local Islamic community; and Jaswant Singh, a local Sikh. The film provides the space for each one of them to explain, directly to the camera, their belief system, their rituals of worship, and the social and familial conventions of their respective faiths. In this sense, the film draws very effectively on the 'think-tape' format used also by Mitchell and Donnellan, insofar as it completely dispenses with the use of an authoritative voiceover commentary and instead foregrounds its subjects' viewpoints. Ormond's 'organic mosaic' poetics serves the film particularly well on this score. The film is duly reverent in its use of every means available to fully and faithfully convey a sense of these religions. We are invited into a Greek church during the Divine Liturgy; the camera movement and speed between cuts slows noticeably in order to convey a sense of respectful awe, while Callinicos whispers a translation of the reading of the Liturgy. After a number of minutes spent here, the film dissolves to a very different place of worship: a small mosque within Sheikh Said's own home. Here Sheikh Said explains to us some of the theological particulars of his faith, and we are offered footage of the daily rituals associated with it: a man performs his ablutions; another sits quietly reading the Qur'an; a group of men face Mecca and kneel to pray. Soon we turn to Singh's place of worship, the local gurdwara, and the film again conveys its respect for this particular style of worship by finding a shooting style appropriate to it: quick editing and camera movement matches the upbeat, rhythmic music; the camera films from floor-level as the worshippers kneel to kiss the ground before the Guru Granth Sahib, their holy text. Ormond thus strives to find in each of these religions something of its *aesthetic* essence: a set of symbols, a style of music, a form of worship. He translates each into filmic content, and in turn each contributes to a sense of his 'mosaic'. It is thus with this pluralist approach in mind that we could suggest this film opens up a space for a multicultural Welsh citizenship. Its subjects are frequently shown to be firmly and comfortably integrated into their community: the first time we meet Callinicos and Sheik Said it is in their respective places of work, Callinicos as he (in a rather contrived way) ends a telephone conversation with a client in the office of his successful shipping firm, Sheik Said as he welds a radiator in a large dockland workshop. We meet each in his own home; in one suggestive shot, the camera pans across a row of houses and locates Singh's own by the sound of Sikh music flooding into the street, as if demonstrating that this form of worship is now a part of local life. In this sense, the film does not essentialise these men by reducing them to mere metonyms of their religious faith; each has his own unique relationship with his faith and with the community in which he lives.

However, the film's poetic pluralism is arguably brought into tension with a relativistic construction of Tiger Bay. Although structured around the distinct qualities of each religion – music, exotic scripture, and religious iconography – the film returns to the same plaintive melody and images of the docks we saw in the opening minutes, along with their attendant connotations of transience, movement and dislocation. These religious identities are framed and exhibited in a way that reminds us that we, as viewers, are engaged in an act of ethnographic viewing of an exceptional community. This tendency is ultimately borne out in the film's ambitious final sequence, where Ormond, in a wordless six-minute montage, attempts to direct the film towards a 'general universal conclusion'. The montage builds quite effectively towards a stirring climax: rousing orchestral music rises and accompanies shots in which solemn acts of worship are counter-pointed with dramatic footage of waves crashing up against the cliffs. The editing quickens and we begin to cut rapidly between the church, the mosque and the gurdwara. The message here is thus a universal one of the enormous human profundity of human migration itself, rather than an endorsement, for instance, of any one particular faith. From here the music and images slow and soften to convey a calmer mood, until we finally fade to black. We find ourselves on an ordinary street in Tiger Bay; a young Greek man sings a song to himself while shaving; next, a pan of the street stops at a 'Continental Grocer' shop, outside which two young boys in turbans listen to a pop song on a portable radio. Again, while on one level the sequence offers an encouraging vision of a new, multicultural generation growing up on the streets of Cardiff, the film frames this footage in such a way that relativises it, viewing the subjects on screen as symbolic of the universal 'song' sung by the sum of all religion in this place.

It is significant too that the film only seeks out footage in Tiger Bay itself. We never see its subjects going about their business in Cardiff city centre, or in any way interacting with the world outside Butetown and the docks. In this sense, the film seems to mirror the social attitudes towards Butetown in 1960s Cardiff, which was in fact, as a number of recent historians have noted, not a reality of tolerance and integration, but frequently one of intolerance and segregation. Martin Johnes notes that the area was at this time 'physically and socially isolated from the rest of the city [. . .] [O]ther Cardiffians thought it a dangerous and disreputable place'.[55] This had, moreover, been the case for some time. Neil Evans suggests in his sobering survey of Welsh racial intolerance that boundaries were drawn after the racial riots that took place in 1919: these 'redrew the boundaries of the black community [. . .]. Those who had settled in areas north of the South Wales Railway bridge were forced to leave their homes.'[56] While there was less outward evidence of racial prejudice and intolerance in the half-century that followed – that is, less than was seen in the Notting Hill and Nottingham riots of the late 1950s, and to which *Song in a Strange Land* is in part a self-satisfied response – this relative harmony hinges upon the fact that Butetown was in fact 'rather cut off from the rest of the inner city'.[57] *Song in a Strange Land* celebrates Wales's credentials as a tolerant nation against those of a racially tense Britain, but in a way that perhaps idealises them, thereby limiting the potential for meaningful symbolic participation. Yet this is arguably where the film's peculiar strength as a *national* documentary lies: in its reification of the mythology of a racially tolerant, humanitarian Wales. The film eloquently portrays a poetic sense of these 'other' ethnicities living within Wales's borders, but leaves no question as to who are the supposed true inhabitants of this 'land'.[58]

THE MORMONS

Borrowed Pasture and *Song in a Strange Land* interpellate a national viewership by poetically constructing a picture of religious and ethnic diversity in Wales that simultaneously circumscribes those ethnicities as 'other'. Ormond's 1965 film on the presence of another religious group in Wales, *The Mormons*, works in a similar way, but extends this ethnographic impulse outwards, finding much of its material abroad by exploring Wales's connections with Salt Lake City. The film itself informs us at length of the Welsh connection with the Church of Latter Day Saints: namely, Merthyr-born Captain Dan Jones's close friendship with its prophet and leader, Joseph Smith. Jones has since been enshrined in Mormon mythology, having allegedly been with Joseph Smith the night before the latter's assassination in an Illinois jail in 1844. On that night, Smith had prophesied that Jones would return to Wales and convert legions of followers to his religion, and this Jones duly did; from his headquarters in Merthyr, Jones converted some 5,000 Welsh people to his faith.[59] Many of these emigrated in the years that followed and became instrumental in the establishment of Salt Lake City. In this sense *The Mormons* is perhaps guilty of a tendency that irritated veteran BBC Wales producer Selwyn Roderick in his essay 'Us Over There',[60] namely, Wales's obsession, in its television programmes, with itself:

> While the French have taken their cameras into the depths of tropical seas, and the West-country English have passed Antarctic seasons recording the frosty matings of polar bears and penguins we, the Welsh, have diligently ventured abroad to film – chiefly – ourselves.[61]

Roderick views this as a weakness, arguing that Welsh broadcasting should seek to 'illuminate the world' from a distinctively Welsh perspective, and look to the international in order to offer Welsh viewers a sense of themselves, rather than allow 'strangers based in London and around the globe' to do it for them.[62] Yet the ways in which Ormond informs (indeed 'informing' seems to be the central intention of this film: its subtitle is *A Film Report by John Ormond*) a Welsh viewership of this often-overlooked chapter in Wales's history is intriguing.

Like *Song in a Strange Land*, *The Mormons* celebrates the exoticism of its subject. In this case, this is the stuff of the American Wild West. The film opens with a cheerfully upbeat country and western tune, and we are greeted with picturesque panning and still shots of the Rocky Mountains. From here the camera pans down the side of a snowy mountain into a small valley, and as a slide banjo takes over to twang the melody on the soundtrack, we cut to shots selected to accompany this Western theme: horses on a small ranch; the local sheriff. We cut to a close up of the sheriff's badge, and then to the logo on the side of his car; the camera pans up, and we see the man himself sitting inside, complete with obligatory dark sunglasses and Stetson hat, coolly lighting a cigarette. We could well be watching a Western, were it not for the film's title – *The Mormons* – earlier displayed on screen in an oddly comic, cartoonish typeface, as if informing us that we are on a jaunt not to be taken too seriously. There is no narrator at this stage, and with images and music alone the film generates wonder and intrigue, leading us to what appears to be a series of large tunnels built into the Rocky Mountains. Again, the scenes that follow

are ambitiously filmic, as opposed to merely expository: the music
fades out and we hear only the sounds of the howling wind; next we
cut to a man spinning a hand-wheel on an enormous vault door, and
now only echoing footsteps are audible. We shortly discover that this
opening sequence's journey into the heart of the mountains has in
fact sought to encapsulate the film's wider project: to delve deep into
the history of the Mormon people and discover the Welsh presence
among them. A spokesman for the Church greets us in a large empty
chamber of an underground vault, and politely explains to us the
purpose of this place: to store vast quantities of microfilmed geneal-
ogy records. Here the commentary cuts in,[63] and confirms for us the
distinctly Welsh perspective that the preceding images have hitherto
only implied:

> In the waiting vaults in the mountains, and among the neat, clinical, grey
> files in Salt Lake City, it's difficult not to feel that they know all about
> us. They've got us tabulated and docketed by the million. [. . .] They've
> got our family histories at their fingertips, and they've got their young
> men in our streets.

These words are dubbed over footage of endless rows of filing cab-
inets: we cut closer to see the labels on some of the drawers: 'Wales
General and Anglesey'; 'Wales Montgomery'; 'Wales Pembrokeshire
Radnorshire'; 'Wales Glamorgan Merioneth'. A young clerical assistant flicks through the reference cards headed by Welsh place-names:
Llanelli, Llanilltern, Llanishen. The film in this way posits a Welsh
viewership by contributing to the powerful process of, in Michael
Billig's phrase, 'flagging the homeland'.[64] This is the process of 'deictic' signalling that, according to Billig, is crucial to the perpetuation
of modern nations, contributing as it does to the everyday 'banal'
normality of the national homeland. This process is clearly at work
in *The Mormons*, in which Wales and its inhabitants (the implied
audience) and the Mormon American 'others' are invariably referred
to in deictic terms: '*they* know all about *us*'; '*they*'ve got *our* family
histories at *their* fingertips'.

   This is not to say that the film refuses to open up a space for a
'Welsh Mormonism' of sorts. The film is not entirely the kind of
'televisual tourism' that Graham Murdock describes: those televisual
images of 'other' nations in which cultural differences are 'constructed
as exotic, picturesque or simply quaint, but [. . .] present no challenge

to our sense of self'.[65] Indeed, a good part of the film's focus is the presence of Mormons in Wales and exploring the reasons for that presence. We meet a dignitary of the Merthyr Church of Latter Day Saints, Ralph Pulman, who explains to us his family's long-held commitment to the church. Pulman's great-grandfather had been converted by Dan Jones himself, and returned with him to Utah in the first wave of Welsh emigration to the Mormon state. We are privy to footage of a church meeting in which members of all ages profess their faith. A young woman addresses the audience: 'I know that this is the true church of Jesus Christ. I know that Joseph Smith was a prophet of God, that he revealed to the world the true church of Jesus Christ.' She is clearly, in her youth, her fashionable dress and her pronounced Merthyr accent intended to symbolise the ongoing, contemporary relevance of the church in a diverse 1960s Wales.

Nevertheless, the final message of *The Mormons* is one of a normative Welsh identity – and that is an identity that is decidedly not Mormon. This is partly indicated by the return of a deictic distancing of the followers of the faith as not quite Welsh: Davies intones that 'two and a half thousand of them here in Wales agree with them'. This is further confirmed by the aesthetic approach Ormond adopts towards this religion; again he seeks out the primarily aesthetic content of Mormonism and visualises it on film in a way that posits a normative 'Welsh' subjectivity. A sequence towards the end of the film illustrates this, in which we are invited to experience a performance by the famous Mormon Tabernacle Choir. Ormond finds an appropriate visual correlative to this rousing choral music: majestic aerial shots of the Rockies. As if lifted by song, the camera glides through the clouds to come upon a vista of the snow-covered mountains, and we spend some time here before cutting to the interior of the Salt Lake Tabernacle itself, where the choir's 375 members sit neatly arranged, singing in perfect unison. The sequence is framed as an invitation into a distinctly American experience: 'on Sunday mornings, as on every Sunday morning for the past thirty-five years, America tunes in coast-to-coast to listen to the famous Mormon Tabernacle Choir'. The film ultimately presents the idea of the faith as a kind of amusing curiosity. The final sequence of the film views two Mormon missionaries going about their work on the streets of Cardiff; their heads are cut out of the frame, as if to emphasise the generality of the image and also the missionaries' permanent marginality: their work is never complete because they could never convert all of Wales. Meanwhile the soundtrack ends with a jaunty folk song by singer Rosalie Sorells, further emphasising the film's – and the audience's – wry amusement. Ormond's choice of singer is pertinent. Sorells was a folk singer from Utah whose satirical songs frequently railed against the Mormon people. In her song 'Brigham Young' she sings, 'He lived with his five-and-forty wives in the city of the great Salt Lake,/ where they breed and swarm like hens on a farm and cackle like ducks to a drake'. The meek-sounding song that ends this film, 'None Can Preach the Gospel Like the Mormons Do', is heavy with irony.

FROM A TOWN IN TUSCANY

From a Town in Tuscany similarly constructs a Welsh viewership through a journey abroad. Filmed in the Tuscan town of Arezzo in 1963, the film's purpose was to visit the hometown of a choir – the Concorso Polifonico Guido d'Arezzo – that was due to perform at the Llangollen International Eisteddfod in the following year.[66] *From a Town in Tuscany* seeks partly to forge a link and find a set of commonalities between Wales and this little town. There is through-out the film a genuine attempt to understand the people of Arezzo, with a particular focus on the choristers' everyday professions. The film emphasises the fact that music, whatever its importance to these people's lives, is necessarily a hobby for most. Finding a topic that choristers in Wales could surely sympathise with, the narrator (here John Darran) explains that 'like the members of most choirs, music is pleasure in the evenings; but all day, a job of work to do'. We visit some of them in their places of work: a jewellery factory, a railway yard. A furniture polisher sings to himself on the doorstep of his business. Even Sylvestro Valdarnini, the choir's conductor, has to make his living as a music teacher. These are ordinary people, then, whatever their extraordinary talents. In this way, the film strongly bears out Selwyn Roderick's remarks on the issue of the importance of Welsh programming finding and forging links with foreign places and cultures.

Ormond's poetic inclinations were perhaps most pronounced in Arezzo, of all places. It was this very excursion to Arezzo in 1963 that Ormond later recounted inspired his surprise return to writing poetry in earnest after nearly twenty years, and a place where, he later wrote, 'long-felt ideas and long-heard musics seem [. . .] to cohere',[67] return-ing there many times in later years. It is not surprising, then, that

Ormond's propensity to use film to 'poeticise' is so strongly apparent in *From a Town in Tuscany*. The film returns more than once to the beautiful sound of the Concorso Polifonico Guido d'Arezzo. Ormond seeks out an appropriately exotic set of 'Italian' images to match these ethereal choral voices, and the result is a strong sense of the film travelogue, with its shots of Arezzo's immaculate Renaissance architecture and scenic footage of the surrounding Tuscan landscape. There is also a rare example of a kind of experiential film-making, of attempting to evoke a foreign experience in this film. A group of folk dancers perform in the town square, and the camera takes part in their festivities by using point-of-view shots to twirl and dance along with them. A sequence in the marketplace adopts a similar technique, with a handheld camera jostling its way through the shoppers and surveying the produce on display. The narrator even addresses the viewer in the second person to reinforce the effect: 'You taste and you try. In time you'll almost certainly buy.' The film lyrically evokes a sense and feeling of the place. Arezzo is celebrated as a richly fertile cultural region, having given birth to some of the key figures of the Renaissance and earlier: Giorgio Vasari, Michelangelo, Petrarch, Guido of Arezzo. Even its modern citizens live alongside these great artists, poets and thinkers; they live, according to the commentary, 'in a place where buildings put up by medieval craftsmen and Renaissance architects are a part of their everyday lives'. *From a Town in Tuscany* thus travels abroad to celebrate an 'other' cultural region in a way that sends a poetic image back to – and thereby reinforces – a Welsh viewership back home.

MUSIC IN MIDSUMMER

Given the internationalising perspective of a film like *From a Town in Tuscany*, it was perhaps inevitable that Ormond should eventually turn to an event that performs this very function within Wales's own borders. *Music in Midsummer* finds its material at the Llangollen International Eisteddfod. This was an ideal topic not only because of the sheer spectacle of a festival of international music and dance, but also because the festival itself shared many of the same post-war Welsh internationalist impulses that were shaping work at the BBC in Wales at that time. The festival at Llangollen, though a product of these wider impulses, had stemmed from the work of one man in particular, Harold Tudor, a journalist and officer of the British Council.

Tudor had sought in the war years to take diplomatic advantage of the presence of exiled Allied governments residing in London by inviting them to the National Eisteddfod. The gesture was calculated to generate a sense of Welsh national sovereignty through the development of international status:

> As a Welshman who believes that his nation should seek to escape from mere provincialism by forging her own direct links with the Continent, the scheme especially appealed to me because it meant that the Allied delegates would be the first official envoys to Wales from other governments since the days of Owain Glyndŵr.[68]

Such a position would undoubtedly have been shared by senior figures at BBC Wales like Alun Oldfield-Davies and Aneirin Talfan Davies, who were interested in raising Wales's cultural profile at home and abroad for the same reason. Tudor's scheme was a success, and set in motion the efforts that resulted in the first International Eisteddfod at Llangollen in 1947. The festival was, from these early days, covered on the Welsh Home Service in short news bulletins and, later, in fully relayed concerts. After the arrival of the Welsh Film Unit in 1957, BBC television cameras were also an annual presence at the festival grounds.[69]

That said, some by the 1960s had grown tired of the extensive BBC coverage of Llangollen – one BBC Audience Research Report on the 1963 coverage of the festival found 'half a dozen' of the sample complain that 'the cultural value doesn't warrant the fuss made. We see far too much of the same thing year after year.'[70] Nevertheless, the BBC did return year after year. Perhaps Ormond felt justified that the earlier grainy black and white footage had not quite captured the full spirit of the event. As Selwyn Roderick has remarked, 'if ever a place was designed for colour television, Llangollen was'.[71] *Music in Midsummer* was filmed in full colour at the 1967 festival, very probably with the intention of broadcasting it soon after on the new all-colour BBC2, which came into service in July of the same year.[72] It was one of very few Welsh contributions to the BBC network because, as John Davies notes, BBC Wales was 'obliged [. . .] to devote its resources to home output'.[73] Evidently the rich and exotic colours of the International Eisteddfod were deemed worthy of the national network. Though, interestingly, many Welsh viewers would have to wait longer to view it in full colour; during these early days the potential coverage of colour broadcasting was estimated at just fifty-two per cent,[74] and as the Wenvoe transmitter – which serviced most of the population of Wales – was not upgraded until 1970, a large part of the Welsh viewership would have been watching *Music in Midsummer* on BBC2 in black and white.[75] The film should therefore be viewed not only as an effort to raise Wales's cultural confidence at home, but also – like the International Eisteddfod itself – as a means of raising Wales's profile elsewhere; in this case, the rest of Britain.

Ormond achieved this in his usual distinctive fashion.[76] Certain striking sequences could be seen as an extension of some of the immersive filming techniques that Ormond experimented with in *From a Town in Tuscany* and *Song in a Strange Land*. The film opens by delving straight into a sequence that attempts to capture something of the raucous multicultural atmosphere of the festival. It is a glorious summer's day; a handheld camera pushes its way through a busy crowd; there is clapping, cheering, singing, but above all the sound of exuberant Arabic music. It becomes clear that the camera is jostling its way to the front of the crowd for a better view of what seems to be an impromptu performance outside the main tent. The camerawork attempts to mimic this lively spontaneity: it zooms in and out, shifts in and out of focus, cuts rapidly between shots of the revelry: a hand bashes out a rhythm on a drum; a mouth blows spiritedly into a *kaba zurna*; feet dance happily through the mud. The intention, clearly, is to use every means available to invite the viewer into this unique experience. Shortly, with the music still on the soundtrack, we cut to footage of a serene pastoral scene that seems altogether more appropriate to a film made in a place like Llangollen. A slow panning shot takes in the perfect calm of the idyllic rural surroundings, and there is a deliberate dissonance between soundtrack and image for some seconds before the song ends and we finally hear the more fitting sound of birds, bees and the wind blowing through bushes on the side of a hill. What is significant about this transition is not so much its stylised juxtaposition – this is common fare for Ormond, who, invariably preferred to communicate his message through the manipulation of sound and image – but rather the fact that the commentary (here read by Ormond himself) must prosaically explain this juxtaposition to the viewer: 'Unlikely sounds, you may think, to hear echoing across a valley in north Wales. But in fact the countryside around Llangollen is familiar ground to thousands of singers and dancers from all over the world.' This intervention is just a small segment of commentary – it lasts only around forty seconds – and constitutes the only voiceover in the film. Judging by the film's predominantly poetic-observational mode, there is the sense that Ormond would have preferred not to use any voiceover commentary at all. For the viewer with prior knowledge of the International Eisteddfod, the film would be perfectly intelligible without it. This short snippet of contextualising information thus signals the fact that *Music in Midsummer* was as much an advert of Wales's cultural cosmopolitanism, intended for a British audience, as a celebration of this on Wales's own terms. Pursuing the observational mode established in the opening sequence, the film's overriding strategy is to offer viewers the experience of visiting this spectacular carnival. The camera wanders the grounds as might the ordinary festival-goer, stumbling across colourful performances of folk music and dance from all over Europe and beyond.[77] Wales is projected to a primetime national BBC2 audience as a culturally confident nation actively engaged in bringing together cultures of all creeds.[78] Much of the early section of the film is concerned with the massive community effort required in order for the festival to go ahead: men of all ages chip in to set up the enormous main tent; women discuss hospitality arrangements; schoolchildren help to carry in the seating. Wales plays the host of the nations.

This filmic experience of Llangollen is a powerful means of contributing to a conception of Wales as a distinct cultural – if not quite political – entity within the British public sphere. It is significant that the film adopts the form of an experience of the festival, as opposed to, for instance, a film report on the festival undertaken by a correspondent from London. This was one of the strengths of having a film unit based in Wales. The film, after all, addresses those outside its realm of experience – 'Unlikely sounds, *you may think*' – and in doing so proves itself to be in the privileged position of being able to invite others in. As with the other films examined in this chapter, *Music in Midsummer* contributes to a sense of Welsh cultural distinctiveness in its capacity to observe and accommodate 'other' cultures. This, of course, underlies the very idea of the International Eisteddfod. But perhaps the most effective way in which it does this is in two interesting final performances, in which the film, rather than emphasising differences, instead draws parallels. Unlike those seen throughout most of *Music in Midsummer*, these final performances are clearly set up specifically for the film. In the first, a section of an American choir sits aboard a small boat being pulled by a mule down the Llangollen canal. They sing the popular American folk song 'Low Bridge, Everybody Down', written by the Tin Pan Alley composer, Thomas S. Allen. This was a song that looked with a melancholy nostalgia at the end of use of mule barges on the Erie Canal, that crucial artery of the American economy in the nineteenth century:

> I've got a mule and her name is Sal
> Fifteen miles on the Erie Canal
> She's a good old worker and a good old pal
> Fifteen miles on the Erie Canal
>
> We hauled some barges in our day
> Filled with lumber, coal and hay
> And every inch of the way we know
> From Albany to Buffalo.

Ormond finds a resonance through which this song, marking the end of an era in American history, rings true for the end of a similar one in Wales. The Welsh canals that were once the mainlines of the Welsh industrial economy now serve – like the Erie Canal – a primarily recreational function, providing, for instance, the scenery for BBC Wales film-makers. From here, the film segues smoothly into a striking final sequence. The American choir finishes its song, and there is a peaceful moment in which the camera faces down at the canal water slowly drifting by; on its surface is reflected the magnificent ruins of Valle Crucis Abbey, the Cistercian abbey built by Madog ap Gruffydd Maelor, Prince of Powys Fadog, at the turn of the thirteenth century. There follows a virtuoso single three-minute take in which the camera somewhat shakily (these were before the days of the Steadicam) but impressively walks us through the abbey while a group of Italian choristers performs a solemn piece. The liturgical music is in keeping with this ancient place of worship nestled in the hills of north-east Wales; the effect is to remind the viewer of Wales's ancient links with Latin Europe. In this way, *Music in Midsummer* serves to showcase a distinctly cosmopolitan, internationalist cultural confidence to both its domestic Welsh audience and the broader British audience viewing on BBC2. The BBC Wales logo brandished proudly at the end of the film's impressive final sequence (beneath, naturally, Ormond's prestigious 'Produced by' credit) would itself have been a statement of Wales's cultural confidence in the late 1960s.

It is therefore important we read television films in more than simply aesthetic terms. These films certainly embody the poetic approach present in all of Ormond's work in verse and on film: the philosophy of the 'organic mosaic' – a belief in the capacity of the creative artefact, forged out of whatever artistic medium is available, to provide meaning in a meaningless world. But such artefacts assume a quite different set of significances in the context of national broadcasting. These significances, as I have attempted to show throughout this book, vary considerably according to the topic at hand: in the case of these documentary studies of 'other' cultures – inside and outside Wales – they, in part, take on an ethnographic function. Broadcasting in Wales is, by definition, part of an attempt to foster a Welsh national public sphere, a Welsh perspective on common and current affairs. As David Morley has suggested, this can be understood as a process of constructing a national 'family', a 'forum of sociability'.[79] While broadly sensitive and accommodating of 'others', Ormond was working within in an ethnographic mode that was distinctly of its time, and, on occasion, aestheticised other cultures and experiences in a way that can be understood – on a symbolic level – to hold them in uneasy tension with an implied Welsh society. That said, these are nevertheless sensitive, meticulously crafted films, valuable on their own terms and as documents of the way a Welsh 'forum of sociability' was constructed by BBC Wales in these decades.

Conclusion: The 'Organic Mosaic'

It has not been possible to examine in detail all of the films produced by John Ormond. Some were programmes produced within the format of established series, and while these are interesting historical documents, they bear few of the hallmarks of his style. *Enquiry: Fitness for Work* (1960) is a study of medical research into work-related illnesses such as pneumoconiosis. *Troubled Waters: Harry Soan Investigates* (1965) looked into fishing rights on the river Teifi. *Meeting Point: Operation Salvation* (1964) examines religious organisations helping the socially excluded. At least one other has been lost, though the production paperwork for *Madawaska Valley* (1967), the film Ormond made during a sabbatical at the National Film Board of Canada, tantalisingly suggests an experimental work very much in his mode. (I have discussed that at length elsewhere.[1]) Details of all of Ormond's known films are contained in the filmography that follows. However, there is one intriguing film that I have not yet discussed.

Alone in a Boat (1966) does not straightforwardly fit into the categories of 'culture', 'history', or 'ethnographic' documentary I have used in this book. Yet in its very unclassifiability, it is perhaps Ormond's most representative work. The film is about Welsh sailor Val Howells's participation in a 1960 solo transatlantic yacht race.[2] Far from the quotidian special-interest documentary we might expect (as did research audiences, for whom 'the film turned out quite differently from what was anticipated'),[3] *Alone in a Boat* is a remarkable and surprising example of Ormond's ekphrastic impulse to portray on screen a unique experience of the world. It is a deeply ruminative film on the nature of solitariness, sociability and the self. Characteristic of Ormond's tendency to create work inspired by and in celebration of others, the film was, according to Howells, 'based on [Ormond's] reading of *Sailing into Solitude*',[4] the sailor's 1966 book about his experiences alone on the open ocean. Howells's book is itself an idiosyncratic and deeply meditative portrayal of a decidedly unusual experience of the world, and this is likely what attracted Ormond to the idea of responding to it on film; indeed he was moved enough also to write a poem alongside, 'Message in a Bottle'. Viewed together, the three texts illuminate one another in ways that encapsulate Ormond's approach to poetry and film.

Consistent with his other poems dedicated to artists, 'Message in a Bottle' borrows unashamedly from the visual, philosophical and lexical vocabulary of its subject's world. The poem is buoyed by the diction of maritime life – 'all your change of rigging, the fine/ Rejigs to jib, genoa, spinnaker/ Are vain',[5] and, in line with this, *Alone in a Boat* uses every filmic means available to portray the subjective – and sometimes disturbingly solitary – experience of Howells's journey.[6] After a few contextual remarks from an external voiceover,[7] the film raises anchor, so to speak, to embark on its own journey. Visually, the film is austere, restricting itself solely to life on the boat and to the ubiquity of the ocean. Howells makes a cup of coffee below deck, checks the rig, trims his beard. The film returns repeatedly to shots of the sheen of the rippling surface of the sea filling the frame; occasionally a distant, empty horizon. The constant bobbing of the camera almost lulls the viewer into a sense of being on the boat. But despite this fluid, unmoored feel, the film does not lack an organising structure. Like Ormond's poem on the same subject, the film loosely responds to the soul-searching pattern of Howells's book. There, Howells encounters no life-threatening storms or major navigational problems: only the formidable antagonism of his own mind. Experimental in form, the book presents the author's expansive physical voyage as a profoundly internal experience. Its formal strategy is close to that of a work of literary modernism; Howells's narrative voice becomes increasingly obscure and fragmented as the psychological trials of the journey begin to take their toll, and the final outcome is a strange blend of poetry, prose and an almost schizophrenic stream of consciousness:

> Hell, I've been at sea thirty days already, and only have not much more than half the distance made good.
>
>   Another thirty days to go.
>   Not only will I be a tail-end Charlie

I'll be fit to be tied when I dock.
If I dock.

. . . you'll dock all right.

How can you be so sure?[8]

Accordingly, the nautical symbolism of Ormond's poem takes on a decidedly personal significance:

> trust old courses
> On interim charts, find reasons for the silence
> On the radio, check your batteries,
> Ignore the sinister becalment threatening
> Your brain.[9]

In the film, the once calming shots of the water's wavering translucence take on a portentous quality as Howells's narration becomes increasingly anxious: 'Nothing between me and the sky, nothing between me and the bottom of the sea.'[10] Mimicking the book's occasional slips into semi-schizophrenic madness, the film more than once adopts the peculiar technique of having Howells in voiceover talking to Howells on screen. In one scene, Howells lies in his cot:

HOWELLS IN VOICEOVER: I feel small out here. How about you?
HOWELLS ON SCREEN: Insignificant I think. Small isn't the word. An irresponsible dot. Not even marking the ocean by our passage.
[. . .]
HOWELLS IN VOICEOVER: A dot. Is a man a dot?

Alone in a Boat, then, is a poetic-filmic rumination on the self. Its title, as with that of Howells's book, *Sailing into Solitude*, points to the philosophical frame of reference within which it operates: a godless one, in which humans are finally alone in the world. This is not to say that these texts end on a nihilistic note; as the title of Ormond's poem hints, they offer a message, a way of seeing and being in a finally unknowable world. In all three, Howells the protagonist reaches a moment of internal crisis, the moment at which, as he states in *Alone in a Boat*, 'the crossing of an ocean [. . .] stretches the imagination perhaps to its breaking point'. Yet this moment is regenerative, perhaps sublime, the point at which the self reaffirms its subjectivity in the face of an almost incomprehensible threat. This humanistic perspective is, significantly, framed in terms of the artist, in which it is the unique vision of the artist that is the ideal. These are the film's closing words:

> I believe that every man can be his own artist. I don't really think you need to have a brush to be an artist. By an artist I mean a man with a freshness of eye, living on distances, though they are close about him. Living, if you like, on the horizon of himself.

The crisis is thus overcome with an affirmation of selfhood, and the film ends with a peaceful calm. Again, shots of the surface of the ocean fills the frame, but this time with barely a ripple on its surface; the only sounds are those of water lapping gently against the side of the boat. While some portions of the audience responded to the film as 'pretentious', on the whole *Alone in a Boat* was 'saluted [. . .] as television cast in an original and refreshing mould'.[11] Watching it today, the success of the film can be understood to come from the way Ormond pushes free of the boundaries of documentary as a straightforwardly informational form to create a film that stands alone as something innovative, reflective and original. Its message is not merely functional or didactic but existentially and creatively affirmative. The film invites us to look afresh at ourselves and the journeys on which we embark.

Dannie Abse once suggested of Ormond that 'however good his films are, it is primarily as a poet that he needs to be profiled.[12] I hope that, by now, it should go without saying that I disagree. This is not to say that he should 'primarily' be profiled as a film-maker – as I have attempted to show, poetry and film were in continuous correspondence with one another throughout Ormond's creative life. Moreover, the two forms were in constant correspondence with a whole range of themes, forms and areas of interest: with the work of other artists and writers, historical themes, people and places in Wales and the wider world. Both his poetry and his film-making were generously humane, giving voice to myriad perspectives, ways of seeing and making sense of a world in which, for him, 'there was plenty to be agnostic about'. *Alone in a Boat* shows that while all Ormond's films can be categorised as television documentaries – documents of that transient and now rapidly diminishing cultural form – they are best viewed on their own terms, as film poems that revel in the possibilities of creative film-making.

'From acute observation of particularities,' Ormond once said, 'you build up a kind of organic mosaic.' If each of his films constitutes a tile, a tessera, then viewed together, they add up to a rich picture of Welsh life in the second half of the twentieth century. Covering a vast range of themes and ideas, they connect and communicate diverse, sometimes uneasily disparate facets of Welsh culture and society, always with style, humour, and humanity. Viewed from different perspectives, they each catch the light in different ways, offering tantalising glimpses of the colours, textures and structures of feeling of a past that continues to inform the present. These films deserve to be viewed today not only as products of a single creative mind, nor as manifestations of a rigid institutional agenda. In a fuller sense, they continue to form organic parts of a lived, living Wales.

NOTES

Chapter 1

1 Gareth Evans, *Dunvant: Portrait of a Community* (Stafford: Stowefields Publications, 1992), p. 10.

2 Rian Evans, 'An Ormond Chronology', in John Ormond, *Collected Poems*, ed. Rian Evans (Bridgend: Seren, 2015), p. 33.

3 John Ormond, 'Ceri Richards: Root and Branch', *Planet*, 10 (1972), 6.

4 Ormond, 'Ceri Richards: Root and Branch', 6.

5 Ormond, 'Ceri Richards: Root and Branch', 6.

6 John Ormond, 'Picturegoers', in Patrick Hannan (ed.), *Wales on the Wireless* (Llandysul: Gomer, 1988), p. 59.

7 Ormond's early poetry bears strongly the mark of the 'Dylan Thomas effect' that James A. Davies speaks of in his essay '"In a different place,/ changed": Dannie Abse, Dylan Thomas, T. S. Eliot and Wales', in Alyce von Rothkirch and Daniel Williams (eds), *Beyond the Difference: Welsh Literature in Comparative Contexts* (Cardiff: University of Wales Press, 2004), p. 225. 'Poem in February' (first published in *Indications*, a shared poetry collection alongside John Bayliss and James Kirkup for the Grey Walls Press in 1943), for instance, brims with grandiloquent Dylanesque phrasings and a concern with the cosmic forces of life.

8 Ormond, 'John Ormond', in Meic Stephens (ed.), *Artists in Wales 2* (Llandysul: Gomer, 1972), p. 157.

9 John Bayliss, James Kirkup and John Ormond, *Indications* (London: Grey Walls Press, 1943).

10 M. Wynn Thomas, 'Ormond, John (1923–1990)', *Oxford Dictionary of National Biography*. Available at *http://www.oxforddnb.com/view/article/61282* (accessed 12 December 2018).

11 Ormond, 'John Ormond', in Meic Stephens (ed.), *Artists in Wales 2* (Llandysul: Gomer, 1973), pp. 160–1.

12   The phrase is BBC producer Norman Swallow's. See Norman Swallow, *Factual Television* (London: Focal Press, 1966).

13   Meic Stephens, 'The Second Flowering', *Poetry Wales*, 3/3 (1963), 2–8.

14   John Ormond, quoted in Richard Poole, 'Conversations with John Ormond', *New Welsh Review*, 2/1 (1989), 42.

15   John Ormond, 'Letter from Tuscany', *Poetry Wales*, 24/1 (1988), 22.

16   Ormond, 'Letter from Tuscany', 22.

17   See Ormond, *Collected Poems*, for a full bibliography.

18   Jeremy Tunstall, *Television Producers* (London: Routledge, 1993), p. 6.

19   On my use of the term 'film'. As James Monaco notes in his book *How to Read a Film*, 4th edn (Oxford: Oxford University Press, 2007), finding a singular term for the 'art of the moving picture' is a tricky process. The names that are usually ascribed to it – 'movies', 'cinema' and 'film' – are not distinct; they each possess different connotations, yet are often used interchangeably. Monaco usefully draws out the broad differences between the three: '"movies", like popcorn, are to be consumed; "cinema" [. . .] is high art, redolent of esthetics; "film" is the most general term we use with the fewest connotations'. Monaco, *How to Read a Film*, p. 252. I have chosen to adopt the term 'film', though I am conscious of the fact that the term is complicated further when used in the context of both documentary and television production. Nevertheless, I find the term 'film' more appropriate than 'television programme' in the context of Ormond's work. Not only does it follow the term preferred by the production unit in which he worked, but further, it seems more aptly to signal the range of artistic and cultural discourses outside broadcasting that contributed to the kind of 'films' Ormond produced. The term 'programme' seems to me to miss some of these important wider connotations.

20   Patrick Russell and James Piers-Taylor (eds), *Shadows of Progress: Documentary Film in Post-War Britain* (London: BFI, 2010), p. 117.

21   Swallow, *Factual Television*, p. 178.

22   Peter Dahlgren, *Television and the Public Sphere: Citizenship, Democracy and the Media* (London: Sage, 1995), p. 25.

23   Dahlgren, *Television and the Public Sphere*, p. 15.

24   Dahlgren, *Television and the Public Sphere*, p. 25.

25   I should make it clear at this point that this is not a study of audience consumption or reception. This was a necessary methodological decision given the fact that there is very little qualitative or quantitative data available to conduct in-depth analyses of audience consumption in Wales in the era in which these films were produced. There are at the BBC Written Archives Centre in Caversham a few audience research reports relating to the films produced in the earliest days of television in Wales, and I will bring these into the discussion where possible. However, most of these date before the creation of BBC Wales proper in 1964, and the research was conducted in London. The material that is available at Caversham relating to post-1964 BBC Wales consists of documentation on programmes relating to the BBC Network, or memoranda sent between Cardiff and the BBC Head Office in London. Internal documentation relating to BBC Wales after this time is stored, uncatalogued, within a vast collection at the National Library of Wales, and deserves further exploration.

26 John Davies, *Broadcasting and the BBC in Wales* (Cardiff: University of Wales Press, 1994), p. ix.

27 Benedict Anderson, *Imagined Communities: Reflections on the Origin and Spread of Nationalism* (London: Verso, 1983), p. 40.

28 Tim Edensor, *National Identity, Popular Culture and Everyday Life* (London: Bloomsbury, 2002), p. 17.

29 Chris Barker, *Television, Globalization and Cultural Identities* (Buckingham: Open University Press, 2000), p. 16.

30 Though conversely it could be said that the close examination of those structures and institutions actually inhibits a full and sophisticated understanding of the complex phenomenon of 'identity'.

31 Jurgen Habermas, *The Structural Transformation of the Public Sphere* (London: Polity, 1989 [1962]).

32 Dahlgren, *Television and the Public Sphere*, pp. 7–8. Monroe E. Price is another theorist who emphasises the centrality of the media in the formation of the public sphere. As he notes in *Television, the Public Sphere and National Identity*, 'no account of the public sphere in the twentieth century would be complete without addressing radio and television. Over time, the electronic media have become so pervasive, so linked not only to political institutions, but to the machinery of debate and decision, so seized with importance, that they suffuse and overwhelm other aspects of public discussion.' Monroe E. Price, *Television, the Public Sphere and National Identity* (Oxford: Oxford University Press, 1995), p. 27.

33 For a selection of critiques of Habermas's work, see Craig Calhoun (ed.), *Habermas and the Public Sphere* (Cambridge: MIT Press, 1993).

34 Price, *Television, the Public Sphere and National Identity*, pp. 11–14.

35 David Morley, 'Broadcasting and the Construction of the National Family', in Robert C. Allen and Annette Hill (eds), *The Television Studies Reader* (London: Routledge, 2004), p. 428.

36 Paddy Scannell and David Cardiff, *A Social History of British Broadcasting 1922–1939* (Oxford: Blackwell, 1991), p. 16.

37 'Plural' is Dai Smith's term, used in *Wales! Wales?* (London: Allen and Unwin, 1984), p. 1. 'Bilateral' is M. Wynn Thomas's, taken from *Corresponding Cultures: The Two Literatures of Wales* (Cardiff: University of Wales Press, 1999), p. 6. 'Tripartite' is a reference to Denis Balsom's 'Three Wales Model', outlined in his chapter 'The Three Wales Model', in John Osmond (ed.), *The National Question Again* (Llandysul: Gomer, 1985), pp. 1–17.

38 David Barlow, Tom O'Malley and Phillip Mitchell, *The Media in Wales: Voices of a Small Nation* (Cardiff: University of Wales Press, 2005), p. 20.

39 Philip Schlesinger, 'The Nation and Communicative Space', in Howard Tumber (ed.), *Media Power, Professionals and Policies* (London: Routledge, 2000), p. 102.

40 Davies, *Broadcasting and the BBC in Wales*, p. ix.

41 For instance, the 1950s, 1960s and 1970s were decades in which internal difference and discontent were intensifying in Wales, and much of the focus of this discontent became focused on the BBC's activities in Wales. In this respect, BBC Wales found itself in an invidious position. Some, such as David

Llewellyn, Conservative MP for Cardiff North, were convinced there was a bias in favour of Welsh nationalism at BBC Wales. See Davies, *Broadcasting and the BBC in Wales*, p. 248. Yet at the same time Welsh intellectuals were anxious about the perceived anglicising influence of broadcasting in Wales. Perhaps the most imaginative protest came from Welsh anthropologist Alwyn D. Rees, whose 1961 letter to the Pilkington Committee on broadcasting invited its recipient to imagine an England some 600 years into the future, in which the Soviet Union had conquered the British Isles and the English language was under threat of extinction. Alwyn D. Rees, *Dear Sir Harry Pilkington: An Open Letter from Alwyn D. Rees* (Carmarthen: Radical Publications, 1961).

42 Broadcasting Council for Wales, *Annual Report 1959–60*, p. 2.

43 Hywel Davies, *The Role of the Regions in British Broadcasting* (London: BBC, 1965), p. 7.

44 Davies, *The Role of the Regions in British Broadcasting*, p. 7.

45 Broadcasting Council for Wales, *Annual Report 1968–69*, p. 2.

46 Broadcasting Council for Wales, *Annual Report 1969–70*, p. 2.

47 See Tony Bianchi, 'R. S. Thomas and his Readers', in Tony Curtis (ed.), *Wales: The Imagined Nation* (Bridgend: Poetry Wales Press, 1986), pp. 69–95.

48 John Davies, *A History of Wales* (London: Penguin, 2007 [1993]), p. 641.

49 A total of 243,048 people voted 'Yes', a mere 20.2 per cent of the vote. Davies, *A History of Wales*, p. 651.

50 Kenneth O. Morgan, *Rebirth of a Nation: A History of Modern Wales* (Oxford: Oxford University Press, 1982), p. 408.

51 Davies, *Broadcasting and the BBC in Wales*, p. 319.

52 Patrick Hannan, 'Introduction', in Patrick Hannan (ed.), *Wales in Vision: The People and Politics of Television* (Llandysul: Gomer, 1990), ix.

53 John Ormond, 'Beginnings', in Hannan (ed.), *Wales in Vision*, p. 1.

54 John Ormond, 'Beginnings', in Hannan (ed.), *Wales in Vision*, p. 2. As I will discuss in the following chapter, it would appear to be to *A Sort of Welcome to Spring* that Ormond was referring when he added, 'We got around this by borrowing somebody else's swing and park.'

55 Davies, *Broadcasting and the BBC in Wales*, p. 209.

56 Things were galvanised by the immediate success of ITV in 1955: as Asa Briggs notes, some seventy-two per cent of viewers were watching this channel rather than the BBC in the late 1950s, and this in spite of the BBC's wider transmission coverage. Asa Briggs, *The History of Broadcasting in the United Kingdom Volume V: Competition* (Oxford: Oxford University Press, 1995), p. 20.

57 Memorandum, 23 April 1958 (BBC Written Archives Centre, Caversham, T16/645).

58 Memorandum, 22 October 1959 (BBC Written Archives Centre, Caversham, T31/79/2).

59 Davies notes that 'during Welsh rugby's great years BBC Wales saw it as an instrument of nation-building' (*Broadcasting and the BBC in Wales*, p. 320.) Furthermore, Martin Johnes suggests that television coverage itself allowed for a new national engagement with the sport, drawing together new allegiances: 'television enabled internationals to become national events that

touched areas outside the game's historic hinterlands, notably in north Wales, traditionally a football area'. Martin Johnes, *Wales Since 1939* (Manchester: Manchester University Press, 2012), p. 282.

60 Steve Blandford has written about the importance of national drama on television, particularly in the context of a national-institutional complex which has historically favoured the 'high' arts: 'What [. . .] television has the capacity to do is transform the old debates much more rapidly and within discourses that can most readily reach out and fire the imaginations of the young in geographical areas not traditionally blessed by the visitations of the Welsh cultural establishment.' Steve Blandford (ed.), *Wales on Screen* (Bridgend: Poetry Wales, 2000), p. 16.

61 Davies, *Broadcasting and the BBC in Wales*, p. 318.

62 Rowland Lucas, *The Voice of a Nation?: A Concise History of the BBC in Wales 1923–1973* (Llandysul: Gomer, 1981), p. 211.

63 John Corner, *Television Form and Public Address* (London: Edward Arnold, 1995), p. 77.

64 John Corner, *The Art of Record: A Critical Introduction to Documentary* (Manchester: Manchester University Press, 1996), p. 15. It is worth noting on this score that the documentary principle found an outlet in mass broadcasting around this time in the radio feature programme of the early 1930s. The radio feature programme can in many ways be viewed as a precursor to the television documentary as it was later to take shape. See Scannell, '"The Stuff of Radio": Developments in Radio Features and Documentaries Before the War', in John Corner (ed.), *Documentary and the Mass Media* (London: Edward Arnold, 1986), pp. 1–28.

65 See Ian Aitken, *Film and Reform: John Grierson and the Documentary Film Movement* (London: Routledge, 1990)

66 John Grierson, quoted in Forsyth Hardy, *John Grierson: A Documentary Biography* (London: Faber, 1979), p. 93.

67 Grierson, quoted in Hardy, *John Grierson: A Documentary Biography*, p. 103.

68 There is, of course, a rich history of narrative cinema in Wales. The authoritative study of this is David Berry's *Wales and Cinema: The First Hundred Years* (Cardiff: University of Wales Press, 1994).

69 On *Today We Live* and *Eastern Valley* as important early filmic representations of Wales, see Gwenno Ffrancon, 'Documenting the Depression in South Wales: *Today We Live* and *Eastern Valley*', *Welsh History Review*, 22/1 (2004), 103–25, and Bert Hogenkamp, '*Today We Live*: The Making of a Documentary in a Welsh Mining Valley', *Llafur: Journal of Welsh Labour History*, 5/1 (1988), 45–52. *David* was produced by Welsh film-maker Paul Dickson for the 1951 Festival of Britain. Dickson later recalled being asked by the Central Office of Information to 'show Wales to the world'. See David Berry, *Wales in Cinema*, p. 249. Yet, as Becky Conekin notes, it was one of a number of films made for the festival that characterised Britain's constitutive nations and regions solely in terms of their productive capacities. See Becky Conekin, *'The Autobiography of a Nation': The 1951 Festival of Britain* (Manchester: Manchester University Press, 2003), p. 7. It was famously Dylan Thomas who provided the script to *Wales: Green Mountain Black Mountain*.

70 Lindsay Anderson, 'Free Cinema', *Universities and Left Review*, 1/2 (1957), 52.

71 Brian Winston, *Claiming the Real II: Documentary: Grierson and Beyond* (Basingstoke: Palgrave Macmillan, 2008 [1995]).

72 André Bazin, *What is Cinema?*, trans. Hugh Gray (Berkeley: University of California Press, 1967), p. 15.

73 Bill Nichols, *Representing Reality: Issues and Concepts in Documentary* (Bloomington: Indiana University Press, 1991), p. 178.

74 Corner, *The Art of Record*, p. 21.

75 Dahlgren, *Television and the Public Sphere*, p. 44.

76 Of the hugely influential and long-running BBC arts documentary series *Monitor* (1958–65), for example, only around four hours of material remain. Similarly, of the important ITV documentary series *This Wonderful World* (1957–65), presented by none other than John Grierson, only one episode remains. See Mary M. Irwin, '*Monitor*: The Creation of the Television Arts Documentary', *Journal of British Cinema and Television*, 8/3 (2011), 322, and Jo Fox, 'From Documentary Film to Television Documentaries: John Grierson and *This Wonderful World*', *Journal of British Cinema and Television*, 10/3 (2013), 501.

77 See Tony Brown, 'At the Utmost Edge: The Poetry of John Ormond', *Poetry Wales*, 23/7 (1990), 31–6; and Thomas, *John Ormond*.

78 Davies, *Broadcasting and the BBC in Wales*, p. 196.

79 Peter Lord, *The Aesthetics of Relevance* (Llandysul: Gomer, 1993), p. 7.

80 Bella Dicks, *Heritage, Place and Community* (Cardiff: University of Wales Press, 2000), p. 79.

81 Wil Aaron, 'Film', in Meic Stephens (ed.), *The Arts in Wales 1950–75* (Cardiff: Welsh Arts Council, 1979), p. 302.

82 Raymond Williams, 'Introduction', in Stephens (ed.), *The Arts in Wales 1950–75*, pp. 1–4.

Chapter 2

1 As I discuss in chapter 3, Ormond had recently completed a film on the life and work of Alun Lewis.

2 It is likely that these were the kinds of things Grierson was saying to students at the Newport Film School around this time. Grierson had been made 'patron and occasional lecturer' at the then recently established school. See David Berry, *Wales and Cinema*, pp. 300–1.

3 See Georgina Born, *Uncertain Vision: Birt, Dyke and the Reinvention of the BBC* (London: Vintage, 2005), p. 72.

4 See Evans, 'An Ormond Chronology', in Ormond, *Collected Poems*, p. 38.

5 Ormond's wife, Glenys, remembers this in an obituary essay in a special issue of *Poetry Wales* the year of Ormond's death: '"J.O." and "Rod"', *Poetry Wales*, 27/3 (1990), 44.

6 Ormond, 'Beginnings', in Hannan (ed.), *Wales in Vision*, p. 10.

7 Norman Swallow, 'Denis Mitchell: Master of Documentary', *The Listener*, 24 April 1975, 551. Swallow was a veteran BBC producer, and judging by the tone of this article, it is clear that by the mid-1970s many within the television

documentary tradition were becoming disillusioned by the circumstances in which they were working. It was also a period in which Ormond took a year's unpaid leave from the BBC (1974–5). See Evans, 'An Ormond Chronology', in Ormond, *Collected Poems*, p. 41.

8   Tony Conran, '*Poetry Wales* and the Second Flowering', in M. Wynn Thomas (ed.), *Welsh Writing in English* (Cardiff: University of Wales Press, 2003), p. 225.

9   Tony Conran, *The Cost of Strangeness: Essays on the English Poets of Wales* (Llandysul: Gomer, 1982), p. 296.

10 Conran, '*Poetry Wales* and the Second Flowering', p. 223. Though it is worth stating that they often had to move to Cardiff.

11 Stephens, 'The Second Flowering', 7.

12 John Ormond, 'Letter from Tuscany', *Poetry Wales*, 24/1 (1988), 21.

13 Conran, '*Poetry Wales* and the Second Flowering', p. 225.

14 John Ormond, 'Introduction', in John Tripp, *Selected Poems* (Bridgend: Seren, 1989), p. 9.

15 Tripp, quoted in Ormond, 'Introduction', in John Tripp, *Selected Poems*, p. 9.

16 James A. Davies, 'Detached Attachment', *New Welsh Review*, 10/3 (1997–8), 37–9.

17 Ormond, 'John Ormond', in Stephens (ed.), *Artists in Wales 2*, p. 162.

18 Ormond, 'John Ormond', in Stephens (ed.), *Artists in Wales 2*, p. 160.

19 Ray Monk, *How to Read Wittgenstein* (London: Granta, 2005), p. 106.

20 Ludwig Wittgenstein, quoted in Ray Monk, *Ludwig Wittgenstein: The Duty of Genius* (London: Vintage, 1991), p. 301.

21 Most critics of Ormond's poetry rightly identify the strain of cosmic uncertainty that fuelled much of his creativity. Richard Poole has argued that for Ormond, 'doubt is paramount' ('Conversations with John Ormond', in *New Welsh Review*, 2/1 (1989), 45). For Tony Brown, 'Ormond's poetry is born of his dissatisfaction' ('At the Utmost Edge: The Poetry of John Ormond', *Poetry Wales*, 27/3 (1990), 36). Randal Jenkins contends that questions '[press] forever on John Ormond's mind' ('The Poetry of John Ormond', *Poetry Wales*, 8/1 (1972), 27).

22 Wittgenstein, quoted in Monk, *How to Read Wittgenstein*, p. 95.

23 Terry Eagleton, 'Wittgenstein's Friends', *New Left Review*, I/135 (1982), 74.

24 Eagleton, 'Wittgenstein's Friends', 74.

25 John Ormond, '*In Place of Empty Heaven: The Poetry of Wallace Stevens*', *W. D. Thomas Memorial Lecture* (Swansea: University College of Swansea, 1983), pp. 18–19.

26 Robert Minhinnick, '"The Echo of Once Being Here": A Reflection on the Imagery of John Ormond', *Poetry Wales*, 27/3 (1990), 52.

27 Frank Kermode, *Wallace Stevens*, 2nd edn (London: Faber, 1989), p. xv.

28 Richard Poole has written on some of the shared thematic and symbolic similarities between Ormond and Stevens in an essay in the special memorial issue of *Poetry Wales* in the year of Ormond's death ('John Ormond and Wallace Stevens: Six Variations on a Double Theme', *Poetry Wales*, 27/ 3 (1990), 16–26).

29 Ormond, 'In Place of Empty Heaven: The Poetry of Wallace Stevens', pp. 18–19.

30 M. Wynn Thomas, *In the Shadow of the Pulpit: Literature and Nonconformist Wales* (Cardiff: University of Wales Press, 2010), p. 24.

31 Wallace Stevens, quoted in Ormond, 'In Place of Empty Heaven', p. 18.

32 Ormond, 'In Place of Empty Heaven', p. 18.

33 Ormond, 'In Place of Empty Heaven', p. 4.

34 Rian Evans, 'Notes to the Poems', in *Collected Poems*, p. 276.

35 John Ormond, 'A Bronze for the Academy', *Picture Post*, 3 May 1947, 24.

36 Ormond, 'A Bronze for the Academy', 24.

37 Ormond, 'A Bronze for the Academy', 24.

38 A number of critics have identified this concern in Ormond's poetry. Michael Collins has argued that the poet's 'concern with craftsmanship' resulted in verse that championed material reality over the metaphysical ('Craftsmanship as Meaning: The Poetry of John Ormond', *Poetry Wales*, 16/2 (1980), 33). Tony Brown views Ormond's existential interest in 'the resilience which causes individuals [. . .] to continue to attempt song, to create fragments of structure and order' to be 'an aspect of the value which Ormond consistently places on human creativity and craftsmanship' ('At the Utmost Edge', 34).

39 Thomas, *John Ormond*, p. 5.

40 Patrick McGuinness, 'Introduction', in John Ormond, *Collected Poems*, ed. Rian Evans (Bridgend: Seren, 2015), p. 29.

41 Ormond, in an autobiographical essay, states that 'at seventeen-and-a-half I badly wanted to try to be an architect'. Yet it was less than a year later that he would stumble across Dylan Thomas and Wilfred Owen, and 'life would never be the same again'. See 'John Ormond', in Stephens (ed.), *Artists in Wales 2*, pp. 156–7.

42 Thomas, *John Ormond*, pp. 5–6.

43 Ormond, 'John Ormond', in Stephens (ed.), *Artists in Wales 2*, p. 163.

44 John Ormond, *Cathedral Builders and Other Poems* (Newtown: Gregynog Press, 1991)

45 Ormond, quoted in Poole, 'Conversations', 40.

46 Stephen Cheeke notes that in debates on ekphrasis 'there is always the fundamental question of which medium comes closest to rendering the "real", and how the very nature of the "real" is contested and described', *Writing for Art: The Aesthetics of Ekphrasis* (Manchester: Manchester University Press, 2008), pp. 4–5.

47 Rush Rhees, *Without Answers* (London: Routledge, 1969), p. 145.

48 Ormond, quoted in Richard Poole, 'Conversations with John Ormond', 41.

49 Ormond, quoted in Richard Poole, 'Conversations with John Ormond', 41.

50 Ormond, quoted in Berry, *Wales and Cinema*, p. 292.

51 This was inspired by Walters's striking portrait of an anonymous coalminer, 'The Welsh Collier', and published in the Swansea University College literary magazine, *Dawn*, in 1942, while Ormond was still a student.

52 This was written alongside Ormond's *Picture Post* piece on the Gower folk singer Phil Tanner in 1949 (*CP*, 77–99).

53 This can be found in Ron Berry, 'What Comes After?', *Poetry Wales*, 27/3 (1990), 54–5.

54 Thomas, *John Ormond*, p. 57.

55 Laura M. Sager Eidt, *Writing and Filming the Painting: Ekphrasis in Literature and Film* (Amsterdam: Rodopi, 2008), p. 19.

56 Dannie Abse, 'John Ormond as Portraitist', *Poetry Wales*, 26/2 (1990), 5–7.

57 Thomas, *John Ormond*, p. 40.

58 David Berry, *Wales and Cinema*, p. 297.

59 Ekphrasis has been identified as a rich seam in Welsh culture. A 1999 touring exhibition, META (curated by Christine Kinsey), for instance, showcased the collaborative work of a variety of Welsh writers and artists, and later resulted in the 2005 anthology of essays, edited by Christine Kinsey and Ceridwen Lloyd-Morgan, *Imaging the Imagination* (Llandysul: Gomer, 2005), which explored the lengthy traditions of collaborative work between writers and artists in Wales. As M. Wynn Thomas noted in his foreword to that book, 'the complex interaction between image and word [. . .] [has been] reproduced across languages, across decades, across genres and right across Wales' (*Imaging the Imagination*, p. 9). Thomas includes Ormond in a long list of Welsh writers in both languages whose work concerns itself with the visual arts, from Glyn Jones and Emyr Humphreys in English to Euros Bowen, Alan Llwyd and R. Gerallt Jones in Welsh. Thomas's recent book on R. S. Thomas, *Serial Obsessive* (Cardiff: University of Wales Press, 2013), contains essays on that poet's often overlooked ekphrastic poetry. Additionally, in an essay in *Imaging the Imagination*, Ceridwen Lloyd-Morgan suggests that the prominence of such ekphrastic work in Welsh culture can in part be attributed to the disproportionate strength of the culture of literacy in Nonconformist Wales: 'The extraordinary status accorded to word-based works, whether written, recited or sung, may help to account for the very close relationship which developed between the two modes of expression within Wales, for even those whose primary career was in visual art could not escape being steeped in the literary culture from childhood onwards' (Ceridwen Lloyd-Morgan, 'A Dual Tradition', in Kinsey and Lloyd-Morgan (eds), *Imaging the Imagination*, pp. 19–36). Such a suggestion perhaps also conversely explains the preoccupation of many Welsh writers with the visual arts, particularly in post-Nonconformist Wales. Ormond, as I have already discussed, can certainly be understood as confirming this; starved of the visual arts in the visually austere Nonconformist culture in which he was brought up, Ormond relished the opportunity to absorb the fruits of European art.

60 Cheeke, *Writing for Art*, p. 4.

61 John Corner, 'Television, Documentary and the Category of the Aesthetic', in Alan Rosenthal and John Corner (eds), *New Challenges for Documentary* (Manchester: Manchester University Press, 2005), p. 48.

62 Corner, 'Television, Documentary, and the category of the aesthetic', in Corner and Rosenthal (eds), *New Challenges for Documentary*, pp. 49–51.

63 Corner, *Television Form*, p. 104. Emphases in original.

64 See for instance Erik Barnouw, *Documentary: A History of the Non-Fiction Film* (Oxford: Oxford University Press, 1993) and Richard Meran Barsam, *Nonfiction Film: A Critical History* (Bloomington: Indiana University Press, 1992).

65 Another notable of the Paris film scene of this era was René Clair, an influential French film-maker who attempted in these early days to achieve what

French contributors to *Cahiers du Cinema* attempted in the 1950s, that is, to view film as a new, discrete art-form of the calibre of any of the traditional arts. Clair's idea of 'pure cinema' was an attempt to move the medium away from its tendency to mimic the traditional narrative and visual arts and to forge a visual vocabulary of its own. See René Clair, *Cinema Yesterday and Today* (New York: Dover, 1972). M. Wynn Thomas has noted that Ormond was an admirer of Clair, and had scribbled notes from the Frenchman's books into his notebook. See Thomas, *John Ormond*, p. 34.

66 Recent historians of the British Documentary Movement, for instance, have sought to highlight the strands of creativity and experimentalism among the films of those working beneath Grierson in the years before and during the Second World War. On the BFI's website, *Screenonline*, for instance, Jamie Sexton notes that Grierson was 'extremely interested in modernist art', and further the modernist 'city symphony' films of Ruttmann and others (Jamie Sexton, 'John Grierson', *http://www.screenonline.org.uk/film/id/439877/* (accessed 12 December 2018)). Another recent book on the topic is Scott Anthony and James G. Marshall (eds), *The Projection of Britain: A History of the GPO Film Unit* (London: BFI, 2011).

67 See Patrick Russell and James Piers Taylor (eds), *Shadows of Progress: Documentary Film in Post-War Britain*.

68 Jamie Sexton, '"Televerité" hits Britain: documentary, drama and the growth of 16mm filmmaking in British television', *Screen*, 44/4 (2003), 435.

69 Swallow, *Factual Television*, p. 176.

70 Swallow, *Factual Television*, p. 190.

71 Ormond, 'Beginnings', p. 10.

72 Though there were considerable developments in the 1970s that restricted many of the freedoms producers like Ormond enjoyed in the 1960s. I will return to this issue in a later chapter.

73 David Berry has called the three men a 'formidable trio of post-war Welsh documentarists'. '*The World Still Sings*: Jack Howells', in Russell and Taylor (eds), *Shadows of Progress: Documentary Film in Post-War Britain*, p. 144.

74 It was at World Wide that Dickson made the two dramatised documentaries that, as critic Leo Enticknap states, 'established his professional reputation' (Leo Enticknap, '"I don't think he did anything after that": Paul Dickson', in Russell and Piers-Taylor (eds), *Shadows of Progress: Documentary Film in Post-War Britain*, p. 156). These were *The Undefeated* (1950), a film that promotes the work of the Ministry of Pensions, and *David* (1951), a film that views the culture of the south Wales valleys through the eyes of school caretaker and poet Dafydd Rhys. The former won Dickson a BAFTA for best documentary film, and the latter, made for the 1951 Festival of Britain, is a key text in post-war screen representations of Wales.

75 Enticknap, '"I don't think he did anything after that"', p. 166. Dickson later went on to teach at the National Film and Television School.

76 Alexander and a number of his colleagues were members of the Communist Party; the company took on a number of commissions on industrial relations from the Board of Trade and, later, the NCB's newsreel *Mining Review* (see Russell and Piers-Taylor (eds), *Shadows of Progress*, pp. 34–5). Howells later proudly recalled the pedigree of this apprenticeship: '[DATA] was an offshoot

of Paul Rotha and in direct line from John Grierson. You couldn't get more purist than that' (quoted in Berry, *Wales and Cinema*, p. 285).

77 It was with his own company that he saw some of his greatest successes, with affecting films on local Welsh culture for HTV (Harlech Television) in the 1970s (in particular *Return to Rhymney* (1972) and *Penclawdd Wedding* (1974)), and, most notably, his Oscar-winning documentary for TWW (Television Wales and West) *Dylan Thomas* (1963), starring Richard Burton. The latter was the first and only Oscar-winning Welsh film (to date).

78 He moved to *Picture Post* after a brief period at the *Brentwood Gazette*. See Evans, 'An Ormond Chronology', in Ormond, *Collected Poems*, p. 35.

79 See Ormond, 'John Ormond', in Stephens (ed.), *Artists in Wales 2*, p. 159.

80 Ormond, 'Letter from Tuscany', 22. This letter in fact contains a small, under-stated sketch similar to those which would illustrate his posthumous Gregynog Press book *Cathedral Builders* (1991).

81 Ormond, 'Letter from Tuscany', 22.

82 Sergei Eisenstein, *The Film Sense*, trans. Jay Leyda (London: Faber, 1943), p. 64.

83 Thomas, *John Ormond*, p. 15.

84 Ormond, 'John Ormond', in Stephens (ed.), *Artists in Wales 2*, p. 161.

85 John Ormond Thomas, 'The Old Singer of Gower', *Picture Post*, 19 March 1949, 32.

86 It was this meeting with Tanner that inspired Ormond's poem, 'Homage to a Folk-Singer'; once again, we see Ormond creative life intersect with his work. (I commented upon this poem in more detail in chapter 1.)

87 Ormond had been invited to contribute to the *News Chronicle* in 1955 by its editor, Tom Hopkinson, the man who had earlier given Ormond a job at *Picture Post*. Rian Evans has noted that when asked to name the most important influence on his life, 'Ormond's response was unequivocal: Tom Hopkinson' (Evans, 'An Ormond Chronology', in Ormond, *Collected Poems*, p. 38). Hopkinson himself fondly remembers Ormond in his auto-biography: 'We knew him as John Ormond Thomas and were sorry when after only a few years he returned to Wales to work for the BBC and to make his name [. . .] as a poet and a television producer.' See Tom Hopkinson, *Of This Our Time: A Journalist's Story 1905–1950* (London: Hutchinson, 1982), p. 237.

88 Thomas, *John Ormond*, p. 28.

89 'Homage to a Folk-Singer' is dedicated to Phil Tanner, and contains a stanza informed by the cadences of the song Tanner had sung in his presence during Ormond's encounter with him.

90 Ormond, 'John Ormond', in Stephens (ed.), *Artists in Wales 2*, p. 161.

91 Ormond, 'John Ormond', in Stephens (ed.), *Artists in Wales 2*, p. 161.

92 Geraint Talfan Davies, *At Arm's Length: Recollections and Reflections on the Arts, Media and a Young Democracy* (Bridgend: Seren, 2008), p. 40.

93 Ormond, 'Beginnings', in Hannan, *Wales in Vision*, p. 5.

94 Ormond, quoted in Poole, 'Conversations', 42.

95 The film was *A Bronze Mask* (1969), in memory of Dylan Thomas. The cromlech was used to illustrate a passage from a posthumous collection of the writings of seventeenth-century metaphysical writer Thomas Traherne,

Centuries of Meditations (1908): 'The corn was orient and immortal wheat, which never should be reaped, nor was ever sown.'

96   This reluctance to reference the unrefined world of television production in a poem is a significant omission; it seems to me to speak volumes about the conflict between Ormond's two creative idioms.

97   Ormond, quoted in Poole, 'Conversations with John Ormond', 42.

98   The unit had until this time been used to provide inserts for network programmes. More on this in the following chapter.

99   Bill Nichols, *Introduction to Documentary* (Bloomington: Indiana University Press, 2001), p. 31.

100 The film was called *A Study of Spring Wild Flowers* (1939). According to the National Film Board of Canada, the producer of the film is not known, since 'at this period filmmakers were not viewed as creators but rather as civil servants employed by the Motion Picture Bureau' (*National Film Board of Canada History, http://www.nfb.ca/historique/about-the-foundation* (accessed 23 April 2013)).

101 Berry, *Wales and Cinema*, p. 291.

102 Memorandum, 16 February 1959 (BBC Written Archives Centre, Caversham, T16/645).

103 Swallow, *Factual Television*, p. 183.

104 Edwards was by this time famous for his roles in radio and cinema. He had performed the part of Mr Waldo in the first production of Dylan Thomas's *Under Milk Wood* (1953), and had acted in a variety of Ealing comedies. Perhaps the most notable of these in a Welsh context was *A Run For Your Money* (1949), in which two happy-go-lucky (and grossly stereotyped) Welshmen win tickets to the Wales–England rugby international at Twickenham.

105 Nichols, *Introduction to Documentary*, p. 31.

106 The film was edited by Terry Laurie.

107 The statue is *Joyance*, by Sir William Goscombe John, situated in Thompson's Park, Cardiff.

108 R. S. Thomas surely had this film in mind when, in a celebrated lecture delivered some years later, he described the capacity for the moving film image to capture such scenes. There Thomas praised film's ability to represent life as it exists in the flow of time, to 'show flowers and the leaves quivering in the breeze, and not still to the point of lifelessness as on a postcard'. R. S. Thomas, 'Abercuawg', trans. Sandra Anstey, in Sandra Anstey (ed.), *R. S. Thomas: Selected Prose* (Bridgend: Poetry Wales Press, 1983), p. 161.

109 BBC Audience Research Report, *A Sort of Welcome to Spring*, 21 April 1960 (BBC Written Archives Centre, Caversham, R9/7/45).

110 Between 1960 and 1975 the number of BBC employees increased from 15,886 to 24,779 (Tom Burns, *The BBC: Public Institution and Private World* (London: Macmillan, 1977), p. 227). These were, of course, the years of expansion in the regions and in the BBC's range of output.

111 Born, *Uncertain Vision*, p. 71.

112 Born, *Uncertain Vision*, p. 72.

113 Burns, *Public Institution and Private World*, p. 211.

114 Burns, *Public Institution and Private World*, p. 212.

115 Richard Collins, 'Seeing is Believing: The Ideology of Naturalism', in John Corner (ed.), *Documentary and the Mass Media* (London: Edward Arnold, 1986), p. 131.

116 Collins, 'Seeing is Believing: The Ideology of Naturalism', in Corner (ed.), *Documentary and the Mass Media*, p. 131.

117 *Principles and Practice in Documentary Programmes* (London: BBC, 1972), p. 18.

118 *Principles and Practice in Documentary Programmes*, p. 23.

119 Swallow, 'Denis Mitchell: Master of Documentary', p. 551. Judging by this article's tone, it seems that by the mid-1970s many in the BBC documentary tradition were becoming disillusioned by the circumstances in which they were forced to work. This was a period in which Ormond took a year's leave from the BBC (1974–5).

120 Ormond, 'Beginnings', in Hannan (ed.), *Wales in Vision*, p. 10.

Chapter 3

1 Matthew Arnold, *Culture and Anarchy* (Cambridge: Cambridge University Press, 1971 [1867]), p. 6.

2 Krishan Kumar, 'Public Service Broadcasting and the Public Interest', in Colin McCabe and Olivia Stewart (eds), *The BBC and Public Service Broadcasting* (Manchester: Manchester University Press, 1986), p. 47.

3 William Haley, 'Broadcasting and British Life', an address to the British Institute of Adult Education, 21 Sept 1946, quoted in Asa Briggs, *The History of Broadcasting in the United Kingdom Volume IV: Sound and Vision* (Oxford: Oxford University Press, 1995), p. 71.

4 Briggs, *The History of Broadcasting in the United Kingdom Volume IV*, p. 70. Briggs quotes Haley's Note for the Governors, 'The Home Programme Policy of the BBC', 4 July 1946.

5 Television licences numbered 343,882 in 1950. By 1955 the number was 4,503,766. See Briggs, *The History of Broadcasting in the United Kingdom Volume IV*, p. 221.

6 *Report of the Committee on Broadcasting* (London: HMSO, 1962), pp. 37–8.

7 Thomas Hajkowski, *The BBC and National Identity in Britain, 1922–53* (Manchester: Manchester University Press, 2010), p. 233.

8 Edensor, *National Identity, Popular Culture and Everyday Life*, p. 4.

9 Paddy Scannell, 'The Origins of BBC Regional Policy', in Sylvia Harvey and Kevin Robins (eds), *The Regions, the Nations and the BBC* (London: BFI, 1993), p. 27.

10 See Davies, *Broadcasting and the BBC in Wales*.

11 Lord, *The Aesthetics of Relevance*, p. 8.

12 Lord, *The Aesthetics of Relevance*, p. 7.

13 Lord takes aim in particular at the National Museum of Wales. See *The Aesthetics of Relevance*, p. 32.

14 Peter Lord, *The Visual Culture of Wales: Industrial Society* (Cardiff: University of Wales Press, 1998), p. 262.

15 The first phrase belongs to M. Wynn Thomas's seminal book on the two literary cultures of Wales, *Internal Difference: Twentieth Century Writing in Wales* (Cardiff: University of Wales Press, 1992).

16 Sarah Rhian Reynolds, 'Aneirin Talfan Davies: Producing a Nation' (unpublished PhD thesis, Swansea University, 2001), 3.

17 Davies, *Broadcasting and the BBC in Wales*, p. 187.

18 Laura Mulvey, 'Introduction: Experimental British Television', in Laura Mulvey and Jamie Sexton (eds), *Experimental British Television* (Manchester: Manchester University Press, 2007), pp. 1–2.

19 *Civilisation* presents Western culture as a narrative of geniuses, unaffected by social pressures, each making their unique mark upon the world around them. However, this view of artists and their work was in the process of being radically undermined by the emergence of new postmodern cultural forms. Accordingly, Clark declares himself 'completely baffled by what is taking place today', and, quoting W. B. Yeats's 'The Second Coming', laments the fact that 'there is still no centre.' His conclusion is gloomy: 'one must concede that the future of civilisation does not look very bright'. See Kenneth Clark, *Civilisation: A Personal View* (London: BBC and John Murray, 1969), pp. 345–6. Though the audience figures upon the first broadcast of *Civilisation* were 'modest', 'its impact', says John Wyver, 'was remarkable'. John Wyver, *Vision On: Film, Television and the Arts in Britain* (London: Wallflower, 2007), p. 36. A book published alongside the series that printed Clark's narration verbatim reached its eighth impression within two years. *Civilisation* has become the standard by which all other arts documentaries are measured, and is regularly repeated on the BBC; indeed, in 2011 the Corporation broadcast a new, digitally remastered HD version of the series.

20 See the special issue of *Journal of British Cinema and Television* on Ken Russell, 12/4 (2015).

21 Wyver, *Vision On*, p. 34.

22 John Read, 'Is There a Documentary Art?', *Sight and Sound*, 17/68 (1948), 157.

23 Wheldon was a BBC producer whose loyalty to that institution left him disinterested with matters of Welsh concern. As Emyr Humphreys has sardonically, but somewhat usefully, remarked: 'why should a man with Wheldon's talent for action tie himself or be tied to the same old scorched stake when there were all those sleek and well-oiled vehicles in the English marshalling yards just waiting for the guiding hand of a thrustful and competent commander?' See 'A Lost Leader', in M. Wynn Thomas (ed.), *Emyr Humphreys: Conversations and Reflections* (Cardiff: University of Wales Press, 2002), pp. 147–8.

24 Angus Wilson, *Tempo: The Impact of Television on the Arts* (London: Headway, 1964), pp. 9–10.

25 Lord, *The Aesthetics of Relevance*, p. 8.

26 Bart Moore-Gilbert and John Seed (eds), *Cultural Revolution? The Challenge of the Arts in the 1960s* (London: Routledge, 2004 [1992]), p. 1. Moore-Gilbert and Seed note in particular a *Time* magazine special published in April 1966 that celebrated such images – the same month that *Horizons Hung in Air* was broadcast.

27 Photography by Tom Friswell, sound by Tony Adkins, editor Tony Lloyd-Jones.

28 Kyffin Williams, *A Wider Sky* (Llandysul: Gomer, 1991), p. 222.
29 Photography by Russ Walker, sound by Mansel Davies and Robin Griffith, editor Tony Jackson.
30 Ormond, quoted in Berry, *Wales and Cinema*, p. 296.
31 Edensor, *National Identity, Popular Culture and Everyday Life*, p. 39.
32 Edensor, *National Identity, Popular Culture and Everyday Life*, p. 37
33 Lord, *Imaging the Nation*, p. 402.
34 Lord, *Imaging the Nation*, p. 292.
35 Mel Gooding, *Ceri Richards* (Moffat: Cameron and Hollis, 2002), pp. 70–2.
36 Ormond wrote on a typescript copy of the poem sent to Ron Berry that it had taken 'off and on four years' to write'. 'Now I won't know what to do in the long winter evenings and week-end' (letter to Ron Berry, n.d., Richard Burton Archives, Swansea University, WWE/1/10/11). Rian Evans notes that the poem was conceived during the production of his 1965 film *Troubled Waters*, covering fishing rights on the River Teifi (see Evans, 'Notes to the Poems', in *Collected Poems*, p. 281).
37 John Ormond, *Rest and Unrest: The Art of Ceri Richards* (BBC Welsh Home Service, 1954).
38 Photography by Bill Greenhalgh, sound by Keith Denton, editor Brian Turvey.
39 A. D. F. Jenkins, 'Richards, Ceri Giraldus (1903–1971)', rev. *Oxford Dictionary of National Biography* (Oxford: Oxford University Press, 2004); May 2011 online edn available at *http://www.oxforddnb.com/view/article/31602* (accessed 12 December 2018).
40 *Piano With Many Strings* was broadcast on Sunday 29 June – two days before the Investiture ceremony. I will return to the other two cultural documentaries, *Bronze Mask* and *The Fragile Universe*, shortly, and to the politics of the Investiture in more detail in the following chapter.
41 John S. Ellis, *Investiture: Royal Ceremony and National Identity in Wales, 1911–1969* (Cardiff: University of Wales Press, 2008), p. 253.
42 Eric Rowan, 'The Visual Arts', in Meic Stephens (ed.), *The Arts in Wales 1950–1975* (Cardiff: Welsh Arts Council, 1979), p. 56.
43 Huw Jones, 'Exhibiting Welshness: Art, Politics and National Identity in Wales 1940–1994' (unpublished PhD thesis, Swansea University, 2007), 213.
44 Jones, 'Exhibiting Welshness', 175.
45 Roger Webster, quoted in Jones, 'Exhibiting Welshness', 145.
46 See Jones, 'Exhibiting Welshness', 176 and 184–5.
47 Lord, *Industrial Society*, p. 237.
48 Lord, *Industrial Society*, p. 237.
49 Josef Herman, *Related Twilights: Notes from an Artist's Diary* (London: Robson, 1975), p. 91.
50 Photography by Robin Rollinson and Russ Walker, sound by Des Bennett, editor Bill Mainman.
51 John Ormond, *Graham Sutherland, O.M.: A Memorial Address* (Cardiff: National Museum of Wales, 1980), p. 5.
52 Peter Lord, *The Visual Culture of Wales: Imaging the Nation* (Cardiff: University of Wales Press, 2000), p. 376.
53 Poole, 'Conversations with John Ormond', 42.

54 Photography by Robin Rollinson, sound by Tony Adkins and Robin Griffith, edited by Michael Hall.

55 Lord, *Imaging the Nation*, p. 376.

56 Graham Sutherland, *Sutherland in Wales* (London: Alistair McAlpine, 1976), p. 7.

57 Welsh Arts Council, *Annual Report 1976* (Cardiff: Welsh Arts Council, 1976).

58 James A. Davies, 'Dylan Thomas and his Welsh Contemporaries', in M. Wynn Thomas (ed.), *Welsh Writing in English* (Cardiff: University of Wales Press, 2003), p. 144.

59 Kathleen Raine, 'Vernon Watkins: Poet of Tradition', *The Anglo-Welsh Review*, 14/33 (1964), 31.

60 Vernon Watkins, 'Rewards of the Fountain', *Affinities* (London: Faber, 1962), p. 15.

61 Watkins, 'Rewards of the Fountain', *Affinities*, p. 15.

62 Photography by John Pike and Bill Greenhalgh, sound by Mansel Davies, editor Brian Tucker.

63 Vernon Watkins, 'Music of Colours – White Blossom', *The Lady with the Unicorn* (London: Faber, 1948), p. 11.

64 Vernon Watkins, quoted in Davies, 'Dylan Thomas and his Welsh Contemporaries', in Thomas (ed.), *Welsh Writing in English*, p. 146.

65 Photography by Charles Beddous and Ken Mackay, editor Brian Tucker.

66 The American sculptor was a friend of Thomas, and had gifted one of his bronze masks to the museum in 1964.

67 See for example Dai Smith, 'The Case of Alun Lewis: A Divided Sensibility', *Llafur*, 3/2 (1981), 14–26; John Pikoulis, *Alun Lewis: A Life* (Bridgend: Seren, 1991 [1984]); and Alan Vaughan Jones, 'Modalities of Cultural Identity in the Writings of Idris Davies and Alun Lewis' (unpublished PhD thesis, Aberystwyth University, 2010).

68 Harri Webb, 'Alun Lewis: The Lost Leader', *Poetry Wales*, 10/3 (1974), 119.

69 Alun Lewis, 'Letter 35, 23 November 1943', in *In the Green Tree* (Cardigan: Parthian, 2006 [1948]), p. 57.

70 See Gareth Evans, 'Welsh Writing in English: Case Studies in Cultural Interaction' (unpublished PhD thesis, Swansea University, 2013).

71 Jones, 'Modalities of Cultural Identity', 4.

72 Gwladys Lewis, quoted in Pikoulis, *Alun Lewis: A Life*, p. 237.

73 Henley Thomas had earlier featured in a 1960 BBC adaptation of Richard Llewellyn's *How Green Was My Valley*, in which he played the role of Huw Morgan.

74 Photography by Charles Beddous, sound by Tony Adkins, editor Chris Lawrence.

75 Lord Chalfont would have been known to the British public in the late 1960s; at the time of filming he was serving as Minister of State in the Foreign and Commonwealth Office.

76 Dai Smith, 'The Case of Alun Lewis', *Llafur*, 27.

77 John Ormond, 'Selections From An Elegy for Alun Lewis', *Wales*, 3/4 (1944), 6.

78 Lewis was buried in a military cemetery in Burma on the afternoon of his death. See Pikoulis, *Alun Lewis: A Life*, p. 233.

79 Pikoulis, *Alun Lewis: A Life*, p. 234.

80 Lewis once wrote that 'Unhappiness swells to the proportions of nightmare at that time and it is hard to overcome it enough to get up and shave and wash and be active'. Quoted in Pikoulis, *Alun Lewis: A Life*, p. 232.

81 Pikoulis, *Alun Lewis: A Life*, p. 235.

82 Thomas was also the subject of a short *Monitor* segment in the 1960s; Ormond's film borrows a short black and white clip from this.

83 Roland Mathias, 'Literature in English', in Meic Stephens (ed.), *The Arts in Wales 1950–75* (Cardiff: Welsh Arts Council, 1979), p. 214. Mathias notes that Thomas's featuring on the programme was the result of 'one of those accidents with which literary history is sprinkled'. One of the presenters of *The Critics*, Alan Pryce-Jones, hailed from a Newtown family, and 'happened to come across' Thomas's work after the poet self-published a book with the Montgomeryshire Printing Company. See Mathias, 'Literature in English', in Stephens (ed.), *The Arts in Wales 1950–75*, p. 214.

84 See John Betjeman, 'Introduction', in R. S. Thomas, *Song at the Year's Turning* (London, Rupert-Hart Davis, 1969 [1955]), p. 11.

85 Tony Brown and M. Wynn Thomas, 'The Problems of Belonging', in M. Wynn Thomas (ed.), *Welsh Writing in English* (Cardiff: University of Wales Press, 2003), p. 175.

86 Brown and Thomas, 'The Problems of Belonging', in Thomas (ed.), *Welsh Writing in English*, p. 175.

87 R. S. Thomas, 'Traeth Maelgwn', in *Collected Poems 1945–1990* (London: Phoenix, 2000), p. 191.

88 R. S. Thomas, 'Reservoirs', in *Collected Poems*, p. 194.

89 R. S. Thomas, 'Y Llwybrau Gynt' ('The Paths Gone By')', trans. Sandra Anstey, in Sandra Anstey (ed.), *R. S. Thomas: Selected Prose* (Bridgend: Poetry Wales Press, 1983), p. 138.

90 Brown and Thomas, 'The Problems of Belonging', in Thomas (ed.), *Welsh Writing in English*, p. 166.

91 R. S. Thomas, 'Y Llwybrau Gynt', in Anstey (ed.), *R. S. Thomas: Selected Prose*, p. 138.

92 See Ned Thomas, 'Introduction', in Anstey (ed.), *R. S. Thomas: Selected Prose*, p. 15.

93 Thomas, 'Introduction', in Anstey (ed.), *R. S. Thomas: Selected Prose*, p. 15.

94 Photography by Bill Greenhalgh, sound by Tony Adkins, editor Bill Lloyd.

95 R. S. Thomas, 'Abercuawg', trans. Sandra Anstey, in Anstey (ed.), *R. S. Thomas: Selected Prose*, p. 161.

96 Thomas, 'Abercuawg', p. 164.

97 Ormond, 'Beginnings', in Hannan (ed.), *Wales in Vision*, p. 7.

Chapter 4

1 Elain Price, *Nid Sianel Gyffredin Mohoni!: Hanes Sefydlu S4C* (Cardiff: University of Wales Press, 2016)

2 Ormond, 'Beginnings', in Hannan (ed.), *Wales in Vision*, p. 1.

3 Dai Smith, 'In the Presence of the Past', in Patrick Hannan (ed.), *Wales in Vision* (Llandysul: Gomer, 1990), p. 39.

4 Smith, 'In the Presence of the Past', in Hannan (ed.), *Wales in Vision*, p. 39.

5 Simon Schama, 'Television and the Trouble with History', in David Cannadine (ed.), *History and the Media* (Basingstoke: Palgrave Macmillan, 2004), p. 20. Schama writes ironically, in defence of his own work on the high-profile BBC history series *A History of Britain* in 2000.

6 Presented by Gwyn Alf Williams and Wynford Vaughan-Thomas, directed by Colin Thomas.

7 Presented by Dai Smith and directed by Selwyn Roderick.

8 E. H. Carr, *What is History?* (London: Penguin, 1985 [1961]), pp. 12–16.

9 Carr, *What is History?*, p. 5. Carr's provocative question was posed in 1961 in order to trigger a debate about the nature of historical enquiry at a time of radical social and cultural change, and the series of lectures that was later published as *What is History?*, delivered at Cambridge University under the name of the great liberal historian, George Macaulay Trevelyan, was in large part a critique of the methodological assumptions upon which historians like Trevelyan had rested since the nineteenth century. Carr revealed these assumptions to be the complacent product of a nineteenth-century liberal order that emphasised economic and technological progress over social critique.

10 Raphael Samuel, *Theatres of Memory Volume 1: Past and Present in Contemporary Culture* (London: Verso, 1994), p. 8.

11 John Fiske and John Hartley, *Reading Television* (London: Methuen, 1978).

12 Daniel Dayan and Elihu Katz, 'Political Ceremony and Instant History', in Anthony Smith (ed.), *Television: An International History*, 2nd edn (Oxford: Oxford University Press, 1998), p. 104.

13 Edgerton, 'Introduction: Television as Historian', in Gary R. Edgerton and Peter C. Rollins (eds), *Television Histories: Shaping Collective Memory in the Media Age* (Lexington: University of Kentucky, 2001), p. 8.

14 See Dafydd Sills-Jones, 'The Teliesyn Co-operative: national broadcasting, production organisation and TV aesthetics', in Ieuan Franklin, Hugh Chignell and Kristin Skoog (eds), *Regional Aesthetics: Mapping UK Media Cultures* (Basingstoke: Palgrave Macmillan, 2015), pp. 169–83.

15 Robert Dillon, *History on British Television: Constructing Nation, Nationality and Collective Memory* (Manchester: Manchester University Press, 2010), p. 36. This rose from 38 programmes between 1946 and 1949, to 765 in the decade 1950–9, on to 2,772 in the following decade and over 4,000 in the 1970s. Dillon, *History on British Television*, p. 70. This was, moreover, the rise in solely factual programmes; these numbers do not take into account the pervasiveness of history in, for instance, costume dramas and literary adaptations.

16 Dillon, *History on British Television*, p. 36.

17 See Davies, *Broadcasting and the BBC in Wales*.

18 *Wales Through the Ages* was a particular success. Each episode in the series invited a specialist to offer their take on the period or theme in question. Topics were chosen by an advisory board consisting of eminent Welsh historians and cultural critics Thomas Parry, Glyn Roberts and David Williams. It also set the precedent for the successful and influential Welsh history books

that stemmed from broadcasting in the 1970s and 1980s (more on which shortly); A. J. Roderick (ed.), *Wales Through the Ages* (1959–60) spanned two volumes and contained the transcripts of every episode in the series.

19 Morgan, *Rebirth of a Nation*, pp. 359– 62.

20 Huw Pryce, *J. E. Lloyd and the Creation of Welsh History: Renewing a Nation's Past* (Cardiff: University of Wales Press, 2011), p. 91.

21 Gwyn A. Williams, *When Was Wales?: A History of the Welsh* (London: Penguin, 1991 [1985]), p. 237.

22 Williams, *When Was Wales?*, p. 232.

23 R. Merfyn Jones, 'Beyond Identity? The Reconstruction of the Welsh', *Journal of British Studies*, 31/4 (1992), 337.

24 Smith, *Wales! Wales?*, p. 1.

25 Morgan, *Rebirth of a Nation*, p. 362. This was due also to the rise in working-class students: the Kelsall Report of 1957 found that forty per cent of students at the University of Wales were children of working-class parents. Morgan, *Rebirth of a Nation*, p. 357.

26 Daryl Leeworthy, *Labour Country: Political Radicalism and Social Democracy in South Wales 1831–1985* (Cardigan: Parthian, 2018), p. 509.

27 Quoted in Davies, *A History of Wales*, p. 636.

28 This book made it abundantly clear that it had the rural Liberal historiographical tradition in its sights: 'One of the most potent and enduring myths of Welsh historiography is that the Welsh radical political tradition derives mainly from the rural areas. The virile and fecund political consciousness of the industrial valleys has, with a few honourable exceptions, had far less than its due.' Glanmor Williams (ed.), *Merthyr Politics: The Making of a Working-Class Tradition* (Cardiff: University of Wales Press, 1966), p. 7.

29 Keith Jenkins, *Re-Thinking History* (London: Routledge, 1991), p. 71.

30 Rhiannon Mason, *Museums, Nations, Identities: Wales and its National Museums* (Cardiff: University of Wales Press, 2007), p. 31.

31 John Davies, 'Wales in the Nineteen-sixties', *Llafur*, 4/4 (1988), 81.

32 Davies, 'Wales in the Nineteen-sixties', 81.

33 Dai Smith, *Aneurin Bevan and the World of South Wales* (Cardiff: University of Wales Press, 1993), p. 5.

34 Morgan, *Rebirth of a Nation*, p. 347.

35 The institute used in the film is the Maindy and Eastern in Ton Pentre, though it is clearly intended to stand in as symbol of any number of institutes across the coalfield.

36 Photography by Bill Greenhalgh, sound by John Lanchester, edited by Mansel Lloyd.

37 In this sense, the film can perhaps be viewed as a precursor to the dialectic structure of *The Dragon Has Two Tongues*, which sees two opposing minds – Wynford Vaughan-Thomas and Gwyn Alf Williams – thrash out aspects of Welsh history.

38 Richard Lewis, *Leaders and Teachers: Adult Education and the Challenge of Labour in South Wales, 1906–1940* (Cardiff: University of Wales Press, 1993), p. xiv.

39 As Hywel Francis has noted, the workmen's institute's role as an educational establishment was in sharp decline by the late 1950s, undermined by municipal

libraries and the changing habits and lifestyles that accompanied the new, better remunerated forms of employment – in particular what Francis calls the 'recreational revolution'. Hywel Francis, 'The Origins of the South Wales Miners' Library', *History Workshop*, 2 (1976), 190.

40 Michael J. Collins is one critic who has identified the strong elegiac strain in Ormond's poetry. See his essay 'The Elegiac Tradition in Contemporary Anglo-Welsh Poetry', *Anglo-Welsh Review*, 26/3 (1976), 46–57.

41 Robert Morgan, 'Miners' Library', in *On the Banks of the Cynon* (Todmorden: Arc Publications, 1975), pp. 8–9.

42 Norman Swallow, 'History by Television', *The Listener*, 2448 (1976), 296. Sadly, this was an approach to television production that was, as I will later discuss, seen far less by the time Swallow was writing here.

43 Davies, *Broadcasting and the BBC in Wales*, p. 90.

44 The film also anticipated the four-part BBC Wales series documenting the Rhondda that was to grace Welsh screens in 1965, Gethyn Stoodley Thomas's *The Long Street*.

45 Robert Graham, 'Television', *Western Mail*, 4 March 1961, 8.

46 BBC Audience Research Report, *Once There Was a Time*, 22 March 1961 (BBC Written Archives Centre, Caversham, R9/7/51).

47 The Broadcasting Council for Wales proudly reported the trip in two successive reports: in 1962 after the footage was recorded, and in 1963 after it had been broadcast. As the latter report states: 'From Patagonia to Perth, from Bardi to Berlin, from California to New York – and all over Wales; this is an indication of the compass of features and talks programmes during the past year.' Broadcasting Council for Wales, *Annual Report 1962–63*, p. 10. Nan Davies is a notable figure in the history of BBC Wales. She began working at the Corporation in the 1930s and became the Welsh Region's first female producer. She was one of only four female employees to reach a position of such standing at the BBC in Wales in the first sixty years of its existence. She retired in 1969. See Davies, *Broadcasting and the BBC in Wales*.

48 After seeing the film he judged it 'interesting' but 'disappointing'. Robert Graham, 'Television', *Western Mail*, 22 December 1962, 8.

49 Prys Morgan, 'Keeping the Legends Alive', in Tony Curtis (eds), *Wales: The Imagined Nation* (Bridgend: Poetry Wales, 1986), p. 36.

50 Davies, 'Wales in the Nineteen-sixties', 81.

51 Saunders Lewis, 'The Fate of the Language', in Alun R. Jones, and Gwyn Thomas (eds), *Presenting Saunders Lewis* (Cardiff: University of Wales Press, 1983), p. 135.

52 A later version of *Y Gymru Bell* utilising much of the same material as the earlier series but condensed into a fifty-minute programme was broadcast in 1965.

53 This effort to translate history into English was deemed an important project for nationalists of this era, and further evidenced in Keidrych Rhys's journal *Wales* in 1959, when a potted history of the colony was published in English, at a time when very few such histories were available. See George Pendle, 'The Welsh in Patagonia', *Wales*, 6/37 (1959), 13–22. Significantly, Pendle acknowledges the need for a factual, written history at a time when oral histories had predominated: 'passed down from one generation of

eloquent patriots to another, [they] have diminished in accuracy in the re-telling' (13).

54 Glyn Williams, *The Welsh in Patagonia: The State and the Ethnic Community* (Cardiff: University of Wales Press, 1991), p. ix.

55 BBC Audience Research Report, *The Desert and the Dream*, 8 January 1963 (BBC Written Archives Centre, Caversham, R9/7/61).

56 R. Bryn Williams, *Gwladfa Patagonia: The Welsh Colony in Patagonia 1865–1965* (Cardiff: University of Wales Press, 1965). Williams's effort to encourage a rapprochement between the two cultures went as far as to 'keep as close as possible to the original' in his English translation 'in order to help those who are learning Welsh as a second language' (p. 5).

57 The titles of the episodes in the original series offer something of the scope of *Y Gymru Bell*'s interests, which range from history to social enquiry: '1: Y Dyddiau Cynnar (The Early Days)'; '2: Wrth Droed yr Andes (At the Foot of the Andes)'; '3: Y Wladfa Heddiw (The Colony Today)'; '4: Pwyso a Mesur (Weighing and Measuring)'.

58 John Corner, 'The Interview as Social Encounter', in Paddy Scannell (ed.), *Broadcast Talk* (London: Sage, 1991), p. 31.

59 Corner, 'The Interview as Social Encounter', in Scannell (ed.), *Broadcast Talk*, pp. 36–40. This was thus close to the strategy of oral history that was gathering interest in academic circles at this time.

60 Photography in both by Bill Greenhalgh, sound by Norman Allen, editor Douglas Mair.

61 Abraham Matthews, a Congregational minister who was one of those who sailed on the *Mimosa* in 1865 (later dubbed the 'bishop of *Y Wladfa*'), had likened the settlers to the Israelites in the desert in his first sermon delivered in Patagonia. See Geraldine Lublin, 'Matthews, Abraham (1832–1899)', *Oxford Dictionary of National Biography* (Oxford: Oxford University Press, 2004); October 2009 edn available at *http://www.oxforddnb.com/view/article/98447* (accessed 22 November 2018).

62 BBC Audience Research Report, *The Desert and the Dream*.

63 The 1965 version of *Y Gymru Bell* ends on a more melancholy note – perhaps, three years after the initial trip, the footage seemed not to fit the reality.

64 John Davies notes that earnings between 1955 and 1970 rose by 140 per cent, while retail prices rose by just 70 per cent. Davies, 'Wales in the Nineteen-sixties', 78.

65 The number of agricultural workers in Wales more than halved between 1931 and 1971, from 92,000 to 45,000. Johnes, *Wales Since 1939*, p. 155. And the number of miners was slashed even more violently: from 106,000 in 1960 to 60,000 in 1970. Morgan, *Rebirth of a Nation*, p. 317.

66 Johnes, *Wales Since 1939*, p. 155.

67 Ellis, *Investiture*, p. 15.

68 Ellis, *Investiture*, p. 15.

69 Queen Elizabeth II, quoted in Anthony Holden, *Charles: A Biography* (London: Bantam, 1998), p. 49.

70 Ellis, *Investiture*, p. 145.

71 Ellis, *Investiture*, p. 163.

72 Ellis, *Investiture*, p. 253.

73 The programme was first broadcast on national BBC1 at 10.50 p.m. on Wednesday 25 June 1969, but was repeated at 10 a.m. on national BBC1 on the morning of the Investiture. Photography by Russell Walker, sound by Tony Adkins, edited by Chris Lawrence.

74 The Audience Research Report noted that while some respondents felt that Edwards's narration was 'attractive' and 'suited to the programme', others felt that he sounded like a 'Welshman, but only just', and that they would 'liked a little more accent'. Nevertheless the Welsh 'exiles' in the research group were 'particularly delighted with it' (Audience Research Report, 5 August 1969 (BBC Written Archives Centre, Caversham, R9/7/99)).

75 Ellis, *Investiture*, p. 164.

76 Dai Smith makes an apt point about television's optimistic vision of the Welsh steel industry in the 1960s in his documentary series *Wales! Wales?* (1984). There he notes that, in the 1960s, 'television correspondents would come [to the steelworks at Port Talbot] to be framed in the future landscape of a heavy industrial base – the old days of depression and unemployment finished.' Unfortunately, the optimism was short-lived; in the ten years after 1973 the number of people employed by the British Steel Corporation in Wales dropped from 65, 981 to 19,199. Davies, *A History of Wales*, p. 657.

77 Johnes, *Wales Since 1939*, p. 282.

78 Martin Johnes notes that 'British coverage [of] Welsh rugby in general, drew heavily on certain national stereotypes [. . .]. The Welsh XVs were described as "magical", "poetic", "rhythmic", "shrewd" and "fighters".' Martin Johnes, *A History of Sport in Wales* (Cardiff: University of Wales Press, 2005), p. 84.

79 Johnes, *A History of Sport in Wales*, p. 84.

80 Daniel Dayan and Elihu Katz, *Media Events: The Live Broadcasting of History* (Cambridge: Harvard University Press, 1992), p. viii.

81 Ellis, *Investiture*, p. 320.

82 In an interview in 2002, Roderick recalls that officials at the BBC were 'colder' to him after his refusal (*Wales Video Gallery*, 'Selwyn Roderick' (2002)). Moreover, with credit to the BBC, it did also address some of the conflicts of opinion; its documentary series *24 Hours* caused a stir after it broadcast an episode that, it was alleged, was biased in favour of those who opposed the ceremony. The Welsh Office were unimpressed, and Ellis notes that some deemed the programme 'anti-investiture propaganda'. Ellis, *Investiture*, p. 296.

83 Ellis, *Investiture*, p. 321.

84 Johnes, *Wales Since 1939*, p. 236.

85 Johnes, *Wales Since 1939*, p. 239.

86 As Johnes notes, in the 1970 general election Plaid Cymru lost twenty-five of its thirty-six deposits. Its vote in Rhondda West dropped from 39.9 per cent in the 1967 by-election to 14.1 per cent in 1970. Johnes, *Wales Since 1939*, pp. 238–9.

87 Ned Thomas, *The Welsh Extremist: Modern Welsh Politics, Literature and Society* (London: Gollancz, 1972), p. 113.

88 Though he doesn't name it in the column, this was *A Bronze Mask* (1969).

89 John Ormond, 'Personal Column', *Western Mail*, 4 March 1974, 9.

90 Alexander Thom was an esteemed engineer who worked in a range of fields and, after retirement from Professorship in Engineering Science at

Oxford in 1961, pursued an interest in megalithic stone circles. His conclusions, which entered popular consciousness in the book Ormond found in Cardiff Central Library (Alexander Thom, *Megalithic Sites in Great Britain* (Oxford: Clarendon, 1967)) and in a BBC documentary presented by Magnus Magnusson, *Chronicle: Cracking the Stone Age Code* (BBC, 1970), caused a storm in archaeological circles and, according to the *Oxford Dictionary of National Biography*, 'remain contentious'. S. S. Wilson, 'Thom, Alexander (1894–1985)', *Oxford Dictionary of National Biography* (Oxford: OUP, 2004). Thom suggested that the builders of these ancient tombs and circles were not improvising but in fact adhering to and experimenting with strict geometrical rules millennia before they were formulised by the Greek mathematicians. Thom actually appears in episode 2 of the first series of *The Land Remembers*, and explains his theory to Gwyn Williams at Moel Ty Uchaf, near Corwen in Denbighshire.

91 Gwyn Williams, *Collected Poems: 1936–1986* (Llandysul: Gomer, 1987), p. xiii.

92 Williams, 'Places in Our Spirit', in *Collected Poems*, p. 100.

93 Dillon, *History on British Television*, p. 43.

94 The first Broadcasting Council for Wales *Annual Report 1954–55* noted that 'in general the output of television programmes from Wales can be classified under three headings of Events (eisteddfodau and festivals); Places (visits to castles, cathedrals); and People (local customs, speech, and talent).'

95 Pryce, *J. E. Lloyd and the Creation of Welsh History*, p. 93.

96 E. Griffiths Jones, 'The Celtic Genius', quoted in Lord, *Imaging the Nation*, p. 292.

97 Lord, 'Improvement: The Visualisation of "y Werin", the Welsh Folk', in *The Meaning of Pictures*, p. 108.

98 Series 1 was photographed by Russ Walker, sound by Ted Doull, edited by John Brewser. Series 2 was photographed by Tom Friswell, sound by Ted Doull, edited by Stan Lane.

99 This is a perspective that Williams made somewhat more explicit in his own writings. In his unusual autobiography, *ABC of (D.) G. W.* (Llandysul: Gomer, 1981) (subtitled *A Kind of Autobiography*), he is scathing on the subject of Cardiff and, it would seem, monoglot anglophone Welsh culture and its national allegiances: 'As a capital city Caerdyf [*sic*] has proved no better than I expected. It satisfies if you think that communication with London is more important than with Aberystwyth or Caernarfon, if you go by population density, if you think that Welsh culture is a tolerable eccentricity so long as it keeps its distance, if you think that the English branch of Yr Academi Gymreig has a likelier future than the original Welsh branch, if rugby is more important to you than poetry, opera more important than penillion singing.'

100 Williams was perhaps thinking of nineteenth-century travel writer Benjamin Malkin's description of the 'Glamorganshire alps', or perhaps Ron Berry's *Flame and Slag* (1968), in which Rees Stevens imagines his psychologist on 'gleaming skis, riding the tip-slide with Olympic verve'. Quoted in Sarah Morse, 'The Black Pastures: The Significance of Landscape in the Work of Gwyn Thomas and Ron Berry' (unpublished PhD thesis, Swansea University, 2010), 104.

101 See D. O. Thomas, 'Price, Richard (1723–1791)', *Oxford Dictionary of National Biography* (Oxford: Oxford University Press, 2004); May 2005 edn available at *http://www.oxforddnb.com/view/article/22761* (accessed 9 October 2013).

102 Richard Price, 'A Discourse on the Love of our Country', in *Political Writings*, ed. D.O. Thomas (Cambridge: Cambridge University Press, 1991), p. 178.

103 In the preface to the most recent edition of their important publication *The Fed*, Hywel Francis and Dai Smith recall a 1970 meeting in Swansea's Bay View Hotel to establish the society. Hywel Francis and Dai Smith, *The Fed: A History of the South Wales Miners in the Twentieth Century* (Cardiff: University of Wales Press, 1998 [1980]), p. xviii.

104 *The South Wales Coalfield History Project: Final Report* (University College, Swansea: Departments of History and Economic History, 1974), p. 1.

105 Hywel Francis, 'The Secret World of the South Wales Miner: The Relevance of Oral History', in David Smith (ed.), *A People and a Proletariat: Essays in the History of Wales 1780–1980* (London: Pluto, 1980), p. 167.

106 Francis, 'The Secret World of the South Wales Miner', in Smith (ed.), *A People and a Proletariat*, p. 179.

107 The exact number is open to some dispute. Francis's most recent count is 206, including all those who volunteered for the International Brigades but did not make it to Spain (having been refused or physically unfit to serve) (Hywel Francis, *Miners Against Fascism: Wales and the Spanish Civil War* (London: Lawrence and Wishart, 2012 [1984]), pp. 300–5). Robert Stradling lists 154 names, which includes those of five who fought with militias other than the International Brigades and one who served with the Nationalist Army, but not those who did not make it to Spain (Stradling, *Wales and the Spanish Civil War: The Dragon's Dearest Cause?* (Cardiff: University of Wales Press, 2004), pp. 183–7).

108 The other was Kim Howells's PhD thesis, titled 'A View From Below: Tradition, Experience and Nationalisation in the South Wales Coalfield 1937–1957' (University of Warwick, 1979).

109 The first major event took place at Mountain Ash on 7 December 1938. Over 7,000 people were present, including the African American actor, singer and political activist Paul Robeson. Francis, *Miners Against Fascism: Wales and the Spanish Civil War*, p. 249. As Daniel G. Williams has noted, Robeson's presence was highly symbolic and, indeed, anticipated what would become his 'talismanic role' in Welsh perceptions of the coalfield for decades to come. Daniel G. Williams, *Black Skin, Blue Books: African Americans and Wales 1845–1945* (Cardiff: University of Wales Press, 2012), p. 150. More recent Welsh engagements with Spain include the Manic Street Preachers' single 'If You Tolerate This Your Children Will Be Next' (1998) (which aptly borrows a quotation from one of the interviews Hywel Francis undertook as part of the Coalfield History Project: 'If I can shoot rabbits then I can shoot fascists'. See Francis, *Miners Against Fascism*, p. xix). On television, the recent BBC Wales programme *Return Journey* (2005) saw one of the men interviewed in Ormond's series, Alun Menai Williams, return to the battlefields on which he fought in Spain.

110 Ormond had read Francis's PhD thesis prior to making *The Colliers' Crusade*.

[111] Francis, *Miners Against Fascism*, p. 156.

[112] Photography by Charles Beddous and Russ Walker, sound by Mansel Davies, Tony Adkins and Robin Griffith, edited by Bill Mainman.

[113] *Principles and Practice in Documentary Programmes*, p. 23.

[114] *Principles and Practice in Documentary Programmes*, p. 24.

[115] Robert Stradling has claimed that Ormond was 'somewhat nonplussed' to turn up to interview Thomas only to find he had not fought for the Republic (*Wales and the Spanish Civil War*, p. 46.) This is not true. As Francis, who worked with Ormond on the series, notes in the most recent edition of *Miners Against Fascism*: 'on the contrary, I had made John Ormond aware of Thomas: he was delighted to have had the opportunity of contrasting Thomas's outlook with those of the International Brigadiers' (Francis, *Miners Against Fascism*, p. xii).

[116] Many of these men had also been prominent in coalfield politics before the outbreak of the Spanish Civil War. Will Paynter, for instance, had been an influential figure within the Communist Party and was in 1936 elected on to the executive council of the South Wales Miners' Federation. He went on to become General Secretary of the National Union of Mineworkers. See Hywel Francis, 'Paynter, Thomas William (1903–1984)', *Oxford Dictionary of National Biography* (Oxford: Oxford University Press, 2004); September 2010 edn available at *http://www.oxforddnb.com/view/article/48653* (accessed 12 December 2018). Jack 'Russia' Roberts had acquired his nickname as an outspoken polemicist during the General Strike of 1926. (Roberts wrote a well-received poem, 'Spain', during his time in on the front line at Brunete that was published in Stephen Spender and John Lehmann's collection *Poems for Spain* (London: Hogarth, 1939). Others, such as Tom Jones, who was pivotal in the creation of the Wales TUC, built political careers after returning home.

[117] The newspaper had, in fact, been a staunch supporter of the Republican government, and even published articles and letters from men serving with the International Brigades. Francis, *Miners Against Fascism*, p. 121. This was in contrast to the conservative *Western Mail*, which is spoken of sardonically as 'jeer[ing]', 'gloat[ing]' elsewhere in the series with regard to its support for the coal owners in the disputes of the 1920s. As it happened the *Western Mail*, having initially shown hostility toward the Republic, shifted its editorial position in support of it after the bombing of Guernica on 26 April 1937. Francis, *Miners Against Fascism*, p. 125.

[118] The series was initially aired as a BBC Wales opt-out in 1979, but was broadcast on the BBC national network in the following year. The *Times* reviewer remarked that it is 'a good job the Welsh are good talkers [. . .] because if they weren't, *The Colliers Crusade* wouldn't be half the programme it is'. Peter Davalle, 'Personal Choice', *The Times*, 6 June 1980, p. 27.

[119] Johnes, *Wales Since 1939*, p. 238.

[120] Hywel Francis, *History on Our Side: Wales and the 1984–85 Miners' Strike* (Ferryside: Iconau, 2009), p. 69.

[121] Dicks, *Heritage, Place and Community*, p. 90. The museum had opened in 1948 as the brainchild of Iorwerth Peate, a poet, scholar, museum curator and staunch supporter of rural, Nonconformist Wales. It was partly modelled on the open-air museum pioneered at Skansen, Sweden.

122 M. Wynn Thomas, *Corresponding Cultures: the Two Literatures of Wales* (Cardiff: University of Wales Press, 1999).

123 Smith, *Wales! Wales?*, p. ix.

124 Smith, *Wales! Wales?*, p. 1.

125 Gwyn A. Williams's work on this subject had earlier been broadcast in the BBC Wales annual lecture of 1979, *When Was Wales?* The later book and his contribution to Colin Thomas's series was an expansion of this earlier exposition.

Chapter 5

1 John Grierson, quoted in Paddy Scannell, "The Social Eye of Television, 1946–1955', *Media, Culture and Society*, 1/1 (1979), 101.

2 Ian Aitken, *Film and Reform: John Grierson and the Documentary Film Movement* (London: Routledge, 1990), pp. 19–20.

3 Grierson had coined the term 'documentary' in a review of Flaherty's *Moana* in a New York newspaper. See Winston, *Claiming the Real*, p. 11.

4 Stuart Hall, 'The Social Eye of Picture Post', in Glenn Jordan, *'Down the Bay': Picture Post, Humanist Photography and Images of 1950s Cardiff* (Cardiff: Butetown History and Arts Centre, 2001), p. 71.

5 Evans, 'An Ormond Chronology', in Ormond, *Collected Poems*, ed. Rian Evans, p. 37.

6 Ien Ang, *Desperately Seeking the Audience* (London: Routledge, 1991), p. 108.

7 Ang, *Desperately Seeking the Audience*, pp. 115–16.

8 Norman Swallow, quoted in Corner, 'Documentary Voices', in Corner (ed.), *Popular Television in Britain*, p. 44.

9 Norman Swallow, quoted in Scannell, 'The Social Eye of Television, 1946–1955', 104.

10 John Corner, 'Television and British Society in the 1950s', in John Corner (ed.), *Popular Television in Britain: Studies in Cultural History* (London: BFI, 1991), p. 11.

11 Scannell, 'The Social Eye of Television, 1946–1955', p. 103.

12 Ieuan Franklin and Paul Long, 'The Overheard and Underprivileged: Uses of Montage Sound in the Post-War BBC Television Documentaries of Denis Mitchell and Philip Donnellan' (unpublished conference paper, *Documentary Now!*, UCL, London, January 2011). Available at *http://www.academia. edu/483597/The_Overheard_and_Underprivileged*, (accessed 10 March 2014), no page number.

13 Though the community was in fact a composite of several different northern communities; Mitchell filmed in the deprived areas of Liverpool, Stockport, Manchester and Salford.

14 Patrick Russell, 'Morning in the Streets', *BFI Screenonline*. Available at *http:// www.screenonline.org.uk/tv/id/1224984/index.html* (accessed 10 January 2013).

15 Philip Donnellan, 'Memories of the Future', *Sight and Sound*, 2/4 (1992), 40. Donnellan's films were guided by an unflinching eye for social injustice, which often got him into trouble with his superiors. *The Irishmen*, for instance, though filmed for the BBC, was never televised. One interesting 1962 BBC

memorandum reveals some of the internal resistance towards the more demo-cratic documentary forms emerging at this time. Stuart Hood, then BBC Controller of Programmes, was responding to the concerns of the North Regional Controller that Donnellan was exacting too much creative freedom: 'I have been enquiring into Donnellan's activities. What he has been engaged on is a pilot programme based on the idea of a prolonged interview with a "man from the people" – in this case a coal miner. From what I hear of it, I do not expect it to be seen on the screen.' Memorandum, 9 April 1962 (BBC Written Archives Centre, Caversham, T16/61/2).

16 Patrick Russell, 'Philip Donnellan', *BFI Screenonline*. Available at *http://www. screenonline.org.uk/people/id/500920/index.html* (accessed 10 January 2013).

17 Randall Hansen, *Citizenship and Immigration in Post-war Britain* (Oxford: Oxford University Press, 2000), p. v.

18 Will Kymlicka, *Multicultural Citizenship* (Oxford: Oxford University Press, 1995), p. 11.

19 Corner, 'Documentary Voices', in Corner (ed.), *Popular Television in Britain*, p. 55.

20 Swallow, *Factual Television*, p. 189.

21 Mitchell, quoted in Swallow, 'Denis Mitchell', *The Listener*, 551.

22 Ormond, 'Beginnings', in Hannan (ed.), *Wales in Vision*, p. 10.

23 Henrietta Lidchi, 'The Poetics and the Politics of Exhibiting Other Cultures', in Stuart Hall (ed.), *Representation: Cultural Representations and Signifying Practices* (London: Sage 1997), p. 161. Author's emphases.

24 James Clifford, *The Predicament of Culture: Twentieth-Century Ethnography, Literature, and Art* (London: Harvard University Press, 1988), p. 13.

25 Broadcasting Council for Wales, *Annual Report 1955–1956*, p. 10.

26 Davies, *Broadcasting and the BBC in Wales*, p. 323.

27 Broadcasting Council for Wales, *Annual Report 1962–1963*, p. 10.

28 Ormond, 'Beginnings', in Hannan (ed.), *Wales in Vision*, p. 5.

29 Burton donated his fee to the two men. Ormond, 'Beginnings', in Hannan (ed.), *Wales in Vision*, p. 8. Burton's diary entry on the day of recording (8 March 1960) simply reads 'John Ormond'. Richard Burton, *The Richard Burton Diaries*, ed. Chris Williams (London: Yale University Press, 2012), p. 73.

30 Swallow, 'Denis Mitchell', *The Listener*, 551. Swallow felt this 'golden age' extended from 1955–1965.

31 Ormond's wife, Glenys, remembers this in an obituary essay in a special issue of *Poetry Wales* the year of Ormond's death: Glenys Ormond , '"J.O." and "Rod"', *Poetry Wales*, 44.

32 Alun Richards, 'Berries on the Tree', in Patrick Hannan (ed.), *Wales in Vision* (Llandysul: Gomer, 1990), p. 46.

33 Robert Graham, 'Radio and Television', *Western Mail*, 21 May 1960.

34 Len Goss, 'Poles Apart', *Evening Post*, 26 May 1960.

35 BBC Audience Research Report, *Borrowed Pasture*, 9 June 1960 (BBC Written Archives Centre, Caversham, R9/7/46). The report quoted numerous positive responses, almost all of whom responded emotionally to the film: 'I found this an inspiring and unforgettable film'; 'We felt extremely moved'; 'I was very moved by the story'; 'It was all so sad'.

36 Ormond, '"J.O." and "Rod"', *Poetry Wales*, 44.

37 Photography by Bill Greenhalgh, edited by Harry Hastings.

38 Ormond, 'Beginnings', in Hannan (ed.), *Wales in Vision*, p. 8.

39 Ormond, quoted in Berry, *Wales and Cinema*, p. 292.

40 David MacDougall, *Transcultural Cinema* (Princeton: Princeton University Press, 1998), p. 246.

41 Colin Holmes, *John Bull's Island: Immigration and British Society 1871–1971* (Basingstoke: Macmillan, 1988), p. 169.

42 Swallow, *Factual Television*, p. 189.

43 Berry, *Wales and Cinema*, p. 532. Gruffydd was a 'veteran radio man' who had been instrumental in the development of Welsh radio in the 1930s and switched to television production in 1954. Davies, *Broadcasting and the BBC in Wales*, p. 208. Perceptions of Polish migrants in south Wales in these years were likely to have been particularly strained following the high-profile trial of Michael Onufrejczyk, the 'Butcher of Cwmdu'. Onufrejczyk, like Okolowicz and Bulaj, had fought with the British Army and been resettled in Wales after 1947, and, under circumstances very similar to the protagonists of Ormond's film, he had purchased a farm in rural Wales with another Polish émigré, Stanislaw Sykut, in an effort to rebuild a life for himself. Yet relations between Onufrejczyk and Sykut soon turned sour, and under suspicious circumstances Sykut disappeared some time in 1953. Onufrejczuk claimed his business partner had taken a trip to London, but after a police investigation found suspicious dark stains on the walls of the farmhouse, he was in 1954 charged with murder. Nathan Bevan, 'A Grisly History of Welsh Murders', 28 January 2008. Available at *http://www.walesonline.co.uk/news/wales-news/grisly-history-welsh-murders-2205058* (accessed 28 February 2014).

44 It was this priest, Father Potoczny, that had introduced Ormond to Okolowicz and Bulaj. See Ormond, 'Beginnings', in Hannan (ed.), *Wales in Vision*, p. 5.

45 There were similar, small communities near the docklands of Liverpool and London.

46 Johnes, *Wales Since 1939*, p. 139.

47 Glenn Jordan, '"We Never Really Noticed You Were Coloured": Postcolonialist Reflections on Immigrants and Minorities in Wales', in Jane Aaron and Chris Williams (eds), *Postcolonial Wales* (Cardiff: University of Wales Press, 2005), p. 59.

48 Glenn Jordan and Chris Weedon, *Cultural Politics: Class, Gender, Race and the Postmodern World* (Oxford: Blackwell, 1995), p. 135. Glenn Jordan has been a social commentator and activist in the Butetown area for many years. He has written extensively on the history of the area and the cultural politics of its representations, and in 1987 helped to set up the Butetown History and Arts Centre.

49 Jordan and Weedon, *Cultural Politics*, p. 138.

50 Jordan, *Down the Bay*, p. 12.

51 Jordan, *Down the Bay*, p. 13.

52 Neil Evans, 'Immigrants and Minorities in Wales, 1840–1990: A Comparative Perspective', in Charlotte Williams, Neil Evans and Paul O'Leary (eds), *A Tolerant Nation?: Exploring Ethnic Diversity in Wales* (Cardiff: University of Wales Press, 2003), p. 20.

53 Photography by John Pike, sound by Tony Adkins, edited by Brian Inglethorpe.

54 This was a familiar trope in images of Tiger Bay around this time. The 1959 feature film set in the area, *Tiger Bay*, draws on precisely the same discourse of permanent transience in its construction of its central character, Korchinsky (played by Horst Buchholz). Korchinsky, a Polish seaman, gets into an altercation with his lover and, in the heat of the moment, shoots her dead. Much of the film's drama is predicated on Korchinsky's unbridled emotionalism and unpredictability as he runs from the law. He rarely stands still throughout the film, and is consistently linked with the tumultuousness of the sea: the first time we see him he stands in line on a ship in dock, waiting for his payment (along with migrants of various other ethnicities), and in the film's final shot he sits dripping wet and shivering, having moments earlier dived into the ocean to rescue his young friend Gillie (played by Hayley Mills).

55 Johnes, *Wales Since 1939*, p. 139.

56 Neil Evans, 'Through the Prism of Ethnic Violence: Riots and Racial Attacks in Wales, 1826–2002', in Charlotte Williams, Neil Evans and Paul O'Leary (eds), *A Tolerant Nation?: Exploring Ethnic Diversity in Wales* (Cardiff: University of Wales Press, 2003), p. 99. Interestingly, another BBC Wales documentary, produced on the same subject a few years later, addressed this issue head-on. Selwyn Roderick's film *A Tamed and Shabby Tiger* (1968) accompanied shots of the railway bridge with a voiceover that stated, 'Above this bridge, on the other side of the tracks, lives the city of Cardiff – civic and suburban, and rather smug; below it, an uninvited community which has coloured the city's reputation around the world.' Such remarks, which more explicitly address the issue, in effect highlight the sense in which Ormond's poeticism to a certain extent masked his films' ethnographic logic: the fact that their poeticism was predicated on an ethnographic distancing – though *A Tamed and Shabby Tiger* is, too, itself undoubtedly guilty of a somewhat idealised and self-serving vision of a tolerant Wales.

57 Evans, 'Immigrants and Minorities in Wales', in Williams, Evans and O'Leary (eds), *A Tolerant Nation?*, p. 28.

58 Indeed, Ormond's use of the phrase from Psalm 137 seems to border riskily on the implication that Wales is a sort of Babylon exhorting its exiles to song.

59 Davies, *A History of Wales*, p. 400.

60 The essay was published in Patrick Hannan's anthology of essays on Welsh broadcasting, *Wales in Vision*, to mark the twenty-fifth anniversary of BBC Wales. The anthology's authorship, consisting entirely of men, alone speaks volumes about the era in which Ormond was working.

61 Selwyn Roderick, 'Us Over There', in Patrick Hannan (ed.), *Wales in Vision* (Llandysul: Gomer, 1990), p. 19.

62 Roderick, 'Us Over There', in Hannan (ed.), *Wales in Vision*, p. 23.

63 The narrator is Hywel Davies, then Head of Programmes at BBC Wales, who had been a pivotal figure in Welsh broadcasting from his employment at the corporation in 1942. For John Davies, he was 'the most outstanding figure in Welsh broadcasting in the post-war years'. Davies, *Broadcasting and the BBC in Wales*, p. 136. Sadly, Hywel Davies passed away the year this film was produced, at the age of forty-four. Photography by Gael Boden and Bill Greenhalgh, edited by Brian Tucker.

64 Michael Billig, *Banal Nationalism* (London: Sage, 1995), p. 93.

65 Graham Murdock, 'Televisual Tourism: National Image-Making and International Markets', in C. W. Thomsen (ed.), *Cultural Transfer or Electronic Imperialism?* (Heidelberg: Carl Winter Universitätsverlag, 1989), p. 173. Murdock's focus is on dramas and nature documentaries that are syndicated abroad, but the same could certainly be said of the travel review programmes that emerged on British television around the late 1960s as a result of improved incomes and affordable foreign travel, such as BBC's *Holiday* (1969–2007) and ITV's (Thames Television) *Wish You Were Here. . .?* (1974–2003).

66 Photography by Russell Walker, sound by Mansel Davies, edited by Harley Jones.

67 Ormond, 'Letter from Tuscany', *Poetry Wales*, 22.

68 Harold Tudor, *Making the Nations Sing: the Birth of the Llangollen International Eisteddfod* (Keele: Keele University Library, 1973), p. 7.

69 The Welsh Home Service was initially reluctant to endorse the first festival. Tudor suggests this apprehension may have been related to the concern of some patrons of the National Eisteddfod, who viewed Llangollen as a threat. (See Tudor, *Making the Nations Sing*, p. 29.) In the end the Welsh Home Service dedicated some airtime to the festival, and Llangollen also became an annual fixture in the coverage of Wales by the BBC Overseas Service (BBC World Service from 1965). (See James Stewart, 'Wales, the wireless and the world – sixty years of Welsh programmes on the BBC World Service', *Cyfrwng: Media Wales Journal*, 10 (2013), 35–52.) The first television coverage was an outside broadcast in 1956 (see Broadcasting Council for Wales's *Annual Reports* of these years). Moreover, Tudor later recalled he '"hawked" the pictorial possibilities of the festival among the cinema news reel companies' in an attempt to generate interest. Only British Movietone News came. Tudor, *Making the Nations Sing*, p. 29.

70 Audience Research Report, *Llangollen International Music Eisteddfod*, 7 August 1963 (BBC Written Archives Centre, Caversham, R9/7/64).

71 Selwyn Roderick, in *Wales Video Gallery: Selwyn Roderick* (2002). However, Ormond's film was not the first 'prestige' film on the Llangollen International Eisteddfod. Fellow Welsh film-maker Jack Howells had produced a colour film (funded privately by Esso) on the festival in 1965, titled *The World Still Sings: An Impression of the Llangollen International Musical Eisteddfod*. Howells had himself talked of the importance of producing a 'prestige' – rather than merely informational – film to combat the standard fare on television: 'The Eisteddfod, after all, has been covered each year on television – much on the lines of an outside broadcast, say, or a test match.' Jack Howells, quoted in Berry, 'The World Still Sings: Jack Howells', in Russell and Piers Taylor (eds), *Shadows of Progress*, p. 148.

72 BBC2 had been broadcasting in monochrome since its inauguration in 1964.

73 Davies, *Broadcasting and the BBC in Wales*, p. 317.

74 Briggs, *The History of Broadcasting in the United Kingdom Volume V: Competition*, p. 858.

75 Some viewers in mid and north Wales would likely have received signals from other transmitters in England already broadcasting in colour. Therefore

John Davies is not entirely accurate when he states that 'the first colour programme made by BBC Wales was [. . .] transmitted on 9 July 1970'. Davies, *Broadcasting and the BBC in Wales*, p. 282. Though the first colour programme *transmitted* by BBC Wales was in 1970 (this too was a programme about Llangollen), the first colour programme *made* by BBC Wales was very likely Ormond's *Music in Midsummer*.

76 Photography by Russell Walker and Ken Mackay, editing by Keith Denton and Bernard Childs. Editor Brian Turvey.

77 In this sense *Music in Midsummer* could be viewed in the manner of some of Ormond's other films that were inspired by the creative works of other artists (see chapter on cultural documentaries). Here the film, in its colourful enthusiasm, bears a striking resemblance to Dylan Thomas's celebrated essay written for the Welsh Home Service in 1953, 'The International Eisteddfod'. Indeed, Ormond would no doubt have had the piece in mind when making this film. Thomas's piece complements Ormond's film nicely: 'Burgundian girls, wearing, on their heads, bird-cages made of velvet, suddenly whisk on the pavement into a coloured dance. A Viking goes into a pub. In black felt feathered hats and short leather trousers, enormous Austrians, with thighs big as Welshmen's bodies, but much browner, yodel to fiddles and split the rain with their smiles. Frilled, ribboned, sashed, fezzed, and white-turbaned, in baggy blue sharavári and squashed red boots, Ukrainians with Manchester accents gopak up the hill. Everything is strange in Llangollen.' In Dylan Thomas, *Quite Early One Morning: Stories, Poems and Essays*, ed. Aneirin Talfan-Davies (London: J. M. Dent, 1971 [1954]), pp. 58–9.

78 The film was aired at 8 p.m. on 4 July 1968. It was also repeated – presumably for those in Wales who could not receive BBC2 at that time – on BBC Wales the following night at 9.35 p.m.

79 Morley, 'Broadcasting and the Construction of the National Family', p. 422.

Chapter 6

1 Kieron Smith, '*Madawaska Valley*: John Ormond's Lost Film and the National Film Board of Canada', *Canadian Journal of Film Studies*, 25/1 (2016), 27–45.

2 This, the OSTAR (*Observer* Single-Handed Trans-Atlantic Race, sponsored by the *Observer* newspaper), was the first solo transatlantic yacht race of its kind.

3 Audience Research Report, *Alone in a Boat*, 4 January 1967 (BBC Written Archives Centre, Caversham, R9/7/84).

4 Email correspondence with Val Howells, September 2011.

5 John Ormond, 'Message in a Bottle', *Selected Poems* (Bridgend: Poetry Wales Press, 1987), p. 24.

6 Much of the photography was by Val Howells himself, with additional footage by Charles Beddous. Sound by Mansel Davies and Keith Denton, edited by John Brewser.

7 The narrator states that 'this film is about the thoughts of a man who is crossing the Western ocean single-handed'. The suggestion that the film is about

the 'thoughts' of a man crossing the ocean as opposed to being about simply 'a man crossing the ocean' is significant.

8 Val Howells, *Sailing into Solitude* (Narberth: Landsker, 2011), p. 128.

9 John Ormond, 'Message in a Bottle', *Selected Poems* (Bridgend: Poetry Wales, 1987), p. 24.

10 Interestingly, viewers seem to have responded well to such sequences, with the audience report noting that it was deemed 'ingenious' in the way it 'match[ed] the visual with the auditory'. Audience Research Report, *Alone in a Boat*.

11 Audience Research Report, *Alone in a Boat*.

12 Interview with Dannie Abse, *In Requiem and Celebration*, dir. Richard Trayler-Smith (BBC Wales, 1995).

Filmography

This is a list of known films produced by Ormond. Ormond also provided commentaries for two series: *Heart of Scotland* (1961) and *Far from Paradise* (1986).

Title	First broadcast	Channel
A Sort of Welcome to Spring	10.45 p.m. Thursday 26 March 1959	Regional opt-out
Borrowed Pasture	9.15 p.m. Wednesday 18 May 1960	BBC Network
Enquiry: Fitness for Work	9.30 p.m. Friday 11 November 1960	BBC Network
Once There Was a Time	10 p.m. Wednesday 1 March 1961	BBC Network
Y Gymru Bell (4 films)	1.10 p.m. Sundays 6 October–27 October 1962	Regional opt-out
The Desert and the Dream	10.20 p.m. Thursday 20 December 1962	BBC Network
From a Town in Tuscany	10.15 p.m. Tuesday 9 July 1963	Regional opt-out
The Mormons	9.25 p.m. Tuesday 18 February 1964	BBC Wales opt-out
Meeting Point: Operation Salvation	6.15 p.m. Sunday 21 June 1964	BBC Network

Title	First broadcast	Channel
Song in a Strange Land	10.15 p.m. Monday 21 December 1964	BBC Wales opt-out
Dylan Thomas: Return Journey	9.50 p.m. Tuesday 27 October 1964	BBC Wales opt-out
Troubled Waters: Harry Soan Investigates	1965	BBC Wales opt-out
My Time Again: Richard Burton	6.30 p.m. Thursday 19 August 1965	BBC1 Network
My Time Again: Harry Secombe	1965	BBC Wales opt-out
Under a Bright Heaven: A Portrait of Vernon Watkins	10.50 p.m. Thursday 13 January 1966	BBC1 Network
Horizons Hung in Air	7 p.m. Wednesday 20 April 1966	BBC Wales opt-out
Alone in a Boat	9.55 p.m. Friday 9 December 1966	BBC Network
Madawaska Valley	1967	Produced for the National Film Board of Canada
Music in Midsummer	8 p.m. Thursday 4 July 1968	BBC2 Network
A Bronze Mask: A Film in Elegy for Dylan Thomas	9.35 p.m. Sunday 8 June 1969	BBC2 Network
The Fragile Universe: A Portrait of Alun Lewis	9.35 p.m. Sunday 15 June 1969	BBC2 Network
The Ancient Kingdoms: A View of Wales	10.50 p.m. Wednesday 25 June 1969	BBC1 Network
Piano with Many Strings: The Art of Ceri Richards	9.35 p.m. Sunday 29 June 1969	BBC2 Network
Private View: Leslie Norris	9.40 p.m. Monday 16 February 1970	BBC Wales opt-out
Private View: Kyffin Williams	9.40 p.m. Monday 9 March 1970	BBC Wales opt-out

Title	First broadcast	Channel
Private View: Dannie Abse	9.45 p.m. Monday 23 March 1970	BBC Wales opt-out
Private View: Robert Graves	9.45 p.m. Monday 13 April 1970	BBC Wales opt-out
Private View: Howard Roberts	10.10 p.m. Monday 27 April 1970	BBC Wales opt-out
Private View: John Grierson	10.10 p.m. Monday 11 May 1970	BBC Wales opt-out
The Land Remembers, Series 1 (6 films)	10.15 p.m. Tuesdays 15 February–21 March 1972	BBC Wales opt-out
R. S. Thomas: Priest and Poet	9.40 p.m. Sunday 2 April 1972	BBC2 Network
The Land Remembers, Series 2 (6 films)	10 p.m. Mondays 4 March–8 April 1974	BBC Wales opt-out
A Day Eleven Years Long	10.45 p.m. Friday 12 September 1975	BBC1 Network
One Man in his Time: W. J. G. Beynon	1975	
The Life and Death of Picture Post	9.55 p.m. Tuesday 30 August 1977	BBC1 Network
Sutherland in Wales	11.05 p.m. Sunday 2 October 1977	BBC Wales opt-out
Fortissimo Jones	8.10 p.m. Friday 8 September 1978	BBC2 Network
Land Against the Light	10.50 p.m. Sunday 24 September 1978	BBC Wales opt-out
The Colliers' Crusade (5 films)	10.45 p.m. Thursdays 29 November–27 December 1979	BBC Wales opt-out
Poems in Their Place: A. E. Housman	10.40 p.m. Thursday 11 March 1982	BBC2 Network
Poems in Their Place: Edward Thomas	10.30 p.m. Friday 12 March 1982	BBC2 Network
Poems in Their Place: Thomas Gray	10.35 p.m. Tuesday 16 March 1982	BBC2 Network

Title	First broadcast	Channel
Poems in Their Place: W. B. Yeats	10.35 p.m. Thursday 18 March 1982	BBC2 Network
Poems in Their Place: Dylan Thomas	10.35 p.m. Monday 29 March 1982	BBC2 Network
Poems in Their Place: Thomas Hardy	10.40 p.m. Wednesday 14 April 1982	BBC2 Network
Poems in Their Place: John Clare	10.35 p.m. Friday 16 April 1982	BBC2 Network
I Sing to you Strangers	7.40 p.m. Thursday 10 November 1983	BBC2 Network

This list was compiled from information contained in the BBC Wales Film Archives at Llandaff, Cardiff; television listings in the *Times*, *Western Mail* and *South Wales Evening Post*; the BBC Genome Project; and Rian Evans's bibliography in John Ormond, *Collected Poems*.

Bibliography

Aaron, Jane, and Chris Williams (eds), *Postcolonial Wales* (Cardiff: University of Wales Press, 2005).

Abse, Dannie, 'John Ormond as Portraitist', *Poetry Wales*, 26/2 (1990), 5–7.

Aitken, Ian, *Film and Reform: John Grierson and the Documentary Film Movement* (London: Routledge, 1990).

Anderson, Benedict, *Imagined Communities: Reflections on the Origin and Spread of Nationalism* (London: Verso, 1983).

Anderson, Lindsay, 'Free Cinema', *Universities and Left Review*, 1/2 (1957), 52.

Ang, Ien, *Desperately Seeking the Audience* (London: Routledge, 1991).

Anstey, Sandra (ed.), *R. S. Thomas: Selected Prose* (Bridgend: Poetry Wales Press, 1983).

Anthony, Scott, and James G. Marshall (eds), *The Projection of Britain: A History of the GPO Film Unit* (London: BFI, 2011).

Arnold, Matthew, *Culture and Anarchy* (Cambridge: Cambridge University Press, 1971 [1867]).

Balsom, Denis, 'The Three Wales Model', in John Osmond (ed.), *The National Question Again: Welsh Political Identity in the 1980s* (Llandysul: Gomer, 1985), pp. 1–17.

Barker, Chris, *Television, Globalization and Cultural Identities* (Buckingham: Open University Press, 2000).

Barlow, David M., Philip Mitchell and Tom O'Malley, *The Media in Wales: Voices of a Small Nation* (Cardiff: University of Wales Press, 2005).

Barnouw, Erik, *Documentary: A History of the Non-Fiction Film* (Oxford: Oxford University Press, 1993).

Barsam, Richard Meram, *Nonfiction Film: A Critical History* (Bloomington: Indiana University Press, 1992).

Bayliss, John, James Kirkup and John Ormond Thomas, *Indications* (London: Grey Walls Press, 1943).

Bazin, André, *What is Cinema?*, trans. Hugh Gray (Berkeley: University of California Press, 1967).

Berry, David, *Wales and Cinema: The First Hundred Years* (Cardiff: University of Wales Press, 1994).

Berry, David, 'The World Still Sings: Jack Howells', in Patrick Russell and James Piers Taylor (eds), *Shadows of Progress: Documentary Film in Post-War Britain* (London: BFI, 2010), pp. 141–55.

Berry, Ron, 'What Comes After?', *Poetry Wales*, 27/3 (1990), 54–5.

Betjeman, John, 'Introduction', in R. S. Thomas, *Song at the Year's Turning* (London, Rupert-Hart Davis, 1969 [1955]), pp. 11–14.

Bianchi, Tony, 'R. S. Thomas and his Readers', in Tony Curtis (ed.), *Wales: The Imagined Nation* (Bridgend: Poetry Wales Press, 1986), pp. 69–95.

Billig, Michael, *Banal Nationalism* (London: Sage, 1995).

Blandford, Steve (ed.), *Wales on Screen* (Bridgend: Poetry Wales, 2000).

Born, Georgina, *Uncertain Vision: Birt, Dyke and the Reinvention of the BBC* (London: Vintage, 2005).

Briggs, Asa, *The History of Broadcasting in the United Kingdom: Volume IV: Sound and Vision* (Oxford: Oxford University Press, 1995).

Briggs, Asa, *The History of Broadcasting in the United Kingdom: Volume V: Competition* (Oxford: Oxford University Press, 1995).

Broadcasting Council for Wales, *Annual Reports*.

Brown, Tony, 'At the Utmost Edge: The Poetry of John Ormond', *Poetry Wales*, 27/3 (1990), 31–6.

Brown, Tony, and M. Wynn Thomas, 'The Problems of Belonging', in M. Wynn Thomas (ed.), *Welsh Writing in English* (Cardiff: University of Wales Press, 2003), pp. 165–202.

Burns, Tom, *The BBC: Public Institution and Private World* (London: Macmillan, 1977)

Burton, Richard, *The Richard Burton Diaries*, ed. Chris Williams (London: Yale University Press, 2012).

Calhoun, Craig (ed.), *Habermas and the Public Sphere* (Cambridge: MIT Press, 1993).

Cannadine, David (ed.), *History and the Media* (Basingstoke: Palgrave Macmillan, 2004).

Carr, E. H., *What is History?* (London: Penguin, 1985 [1961]).

Cheeke, Stephen, *Writing for Art: The Aesthetics of Ekphrasis* (Manchester: Manchester University Press, 2008).

Clair, René, *Cinema Yesterday and Today* (New York: Dover, 1972).

Clark, Kenneth, *Civilisation: A Personal View* (London: BBC and John Murray, 1969).

Clifford, James, *The Predicament of Culture: Twentieth-Century Ethnography, Literature, and Art* (London: Harvard University Press, 1988).

Collins, Michael J., 'The Elegiac Tradition in Contemporary Anglo-Welsh Poetry', *Anglo-Welsh Review*, 26/3 (1976), 46–57.

Collins, Michael J., 'Craftsmanship as Meaning: the Poetry of John Ormond', *Poetry Wales*, 16/2 (1980), 25–33.

Collins, Richard, 'Seeing is Believing: The Ideology of Naturalism', in John Corner (ed.), *Documentary and the Mass Media* (London: Edward Arnold, 1986), pp. 125–40.

Conekin, Becky, *'The Autobiography of a Nation': The 1951 Festival of Britain* (Manchester: Manchester University Press, 2003).

Conran, Anthony, *The Cost of Strangeness: Essays on the English Poets of Wales* (Llandysul: Gomer, 1982).

Conran, Tony, 'Poetry Wales and the Second Flowering', in M. Wynn Thomas (ed.), *Welsh Writing in English* (Cardiff: University of Wales Press, 2003), pp. 222–54.

Corner, John (ed.), *Documentary and the Mass Media* (London: Edward Arnold, 1986).

Corner, John, 'Television and British Society in the 1950s', in John Corner (ed.), *Popular Television in Britain: Studies in Cultural History* (London: BFI, 1991), pp. 1–21.

Corner, John, 'Documentary Voices', in John Corner (ed.), *Popular Television in Britain: Studies in Cultural History* (London: BFI, 1991), pp. 42–59.

Corner, John, 'The Interview as Social Encounter', in Paddy Scannell (ed.), *Broadcast Talk* (London: Sage, 1991), pp. 31–47.

Corner, John, *Television Form and Public Address* (London: Edward Arnold, 1995).

Corner, John, *The Art of Record: A Critical Introduction to Documentary* (Manchester: Manchester University Press, 1996).

Curtis, Tony (eds), *Wales: The Imagined Nation* (Bridgend: Poetry Wales, 1986).

Dahlgren, Peter, *Television and the Public Sphere: Citizenship, Democracy and the Media* (London: Sage, 1995).

Davies, Hywel, *The Role of the Regions in British Broadcasting* (London: BBC, 1965).

Davies, James A., 'Detached Attachment', *New Welsh Review*, 10/3 (1997–8), 37–9.

Davies, James A., 'Dylan Thomas and his Welsh Contemporaries', in M. Wynn Thomas (ed.), *Welsh Writing in English* (Cardiff: University of Wales Press, 2003), pp. 120–64.

Davies, James A., "In a different place,/ changed': Dannie Abse, Dylan Thomas, T. S. Eliot and Wales', in Alyce von Rothkirch and Daniel Williams (eds), *Beyond the Difference: Welsh Literature in Comparative Contexts* (Cardiff: University of Wales Press, 2004), pp. 223–36.

Davies, John, 'Wales in the Nineteen-sixties', *Llafur*, 4/4 (1988), 78–88.

Davies, John, *Broadcasting and the BBC in Wales* (Cardiff: University of Wales, 1994).

Dayan, Daniel and Elihu Katz, *Media Events: The Live Broadcasting of History* (Cambridge: Harvard University Press, 1992).

Dayan, Daniel, and Elihu Katz, 'Political Ceremony and Instant History', in Anthony Smith (ed.), *Television: An International History*, 2nd edn (Oxford: Oxford University Press, 1998), pp. 97–106.

Dicks, Bella, *Heritage, Place and Community* (Cardiff: University of Wales Press, 2000).

Dillon, Robert, *History on British Television: Constructing Nation, Nationality and Collective Memory* (Manchester: Manchester University Press, 2010).

Donnellan, Philip, 'Memories of the Future', *Sight and Sound*, 2/4 (1992), 40.

Dover, Caroline, '"Crisis" in British Documentary Television: the End of a Genre?', *Journal of British Cinema and Television*, 1/2 (2004), 242–59.

Eagleton, Terry, 'Wittgenstein's Friends', *New Left Review*, I/135 (1982), 64–90.

Edensor, Tim, *National Identity, Popular Culture and Everyday Life* (London: Bloomsbury, 2002).

Edgerton, Gary R., 'Introduction: Television as Historian: A Different Kind of History Altogether', in Gary R. Edgerton and Peter C. Rollins (eds), *Television Histories: Shaping Collective Memory in the Media Age* (Lexington: University Press of Kentucky, 2001), pp. 1–16.

Eisenstein, Sergei, *The Film Sense*, trans. Jay Leyda (London: Faber, 1943).

Ellis, John S., *Investiture: Royal Ceremony and National Identity in Wales, 1911–1969* (Cardiff: University of Wales Press, 2008).

Enticknap, Leo, '"I don't think he did anything after that": Paul Dickson', in Patrick Russell and James Piers Taylor (eds), *Shadows of Progress: Documentary Film in Post-War Britain* (London: BFI, 2010), pp. 156–75.

Evans, Gareth, *Dunvant: Portrait of a Community* (Stafford: Stowefields Publications, 1992).

Evans, Gareth, 'Welsh Writing in English: Case Studies in Cultural Interaction' (unpublished PhD thesis, Swansea University, 2013).

Evans, Neil, 'Immigrants and Minorities in Wales, 1840–1990: A Comparative Perspective, in Charlotte Williams, Neil Evans and Paul O'Leary (eds), *A Tolerant Nation?: Exploring Ethnic Diversity in Wales* (Cardiff: University of Wales Press, 2003), pp. 14–34.

Evans, Neil, 'Through the Prism of Ethnic Violence: Riots and Racial Attacks in Wales, 1826–2002', in Charlotte Williams, Neil Evans and Paul O'Leary (eds), *A Tolerant Nation?: Exploring Ethnic Diversity in Wales* (Cardiff: University of Wales Press, 2003), pp. 93–108.

Evans, Rian, 'An Ormond Chronology', in John Ormond, *Collected Poems*, ed. Rian Evans (Bridgend: Seren, 2015), p. 33.

Ffrancon, Gwenno, 'Documenting the Depression in South Wales: Today We Live and Eastern Valley', *Welsh History Review*, 22/1 (2004), 103–25.

Fiske, John and John Hartley, *Reading Television* (London: Methuen, 1978).

Fox, Jo, 'From Documentary Film to Television Documentaries: John Grierson and *This Wonderful World*', *Journal of British Cinema and Television*, 10/3 (2013), 498–523.

Francis, Hywel, 'The South Wales Miners and the Spanish Civil War: A Study in Internationalism' (unpublished PhD thesis, University of Wales, 1977).

Francis, Hywel, 'The Origins of the South Wales Miners' Library', *History Workshop*, 2 (1976), 183–205.

Francis, Hywel, 'The Secret World of the South Wales Miner: The Relevance of Oral History', in David Smith (ed.), *A People and a Proletariat: Essays in the History of Wales 1780–1980* (London: Pluto, 1980), pp. 166–80.

Francis, Hywel, *Miners Against Fascism: Wales and the Spanish Civil War* (London: Lawrence and Wishart, 2012 [1984]).

Francis, Hywel, 'Paynter, Thomas William (1903–1984)', *Oxford Dictionary of National Biography*, (Oxford: Oxford University Press, 2004); September 2010 online edn available at *http://www.oxforddnb.com/view/article/48653* (accessed 12 December 2018).

Francis, Hywel, and Dai Smith, *The Fed: A History of the South Wales Miners in the Twentieth Century*, 2nd edn (Cardiff: University of Wales Press, 1998 [1980]).

Franklin, Ieuan, and Paul Long, 'The Overheard and Underprivileged: Uses of Montage Sound in the Post-War BBC Television Documentaries of Denis Mitchell and Philip Donnellan' (unpublished conference paper, 'Documentary Now!', UCL, London, January 2011). Available at *http://www.academia.edu/483597/The_Overheard_and_Underprivileged* (accessed 10 March 2014).

Franklin, Ieuan, Hugh Chignell and Kristin Skoog (eds), *Regional Aesthetics: Mapping UK Media Cultures* (Basingstoke: Palgrave Macmillan, 2015).

Gooding, Mel, *Ceri Richards* (Moffat: Cameron and Hollis, 2002).

Habermas, Jurgen, *The Structural Transformation of the Public Sphere* (London: Polity, 1989 [1962]).

Hajkowski, Thomas, *The BBC and National Identity in Britain, 1922–53* (Manchester: Manchester University Press, 2010).

Hall, Stuart, 'The Social Eye of *Picture Post*', in Glenn Jordan, *'Down the Bay':* Picture Post*, Humanist Photography and Images of 1950s Cardiff* (Cardiff: Butetown History and Arts Centre, 2001), pp. 67–72.

Hannan, Patrick (ed.), *Wales in Vision: The People and Politics of Television* (Llandysul: Gomer, 1990).

Hansen, Randall, *Citizenship and Immigration in Post-war Britain* (Oxford: OUP, 2000).

Hardy, Forsyth, *John Grierson: A Documentary Biography* (London: Faber, 1979).

Herman, Josef, *Related Twilights: Notes from an Artist's Diary* (London: Robson, 1975).

Hogenkamp, Bert, 'Today We Live: The Making of a Documentary in a Welsh Mining Valley', *Llafur: Journal of Welsh Labour History*, 5/1 (1988), 45–52.

Holden, Anthony, *Charles: A Biography* (London: Bantam, 1998).

Holmes, Colin, *John Bull's Island: Immigration and British Society 1871–1971* (Basingstoke: Macmillan, 1988).

Howells, Kim, 'A View From Below: Tradition, Experience and Nationalisation in the South Wales Coalfield 1937–1957' (unpublished PhD thesis, University of Warwick, 1979).

Humphreys, Emyr, 'A Lost Leader', in M. Wynn Thomas (ed.), *Emyr Humphreys: Conversations and Reflections* (Cardiff: University of Wales Press, 2002).

Irwin, Mary M., '*Monitor*: The Creation of the Television Arts Documentary', *Journal of British Cinema and Television*, 8 (2011), 322–36.

Jenkins, A. D. F., 'Richards, Ceri Giraldus (1903–1971)', rev. *Oxford Dictionary of National Biography* (Oxford : Oxford University Press, 2004); May 2011 online edn available at *http://www.oxforddnb.com/view/ article/31602* (accessed 14 January 2014).

Jenkins, Keith, *Re-Thinking History* (London: Routledge, 1991).

Jenkins, Randal, 'The Poetry of John Ormond', *Poetry Wales*, 8/1 (1972), 17–28.

Johnes, Martin, *A History of Sport in Wales* (Cardiff: University of Wales Press, 2005).

Johnes, Martin, *Wales Since 1939* (Manchester: Manchester University Press, 2012).

Jones, Alun R., and Gwyn Thomas (eds), *Presenting Saunders Lewis* (Cardiff: University of Wales Press, 1983).

Jones, Huw, 'Exhibiting Welshness: Art, Politics and National Identity in Wales 1940–1994' (unpublished PhD thesis, Swansea University, 2007).

Jones, R. Merfyn, 'Beyond Identity? The Reconstruction of the Welsh', *Journal of British Studies*, 31/4 (1992), 330–57.

Jordan, Glenn, *'Down the Bay':* Picture Post, *Humanist Photography and Images of 1950s Cardiff* (Cardiff: Butetown History and Arts Centre, 2001).

Jordan, Glenn, '"We Never Really Noticed You Were Coloured": Postcolonialist Reflections on Immigrants and Minorities in Wales', in Jane Aaron and Chris Williams (eds), *Postcolonial Wales* (Cardiff: University of Wales Press, 2005), pp. 55–81.

Jordan, Glenn, and Chris Weedon, *Cultural Politics: Class, Gender, Race and the Postmodern World* (Oxford: Blackwell, 1995).

Kermode, Frank, *Wallace Stevens*, 2nd edn (London: Faber, 1989).

Kinsey, Christine, and Ceridwen Lloyd-Morgan (eds), *Imaging the Imagination* (Llandysul: Gomer, 2005), pp. 7–11.

Kumar, Krishan, 'Public Service Broadcasting and the Public Interest', in Colin McCabe and Olivia Stewart (eds), *The BBC and Public Service Broadcasting* (Manchester: Manchester University Press, 1986).

Kymlicka, Will, *Multicultural Citizenship* (Oxford: Clarenden, 1995).

Leeworthy, Daryl, *Labour Country: Political Radicalism and Social Democracy in South Wales 1831–1985* (Cardigan: Parthian, 2018).

Lewis, Alun, *In the Green Tree* (Cardigan: Parthian, 2006 [1948]).

Lewis, Richard, *Leaders and Teachers: Adult Education and the Challenge of Labour in South Wales, 1906–1940* (Cardiff: University of Wales Press, 1993).

Lewis, Saunders, 'The Fate of the Language', in Alun R. Jones, and Gwyn Thomas (eds), *Presenting Saunders Lewis* (Cardiff: University of Wales Press, 1983), pp. 127–41.

Lidchi, Henrietta, 'The Poetics and the Politics of Exhibiting Other Cultures', in Stuart Hall (ed.), *Representation: Cultural Representations and Signifying Practices* (London: Sage 1997), pp. 152–222.

Lord, Peter, *The Aesthetics of Relevance* (Llandysul: Gomer, 1993).

Lord, Peter, *The Visual Culture of Wales: Industrial Society* (Cardiff: University of Wales Press, 1998).

Lord, Peter, *The Visual Culture of Wales: Imaging the Nation* (Cardiff: University of Wales Press, 2000).

Lord, Peter, *The Meaning of Pictures: Images of Personal, Social and Political Identity* (Cardiff: University of Wales Press, 2008).

Lublin, Geraldine, 'Matthews, Abraham (1832–1899)', *Oxford Dictionary of National Biography* (Oxford: Oxford University Press, 2004), October 2009 online edn available at *http://www.oxforddnb.com/view/article/98447* (accessed 22 November 2018).

Lucas, Rowland, *The Voice of a Nation? A Concise Account of the BBC in Wales 1923–1973* (Llandysul: Gomer, 1981).

Mason, Rhiannon, *Museums, Nations, Identities: Wales and its National Museums* (Cardiff: University of Wales Press, 2007).

McCabe, Colin, and Olivia Stewart (eds), *The BBC and Public Service Broadcasting* (Manchester: Manchester University Press, 1986).

McGuinness, Patrick, 'Introduction', in John Ormond, *Collected Poems*, ed. Rian Evans (Bridgend: Seren, 2015), pp. 13–30.

Minhinnick, Robert, '"The Echo of Once Being Here": A Reflection on the Imagery of John Ormond', *Poetry Wales*, 27/3 (1990), 51–3.

Monaco, James, *How to Read a Film: Movies, Media and Beyond*, 4th edn (Oxford: Oxford University Press, 2009).

Monk, Ray, *Ludwig Wittgenstein: The Duty of Genius* (London: Vintage, 1991).

Monk, Ray, *How to Read Wittgenstein* (London: Granta, 2005).

Moore-Gilbert, Bart, and John Seed (eds), *Cultural Revolution? The Challenge of the Arts in the 1960s* (London: Routledge, 2004 [1992]).

Morgan, Prys, 'Keeping the Legends Alive', in Tony Curtis (eds), *Wales: The Imagined Nation* (Bridgend: Poetry Wales, 1986), pp. 19–41.

Morgan, Robert, *On the Banks of the Cynon* (Todmorden: Arc Publications, 1975).

Morley, David, 'Broadcasting and the Construction of the National Family', in Robert C. Allen and Annette Hill (eds), *The Television Studies Reader* (London: Routledge, 2004), pp. 418–41.

Morse, Sarah, 'The Black Pastures: The Significance of Landscape in the Work of Gwyn Thomas and Ron Berry' (unpublished PhD thesis, Swansea University, 2010).

Mulvey, Laura, and Jamie Sexton (eds), *Experimental British Television* (Manchester: Manchester University Press, 2007).

Murdock, Graham, 'Televisual Tourism: National Image-Making and International Markets', in C. W. Thomsen (ed.), *Cultural Transfer or Electronic Imperialism?* (Heidelberg: Carl Winter Universitätsverlag, 1989), pp. 171–84.

Nichols, Bill, *Introduction to Documentary* (Bloomington: Indiana University Press, 2001).

Ormond Thomas, John, 'The Old Singer of Gower', *Picture Post*, 19 March 1949, 30–3.

Ormond, Glenys, '"J.O." and "Rod"', *Poetry Wales*, 27/3 (1990), 42–5.

Ormond, John, 'Selections From An Elegy for Alun Lewis', *Wales*, 3/4 (1944), 5–6.

Ormond, John, 'A Bronze for the Academy', *Picture Post*, 3 May 1947, 21–4.

Ormond, John, *Requiem and Celebration* (Swansea: Christopher Davies, 1969).

Ormond, John, 'A Music Restored', *Planet*, 7 (1971), 75–7.

Ormond, John, 'Ceri Richards: Root and Branch', *Planet*, 10 (1972), 3–11.

Ormond, John, 'Ceri Richards', in *Ceri Richards: Memorial Exhibition* (Cardiff: National Museum of Wales/Welsh Arts Council, 1973).

Ormond, John, 'John Ormond', in Meic Stephens (ed.), *Artists in Wales 2* (Llandysul: Gomer, 1973), pp. 153–64.

Ormond, John, *Definition of a Waterfall* (Oxford: Oxford University Press, 1973).

Ormond, John, 'Personal Column', *Western Mail*, 4 March 1974, 9.

Ormond, John, *Graham Sutherland, O.M.: A Memorial Address* (Cardiff: National Museum of Wales, 1980).

Ormond, John, *'In Place of Empty Heaven: The Poetry of Wallace Stevens'*, *W. D. Thomas Memorial Lecture* (Swansea: University College Swansea, 1983).

Ormond, John, 'There you are, he's an artist', in *Ceri Richards: An Exhibition to Inaugurate the Ceri Richards Gallery* (Swansea: University College of Swansea, 1984), pp. 22–4.

Ormond, John, *Selected Poems* (Bridgend: Poetry Wales Press, 1986).

Ormond, John, 'Introduction', in *Kyffin Williams R.A.* (Cardiff: National Museum of Wales, 1987).

Ormond, John, 'Letter from Tuscany', *Poetry Wales*, 24/1 (1988), 20–4.

Ormond, John, 'Picturegoers', in Patrick Hannan (ed.), *Wales on the Wireless* (Llandysul: Gomer, 1988), pp. 58–60.

Ormond, John, 'Introduction', in John Tripp, *Selected Poems* (Bridgend: Seren, 1989), pp. 9–13.

Ormond, John, 'Beginnings', in Patrick Hannan (ed.), *Wales in Vision: The People and Politics of Television* (Llandysul: Gomer, 1990), pp. 1–10.

Ormond, John, *Cathedral Builders and Other Poems* (Newtown: Gregynog Press, 1991).

Pendle, George, 'The Welsh in Patagonia', *Wales*, 6/37 (1959), 13–22.

Pikoulis, John, *Alun Lewis: A Life* (Bridgend: Seren, 1991 [1984]).

Poole, Richard, 'Conversations with John Ormond', *New Welsh Review*, 2/1 (1989), 38–46.

Poole, Richard, 'John Ormond and Wallace Stevens: Six Variations on a Double Theme', *Poetry Wales*, 27/3 (1990), 16–26.

Price, Elain, *Nid Sianel Gyffredin Mohoni!: Hanes Sefydlu S4C* (Cardiff: University of Wales Press, 2016).

Price, Monroe E., *Television, the Public Sphere, and National Identity* (Oxford: Oxford University Press, 1995).

Price, Richard, *Political Writings*, ed. D. O. Thomas (Cambridge: Cambridge University Press, 1991).

Principles and Practice in Documentary Programmes (London: BBC, 1972).

Pryce, Huw, *J. E. Lloyd and the Creation of Welsh History: Renewing a Nation's Past* (Cardiff: University of Wales Press, 2011).

Raine, Kathleen, 'Vernon Watkins: Poet of Tradition', *Anglo-Welsh Review*, 14/33 (1964), 20–39.

Read, John, 'Is There a Documentary Art?', *Sight and Sound*, 17/68 (1948), 156–8.

Rees, Alwyn D., *Dear Sir Harry Pilkington: An Open Letter from Alwyn D. Rees* (Carmarthen: Radical Publications, 1961).

Report of the Committee on Broadcasting (London: HMSO, 1962).

Reynolds, Sarah Rhian, 'Aneirin Talfan Davies: Producing a Nation' (unpublished PhD thesis, Swansea University, 2001).

Rhees, Rush, *Without Answers* (London: Routledge, 1969).

Richards, Alun, 'Berries on the Tree', in Patrick Hannan (ed.), *Wales in Vision* (Llandysul: Gomer, 1990), pp. 40–6.

Roderick, A. J., *Wales Through the Ages, Volume 1, From the Earliest Times to 1485* (Llandybie: Christopher Davies, 1959).

Roderick, A. J., *Wales Through the Ages, Volume 2, Modern Wales* (Llandybie: Christopher Davies, 1960).

Roderick, Selwyn, 'Us Over There', in Patrick Hannan (ed.), *Wales in Vision: The People and Politics of Television* (Llandysul: Gomer, 1990), pp. 17–23.

Rosenthal, Alan and John Corner (eds), *New Challenges for Documentary* (Manchester: Manchester University Press, 2005).

Rowan, Eric, 'The Visual Arts', in Meic Stephens (ed.), *The Arts in Wales 1950–1975* (Cardiff: Welsh Arts Council, 1979), pp. 51–85.

Russell, Patrick, 'Morning in the Streets', BFI Screenonline, *http://www.screenonline.org.uk/tv/id/1224984/index.html* (accessed 12 December 2018).

Russell, Patrick, 'Philip Donnellan', BFI Screenonline, *http://www.screenonline.org.uk/people/id/500920/index.html* (accessed 12 December 2018).

Russell, Patrick, and James Piers Taylor (eds), *Shadows of Progress: Documentary Film in Post-War Britain* (London: BFI, 2010).

Sager Eidt, Laura M., *Writing and Filming the Painting: Ekphrasis in Literature and Film* (Amsterdam: Rodopi, 2008).

Samuel, Raphael, *Theatres of Memory Volume 1: Past and Present in Contemporary Culture* (London: Verso, 1994).

Scannell, Paddy, 'The Social Eye of Television, 1946–1955', *Media, Culture and Society*, 1/1 (1979), 101.

Scannell, Paddy, '"The Stuff of Radio": Developments in Radio Features and Documentaries Before the War', in John Corner (ed.), *Documentary and the Mass Media* (London: Edward Arnold, 1986), pp. 1–26.

Scannell, Paddy (ed.), *Broadcast Talk* (London: Sage, 1991).

Scannell, Paddy, 'The Origins of BBC Regional Policy', in Sylvia Harvey and Kevin Robins (eds), *The Regions, the Nations and the BBC* (London: BFI, 1993), pp. 27–37.

Scannell, Paddy, and David Cardiff, *A Social History of British Broadcasting 1922–1939* (Oxford: Blackwell, 1991).

Schama, Simon, 'Television and the Trouble with History', in David Cannadine (ed.), *History and the Media* (Basingstoke: Palgrave Macmillan, 2004), pp. 20–33.

Schlesinger, Philip, 'The Nation and Communicative Space', in Howard Tumber (ed.), *Media Power, Professionals and Policies* (London: Routledge, 2000), pp. 99–115.

Sexton, Jamie, 'John Grierson', *http://www.screenonline.org.uk/people/id/454202/index.html* (accessed 12 December 2018).

Sexton, Jamie, '"Televerite" hits Britain: documentary, drama and the growth of 16mm film-making in British television', *Screen*, 44/4 (2003), 435.

Sills-Jones, Dafydd, 'The Teliesyn Co-Operative: national broadcasting, production organisation and TV aesthetics', in Ieuan Franklin, Hugh Chignell and Kristin Skoog (eds), *Regional Aesthetics: Mapping UK Media Cultures* (Basingstoke: Palgrave Macmillan, 2015), pp. 169–83.

Smith, Anthony (ed.), *Television: An International History*, 2nd edn (Oxford: Oxford University Press, 1998).

Smith, Dai, ' A Cannon off the Cush', *Arcade*, 14 (1980), 13–14.

Smith, Dai, 'The Case of Alun Lewis: A Divided Sensibility', *Llafur*, 3/2 (1981), 14–26.

Smith, Dai, *Wales! Wales?* (London: Allen and Unwin, 1984).

Smith, Dai, 'In the Presence of the Past', in Patrick Hannan (ed.), *Wales in Vision* (Llandysul: Gomer, 1990), pp. 32–40.

Smith, Dai, *Aneurin Bevan and the World of South Wales* (Cardiff: University of Wales Press, 1993).

Smith, Kieron, 'Madawaska Valley: John Ormond's Lost Film and the National Film Board of Canada', *Canadian Journal of Film Studies*, 25/1 (2016), 27–45.

Stephens, Meic, 'The Second Flowering', *Poetry Wales*, 3/3 (1963), 2–8.

Stephens, Meic (ed.), *The Arts in Wales 1950–75* (Cardiff: Welsh Arts Council, 1979).

Stewart, James, 'Wales, the wireless and the world – sixty years of Welsh programmes on the BBC World Service', *Cyfrwng: Media Wales Journal*, 10 (2013), 35–52.

Stradling, Robert, *Wales and the Spanish Civil War: The Dragon's Dearest Cause?* (Cardiff: University of Wales Press, 2004).

Sutherland, Graham, *Sutherland in Wales* (London: Alistair McAlpine, 1976).

Swallow, Norman, *Factual Television* (London: Focal Press, 1966).

Swallow, Norman, 'Denis Mitchell: Master of Documentary', *The Listener*, 24 April 1975, 551.

Swallow, Norman, 'History by Television', *The Listener*, 2448 (1976), 296–7.

Talfan Davies, Geraint, *At Arm's Length: Recollections and Reflections on the Arts, Media and a Young Democracy* (Bridgend: Seren, 2008).

Thom, Alexander, *Megalithic Sites in Great Britain* (Oxford: Clarendon, 1967).

Thomas, D. O., 'Price, Richard (1723–1791)', *Oxford Dictionary of National Biography* (Oxford: Oxford University Press, 2004), May 2005 online edn available at *http://www.oxforddnb.com/view/article/22761* (accessed 30 November 2018).

Thomas, Dylan, *Quite Early One Morning*, ed. Aneirin Talfan-Davies (London: Dent, 1971).

Thomas, M. Wynn, *John Ormond* (Cardiff: University of Wales Press, 1997).

Thomas, M. Wynn, *Corresponding Cultures: The Two Literatures of Wales* (Cardiff: University of Wales Press, 1999).

Thomas, M. Wynn (ed.), *Emyr Humphreys: Conversations and Reflections* (Cardiff: University of Wales Press, 2002).

Thomas, M. Wynn (ed.), *Welsh Writing in English* (Cardiff: University of Wales Press, 2003).

Thomas, M. Wynn, 'Ormond, John (1923–1990)', *Oxford Dictionary of National Biography* (Oxford: Oxford University Press, 2004). Available at *http://www.oxforddnb.com/view/article/61282* (accessed 12 December 2018).

Thomas, M. Wynn, 'Foreword', in Christine Kinsey and Ceridwen Lloyd-Morgan (eds), *Imaging the Imagination* (Llandysul: Gomer, 2005), pp. 7–11.

Thomas, M. Wynn, *In the Shadow of the Pulpit: Literature and Nonconformist Wales* (Cardiff: University of Wales Press, 2010).

Thomas, M. Wynn, *R. S. Thomas: Serial Obsessive* (Cardiff: University of Wales Press, 2013).

Thomas, Ned, *The Welsh Extremist: Modern Welsh Politics, Literature and Society* (London: Gollancz, 1971).

Thomas, R. S., *Song at the Year's Turning* (London, Rupert-Hart Davis, 1969 [1955]).

Thomas, R. S., 'Abercuawg', trans. Sandra Anstey, in Sandra Anstey (ed.), *R. S. Thomas: Selected Prose* (Bridgend: Poetry Wales Press, 1983), pp. 155–66.

Thomas, R. S., 'Y Llwybrau Gynt' (The Paths Gone By)', trans. Sandra Anstey, in Sandra Anstey (ed.), *R. S. Thomas: Selected Prose* (Bridgend: Poetry Wales Press, 1983), pp. 129–46.

Thomas, R. S., *Collected Poems 1945–1990* (London: Phoenix, 2000).

Tudor, Harold, *Making the Nations Sing: The Birth of the Llangollen International Eisteddfod* (Keele: Keele University Library, 1973).

Tunstall, Jeremy, *Television Producers* (London: Routledge, 1993).

Vaughan Jones, Alan, 'Modalities of Cultural Identity in the Writings of Idris Davies and Alun Lewis' (unpublished PhD thesis, Aberystywth University, 2010).

Watkins, Vernon, *The Lady with the Unicorn* (London: Faber, 1948).

Watkins, Vernon, *Affinities* (London: Faber, 1962).

Webb, Harri, 'Alun Lewis: The Lost Leader', *Poetry Wales*, 10/3 (1974), 118–23.

Welsh Arts Council, *Annual Report 1976* (Cardiff: Welsh Arts Council, 1976).

Williams, Charlotte, Neil Evans and Paul O'Leary (eds), *A Tolerant Nation?: Exploring Ethnic Diversity in Wales* (Cardiff: University of Wales Press, 2003).

Williams, Daniel G., *Black Skin, Blue Books: African Americans and Wales 1845–1945* (Cardiff: University of Wales Press, 2012).

Williams, Glanmor (ed.), *Merthyr Politics: The Making of a Working-Class Tradition* (Cardiff: University of Wales Press, 1966).

Williams, Glyn, *The Welsh in Patagonia: The State and the Ethnic Community* (Cardiff: University of Wales Press, 1991).

Williams, Gwyn, *ABC of (D.)G.W.* (Llandysul: Gomer, 1981).

Williams, Gwyn, *Collected Poems: 1936–1986* (Llandysul: Gomer, 1987).

Williams, Gwyn A., *When Was Wales?: A History of the Welsh* (London: Penguin, 1991 [1985]).

Williams, Kyffin, *A Wider Sky* (Llandysul: Gomer, 1991).

Williams, Raymond, 'Introduction', in Meic Stephens (ed.), *The Arts in Wales 1950–75* (Cardiff: Welsh Arts Council, 1979), pp. 1–4.

Williams, R. Bryn, *Gwladfa Patagonia: The Welsh Colony in Patagonia 1865–1965* (Cardiff: University of Wales Press, 1965).

Wilson, Angus, *Tempo: The Impact of Television on the Arts* (London: Headway, 1964).

Wilson, S. S., 'Thom, Alexander (1894–1985)', *Oxford Dictionary of National Biography* (Oxford: Oxford University Press, 2004).

Winston, Brian, *Claiming the Real II: Documentary: Grierson and Beyond* (London: Palgrave Macmillan, 2008 [1995]).

Wyver, John, *Vision On: Film, Television and the Arts in Britain* (London: Wallflower, 2007).

INDEX